PUBLICATION OF THE AMERICAN DIALECT SOCIETY

Number 2

WORD-LISTS FROM THE SOUTH

Published by the
AMERICAN DIALECT SOCIETY
November, 1944

Obtainable from the Secretary-Treasurer
Woman's College of the
University of North Carolina
Greensboro, North Carolina

Continued on Cover 3

PUBLICATION OF THE AMERICAN DIALECT SOCIETY
12/

Number 2

WORD-LISTS FROM THE SOUTH

Published by the
AMERICAN DIALECT SOCIETY
November, 1944

Obtainable from the Secretary-Treasurer
Woman's College of the
UNIVERSITY OF NORTH CAROLINA
Greensboro, North Carolina

INTRODUCTION

The eight word-lists which follow contain representative samplings of words, grammatical usages, word order, pronunciations, and proverbs and sayings, selected from the material of a few collectors. Some of the items included are rare and, as far as the Editor knows, have not appeared in any printed glossary in America. Certainly this type of material should be collected and printed. Some other items have appeared in word-lists, especially in those in *Dialect Notes*; for such inclusion, see the Editor's prefatory remarks to Dr. Dennis's list from Alabama. A few words are repeated in more than one list. The reason for repeating these words is that they show that certain words with the same meaning and the same pronunciation are found in different localities, or that the same words with different meanings and different pronunciations (or the same pronunciations) are found in different localities. In labeling a usage as being found in a certain locality, the contributor does not by that labeling declare that the usage is confined to a certain community. (Sometimes the Editor has specified or "reported" other locales, meanings, or pronunciations than those given by the collector. This he has done not as a criticism but as a slight enlargement of information.) Some usages are included which the contributor and the Editor may suspect to be local creations. But every experienced collector of folklore, proverbs, and dialect sometimes happily discovers that he was in error—that what he thought was a family creation later proved to be older and more widespread.

If some of the contributors have made no effort to show whether the expressions they contribute are found in the *Oxford English Dictionary*, the *English Dialect Dictionary*, and other lexicographical works or glossaries, it must be remembered that they were not asked to do so, even though such information is desirable. It should also be remembered that most persons who collect linguistic phenomena do so for love and not for money, and that their collecting is done on time borrowed from a busy schedule. Dr. Hans Kurath has kindly looked over some of the lists and pointed out words in them which are also found in the *Linguistic Atlas*. These are marked "LA."

The specimens presented in this issue of the *Publication of the American Dialect Society* may serve a number of purposes. Among them are:

1. To record some valuable dialect material found in the Southern states;
2. To indicate the locales, the frequency of appearance, the levels of usage, the variations in meaning, form, and pronunciation of certain expressions;
3. To illustrate different types of regional or local material that may be collected and sent in;
4. To stimulate other collectors in both the United States and Canada to collect and send in material of whatever type they can find and happen to be interested in;
5. To induce discussion and clarification of some of the material given here.

The reader will observe that the style obtaining among the lists is not completely uniform. This is to be accounted for on two grounds: First, the *Instructions to Collectors of Dialect* had not been printed and distributed when the contributions were sent in. Second, the Editor feels that every contributor is an individual and that a work such as this should retain some marks of the individual. Frequently a narrative-descriptive style brings out the meaning better than does a terse lexicographical style. But the Editor has attempted to bring about some uniformity. The contents of the *Dialect Dictionary of the United States and Canada* will, of course, be made uniform in its style.

When the pronunciation of a word has no point or when the pronunciation is obvious, no pronunciation is given. This was done to save time and money.

It is hoped that persons who can throw additional light on any expressions here will write either the Editor or the contributor. If these comments are made on slips of paper 4 x 6 inches, this method will prove most helpful, for these slips can be placed with the original slips now on file. Persons good enough to assist in this way should put their full name and address at the bottom of each slip. If such comments are sufficiently enlightening, they will appear, with proper credit, in some subsequent issue of the *Publication*.

Editorial comments are placed in double parentheses.

The Editor is deeply indebted to his Associate Editors, Dr. Kemp Malone and Dr. Elliott V. K. Dobbie, for reading the manuscript of this issue and making valuable suggestions and corrections.

GEORGE P. WILSON

Chairman of the Committee on
Regional Speech and Localisms
and
Secretary of the Society

I. A WORD-LIST FROM ALABAMA AND SOME OTHER SOUTHERN STATES

LEAH A. DENNIS

Alabama College

The words in this list are part of a collection which Dr. Dennis sent the Secretary about three years ago, when he was chairman of a committee on Southern dialect. She sent her collection, at his request, to go towards making a dialect dictionary, and not to be published in this form. That she did not check her words against those of L. W. Payne, Jr., *Dialect Notes*, III, 279–328, 342–391 (1908), is not to be charged against her; such work would be done by the editors of a dialect dictionary.

It is important that collectors send in not only new words but also old ones even though the old ones have been reported before. Reporting old words is valuable in determining locales, date of usage, frequency of appearance, and classes of persons using the expressions. Payne's list is now nearly forty years old.—The Editor

A. GLOSSARY

aim to: *vb.* + infin. To intend to. "He wasn't *aiming to hurt* you." Deep South. DAE.

and: *conj.* The inclusion of *and* between hundreds and the following ten: "nineteen hundred *and* forty-two." Miss., Tenn., Va. Common.

bait: *n.* ((A large amount (of food).)) "He ate himself a plumb *bait* of pie." Chickasaw Co., Miss. ((Also Va., N. C., Tenn., and probably all other Southern states.))

be: *vb.* The forms *is* and *are* are used interchangeably for any person or number by Negroes over much of the South. In Alabama *am* is frequently used as third person singular as well as first person. LA.

bitty bit: *n.* A very small amount. "Just a wee little *bitty bit*, thank you." Ala., Miss. Chiefly feminine.

blue-John, less often **blue-Johnny**: *n.* Milk, skimmed (hence blue) and slightly sour. Ala., ((also S. C., mid. Tenn., Ky.)).

blinky ['blɪŋkɪ]: *adj.* Slightly sour; said of milk. Rabun Co., Ga. ((Common in mountains of N. C. and Tenn. and perhaps other Southern mountainous sections.))

6

brung: pret. and p. p. of *bring*. Ala. Vulgar. ((Common in South among uneducated.))

bump: *n.* A euphemism for a pimple. Deep South. General.

bunny hop: *n.* A side road. Ala. Infrequent. Low popular. Reported.

carry: *tr. vb.* To conduct, escort, take with one someone or something even under its own motive power. *Carry a girl to a dance*, with or without a conveyance; *carry a horse to market, a car to a garage.* "*Carry me* back to ole Virginny." ((Widely used in the South. Cf. Henry Carey, "Sally in our Alley": "My master *carries me* to church"; Pepys: " . . . and so I took them up in a coach, and *carried the ladies* to Paul's." Also: *Lev.* 4, 21; *II Chr.* 14, 15; *Jere.* 39, 14.)) OED, EDD, CD, DAE, LA.

Chicken brissel: *n.* A chicken barbecue. Greenville, Ala. Reported.

Christmas Eve: *n.* The twenty-four hours preceding Christmas, usually supplemented with *day* or *night* to specify. "Generally we left home early on *Christmas Eve* day to go to my grandfather's." Ala. General. ((Also other sections of the South.))

chunk: *tr. vb.* To throw, hurl, toss with a short throw with little elevation. Deep South. Popular. ((Also s. Va., e. N. C., upper S. C.)) LA.

clay gall: *n.* (From *gall*, a sore from chafing?) Clay land from which the good soil has been washed. "It's a strange thing that the cotton on the rich lands this year is poor, but that on the *clay galls* is excellent." Cent. Ala. Rural. Reported. ((Also Va., N. C.)) LA.

clean up (your) **duty:** *phr.* Complete (your) assignment. Okla. Reported. ((Also reported from upper S. C.))

clumb: pret. and p. p. of *climb*. Deep South, ((also other sections of the South)). Low popular. LA.

cooter ['kutə, -ɚ]: *n.* A turtle. Ala., Miss., ((also Va., N. C., S. C., Ga.)). OED, DAE, LA.

country, to drive through: *phr.* To go by automobile ((or any other vehicle)), especially as contrasted with travel by train or bus. N. C., Deep South, ((also Va.)).

country, to give down the: *phr.* To "lecture" someone thoroughly. Ala., ((also Va., N. C., S. C.)). Colloquial, jocular.

critter: *n.* A horse. Rabun Co., Ga. Reported. ((Also elsewhere in the South.)) LA.

did: p. p. of *do*. Slightly less frequent than *done*. "It's already *did*." Over much of the South. Negro.

dinner on the ground: *n*. The co-operative picnic meal served at an all-day singing ((preaching or other meeting)). N. Ala. Reported. ((Also other Southern states.))

directly [dɪˈrɛklɪ, ˈdrɛklɪ, ˈtrɛklɪ]: *adv*. Presently, in a little while. Over wide areas of the South. Popular. DAE, EDD.

do: *tr. vb*. To treat; ill-treat, but without general slang notion of cheating. ((Usually stressed.)) "I think it's awful for you to *do* me that way." Ala., ((also other Southern states)). General, up to high popular use.

dog, to run like a scalded: *phr*. To run exceedingly fast. Ala. Low popular. Reported. ((Also Va., N. C.))

dog-trot, also called **breeze-way:** *n*. A wide, floored passage-way running between two halves of a house, built, except for a common roof and floor level, as two separate structures. Being open at both ends, the passage-way is cool, and many of the household activities are carried on there. This type of structure is common in retired parts of the South where the building was done by the owner and neighbors. Deep South. Rural. LA.

done: aux. of perf. tense of *do*. "I *done* seen him." Pleonastically with *has*, contracted: "I's *done* seen him." As perfect passive auxiliary, usually with *is*: "It's *done did*." Over much of the South. Negro.

draw up: *vb*. To shrink. "When my blue dress was washed, it *drew up* dreadfully; now I can't wear it." Ala., ((also Va., N. C., S. C., Tenn.)). General.

drop by: To drop in, "stop by"; to drop (someone) in passing by; to let (someone) out of a vehicle. "Mrs. Weston was going to *drop* Jane *by* in her carriage." Deep South, ((also Va., N. C., S. C.)).

drug: pret, and p. p. of *drag*. Deep South. High popular. ((Also Va., N. C. Low popular.)) EDD, LA.

dumb chill: *n*. A chill acompanied by shaking. Miss., Ala. Lay use. Popular. Reported. ((Also Va., N. C.)) LA.

evening: *n*. Afternoon, commonly the time of day between the midday and the end-of-day meals. *Good evening* is the common Southern salutation in the afternoon. ((Also Va., N. C. Popular. Also, reported from Tenn., La.)) EDD, LA.

fall off: *vb*. To lose weight. Ala., ((also elsewhere in the South)).

fire, to put fire to: *phr.* To burn up. "This evening we'll *put fire to* that pile of trash." Rabun Co., Ga.; ((also Va., N. C.)).

fit: pret. and p. p. of *fight.* Ala. ((Also Va., N. C., S. C. In Harnett Co., N. C.: *fought* [faʊt]. Uneducated.))

fix: *tr. vb.* To prepare (a meal): *fix breakfast*; equivalent of General American *get* in the same sense. Deep South. Common. ((Also other Southern states.)) LA.

fixing to ['fɪksn̩ tu]: In progressive tense system, followed by infinitive, an auxiliary. 1. Of immediate attention. About to, on the point of. "I was just *fixin'* to call on you." Ala. Popular colloquial. ((Also Va., N. C., upper S. C., Tenn.)) 2. Of more immediacy. "Look at that child! He's *fixin'* to fall!" Ala. Popular. ((Also Va., N. C., upper S. C., Tenn.)) LA.

flitting ['flɪtɪŋ, *not* -ɪn]: *n.* Interpretative dancing; courses in interpretative dancing. Alabama College slang of at least fifteen years' standing.

frog [froᵛg]: *n.* A toad. Ala. Common. ((Also other Southern states.)) LA.

get along: *vb.* "How are you *getting along*?" Common salutation of popular level in wide areas of the South. Low popular: "How ye *gittin' 'long*?" ((Also Va., N. C., upper S. C., mid. Tenn.)) LA.

grabble ['græbl̩, 'grævl̩]: *tr. vb.* To take a few potatoes from the hill without disturbing the rest. Cent. Ala. Rural. ((Also Va., N. C.)) Also *scratch* in same sense. Reported.

hey [heɪ]: *interj.* The common term of familiar salutation of children and young people in most of the South; *hello* seems to them either semiformal or archaic. On many Northern and Western campuses the term is *hi* [haɪ]. ((In Va., N. C.: [hɛ, heɪ].))

hog, since the hog et grandma (my little brother): Expressive of great amusement. "I haven't laughed so much *since the hog et grandma.*" Ala. Low popular. ((Also, reported from S. C.))

kind, some kind of: *adv.* Remarkably, extraordinarily. "She's *some kind of* smart." Phrase strongly stressed. N. C., Ala. Reported. ((Also Va.))

leave out of here: *phr.* To get out, leave. Ala. Low popular. Reported. ((Also Va., N. C., S. C., Tenn.))

light-bread: *n.* Yeast-raised wheat-bread in a loaf. 1940, Cather, *Sapphira and the Slave Girl*, 99: "Mrs. Blake will tell you how many loaves of *light bread* to bake." (Footnote to same: " '*Light*' *bread* meant bread of wheat flour, in distinction from corn bread.") Standard use over much of the South. LA.

light rolls: *n.* Yeast-raised rolls.

like: *intr. vb.* "You go to —— College? How do you *like*?" "I *like* fine." Ala., Ga., ((also Va., N. C.)).

like: after a number of verbs, such as *seem, look, feel, like* is felt as part of the verb; followed by clause without or (rarely) with *that.* "He was in a dreadful hurry, seemed *like*." " . . . until we feel *like* (*that*) we are traveling . . ." Used by many standard speakers in much of the South. ((Also Indiana. Farmers.))

little old ['lɪt lo, 'lɪl lo]: *adj.* Term of affection, derogation, or diminution—irrespective of age. Ala. Low popular. ((Also other Southern states.))

make (**out**) **like:** *phr.* To pretend, make it appear that. "Don't *make out like* you don't know me." Deep South, ((also Va., N. C., upper S. C.)). LA.

may can: *vb. phr.* May be able to. Treated as compound modal auxiliary. Preterit, usually preterit of speculation or unreality: *might could.* "I *may can* come tomorrow." "I *might could* get to it next week." Ala. Colloquial with some speakers. ((Also Va., N. C., S. C., Tenn.)) LA.

medinary ['midɪˌnɛrɪ, 'midn̩ˌɛrɪ]: *adj.* Of indifferent qualities; said of a horse or mule or crop, etc. Cent. Ala. Rural. Rare.

middlin' meat or **middlin':** *n.* The meat ((of the pig or hog)) between shoulder and haunch, hence the middle portion of the animal; "sow belly." 1940, Cather, *Sapphira and the Slave Girl*, 99: "You are to boil a ham and fry up plenty of *middling meat*." Va., cent. Ala., ((also N. C., upper S. C.)). LA.

might nigh ['maɪt 'naɪ]: *adv.* Very nearly, almost. Ala., ((also Va., N. C., upper S. C.)). Negro. Low popular. LA.

mind, to pay (me) **some** (any): *phr.* To give attention to (me). "I talked with enthusiasm, but he didn't *pay me any mind*." N. C., Ala., ((also Va., S. C., Tenn.)). LA.

misery ['mɪzrɪ]: *n.* Pain from rheumatism, arthritis, sciatica, etc. Over much of the South. Negro and older uneducated whites. ((Cf. Carlyle, *Past and Present*, I, iv:" . . . if we had Morrison's Pill . . . which men could swallow, . . . and then go on their old courses, cleared from all *miseries* and mischiefs.")) LA.

mort [mɔ(ə)t]: *n.* A quantity. 1941, Glasgow, *In This Our Life*, 317: "It was the blessed truth, Minerva reminded herself, that she had a *mort* of things to be thankful for." ((Va., N. C., Tenn.))

mule, suck-egged: Superlative of surprise or astonishment. "Well, I'll be a *suck-egged mule* . . . " Ala., Miss. Low popular. Reported. ((Cf. *suck-egg dog* in some sections of the South, a term of contempt.))

nervous salad: *n.* Any gelatine salad. Alabama College slang. In use for at least ten years.

on: *prep.* Substituted for *in* or *at* in some phrases; specifically, *ride on a car* (automobile) *sick on his stomach*. Dothan area, Ala., and probably other districts. Popular. Reported. LA.

one: *alternative pron.* Not followed by *or the other*, but with that meaning. "She will go home or to Florida, *one*." N. C., Ala., ((also Va., upper S. C.)). General.

overplus of food: *n.* Unneeded food that might be given away. Ala. Negro. Reported.

Pat, as long as Pat stayed in the army: Figurative for a very short time. Ala. Low popular. Reported. ((Also Va.))

piece: *n.* Part of the way. *Go (walk) a piece with* (someone): accompany (someone) part of the way. Deep South, parts of Mo., ((also Va., N. C., upper S. C.)). Popular. In some Southern states: *a piece-ways*. LA.

pig-trail: *n.* A side-road. Ala. Popular. Reported.

play like ['ple'laɪk, plaɪk]: *tr. vb.* A child's word. To play. ((To pretend.)) Used of imaginative games without rules. "Let's *play like* we're Indians." Ala. ((Also, reported from upper S. C.)) *Adj.* In play. 1940, McCullers, *The Heart Is a Lonely Hunter*, 114–115: "Freshmen in Vocational all dressed up for a real prom party and acting just like kids. It was half *play-like* and half not *playlike* at all."

proud: *adj.* Glad, pleased. Ala. Popular. EDD, LA.

pump-knot: *n.* A swelling, such as that produced—"pumped up"—by a bump or blow, or the sting of a bee or wasp. Rabun Co., Ga., in the Blue Ridge. Reported.

pup, pretty as a speckled pup under a red wagon (buggy): Very pretty. N. Ala. Reported. ((Also Va., N. C., S. C.))

rat: *n.* 1. A mouse. ((Most of the South.)) 2. A freshman, especially in some Southern colleges where hazing is permitted.

reckon [rɛkn̩], ((['rɛkn̩])) *tr. vb.* and *intrans. vb.* An equivalent of *think* in its loosest sense. "Reckon so?" = "Do you think so?" Over wide areas of the South. Generally colloquial. LA.

retch [rɛtʃ]: pret. and p. p. of *reach*. Deep South. Vulgar. ((Also other Southern states.))

rising: *n.* A boil. Ala., ((also other Southern states)). General lay term. OED, EDD. LA.

roasting-ear [ˈroᵘstn̩ˌɪə] ((in Va., N. C. [ˈrosnjɛə])): *n.* Ear of green corn, well filled out and suitable for cooking, chiefly by boiling, served with the grain on the ear. ((Still roasted in Va. and N. C. in hot ashes, over hot coals, in a stove, or in the "flue" or the "furnace" of the tobacco barn.)) Over much of the South. Popular. LA.

salat [ˈsælɪt]: *n.* Cooked greens, as *turnip salat*. Cent. Va. Turnip greens. Rabun Co., Ga. Somewhat archaic. ((Also Va., N. C., S. C., Tenn.)) LA.

scrouge [skraᵘdʒ]: *tr. vb.* To crowd, pack together, squeeze into or out of. "He just *scrouged* them into the wagon." "They *scrouged* me out of the bus." E. cent. Ala.; Rabun Co., Ga.; n. Miss. Popular. ((Also Va., N. C., S. C.)) [skrutʃ, skrudʒ]: *intr. vb.* To squeeze into small space, crouch. Used chiefly of people, with *up* or *down* indicating posture. 1940, McCullers, *The Heart Is a Lonely Hunter*, 167: "Father, you been *scrouched* over that desk since five o'clock." Negro: *ibid.*, 179. The distinction between pronunciation and meaning is not clearly maintained. Rabun Co., Ga.; e. cent. Ala.; n. Miss. Rural. Popular. LA.

shut-mouth: *n.* One who says little about his own or others' personal affairs. Ala. ((Common in South.)) Popular.

smart, right: *adj.* Long, large, extensive. "It's a right smart distance to town." Deep South, ((other Southern states)). Popular.

snuck [snʌk]: pret. and p p. of *sneak*. Ala. Low popular. ((Obsolescent in Va., N. C.; often used jocosely by the educated. Also, reported from S. C., Tenn., La.))

sobby [ˈsɑbɪ]: *adj.* Soggy, heavy, underdone. Said of biscuit, bread, pie-crust, cake. Corruption of *soggy*? "I do want a biscuit cooked quick; if there's anything I can't stand, it's an old *sobby* biscuit." Cent. Ala. Negro ((also whites)). ((Also Va., N. C., S. C., Tenn. In Va., N. C.: *sobbing, sobbing wet*. Wet; that is, heavy from being wet. "My feet are *sobbing wet*." "That log in the pond is right *sobby*.")) LA.

sorry [ˈsɑrɪ] ((frequently [ˈsɒrɪ])): *adj.* Inferior, of low quality or standard; squalid. A *sorry crop*, or *mule*, or *carpenter*, etc.; a *sorry sight.* Frequently combined with *looking:* a *sorry-looking nag.* Ala., sections of Mo. ((very common in the South)). Colloquial. General. EDD.

sow belly: *n.* Pork from the belly or sides of the animal, fried or used to cook with vegetables. Negro, vulgar white. LA.

sparrow-hawk, weak as a sparrow-hawk sitting on a pole: Figurative for very weak. Ala. Low popular.

stoop: *n.* The steps of a porch. S. and cent. Ala. ((In some parts of Texas: a porch. Reported from S. C.: a small roofless porch at the back of a house.)) LA.

stop by: *vb.* To stop in passing by, to call for. Over wide areas of the South. General colloquial.

sure is [ʃoˈɪz]: It certainly is. Term of assent. Deep South. Negro. Low popular.

swole [swol]: pret. and p. p. of *swell.* Deep South. Low popular. ((Also, reported from S. C., Tenn.)) LA.

taken: pret. of *take.* Franklin Co., Tenn. Rural. (("The Editor feels that this form is one that is imported into a dialect district," a comment on an edited draft sent to Dr. Dennis some months ago. To this she replied: "I would classify the use as a mountain use, not an illiteracy. . . . . I am not suggesting that you remove your editorial comment. I think that it may produce some interesting information." See Hays's list.))

the, sick in the bed: *idiom.* Other American dialects omit the article. Ala. General.

till, until: *conj.* with degree-result clauses. " . . . the necessity of the peasants' working so hard *till* they almost drop." Deep South. Up to high popular level. ((Also, reported from upper S. C., mid. Tenn.))

toad-frog: *n.* 1. A tree-toad. Marshall Co., Ala.; sections of Mo. 2. Almost any kind of toad or frog except the bullfrog. (Also *toady-frog.*) Deep South. LA.

tote [toᵘt]: *tr. vb.* 1. To carry with effort. E. and cent. Va., N. C.; rated vulgar in Ala. 2. *tr. vb.* or *intr. vb.* To take home (left-overs of food). Said of the practice of some Negro servants, permitted or not. LA.

toting: *n.* The practice of taking home food from the employer's kitchen. "I don't allow *toting,* remember." ((In a number of Southern states.))

tough: *vb.* with impersonal object. "It was hard for him, but he *toughed it* out." ((In a number of Southern states.))

trod: pret. form of *tread* used for the present. "Do not *trod* on the grass." Cent. and n. Ala. Occasional high popular.

try to: *vb.* To be on the point of, about to. Followed by infinitive auxiliary of near future without idea of intention. "Look at that girl's arms; she's trying to catch pneumonia." Ala. Popular colloquial. ((The Editor has heard the expression used in an ironical rebuking sense: Va., N. C., S. C., Tenn.))

wait on: *vb.* Equivalent of General English *wait for.* Ala., ((also Va., N. C., S. C., Tenn., La.)). High popular. LA.

wa'n't [wɑnt]: ((Contraction of *was* + *not* and, by analogy, *were* + *not.*)) Ala. Used even by some high popular speakers. ((Also mid. and e. Va. and N. C. Common. [wont] more frequent than [wɑnt]. Also, reported from upper S. C., mid. Tenn., N. E.)) LA.

washwoman: *n.* A washerwoman. Ala., ((also Va., N. C., upper S. C., Ga., Miss., Tenn.)).

week, (Tuesday) (a) week: A week from the following (Tuesday). Over much of the South. Standard. LA.

week, (Tuesday) was a week ago; or a week ago (Tuesday): "The first time I came to see you, *Tuesday was a week ago,* you were away." Ga., Ala., ((also S. C.)). Popular. LA.

white-eye: *intr. vb.* To become exhausted, to faint from exhaustion. "I almost *white-eyed.*" Ala. Rural. Sometimes used by standard speakers jocularly. Reported. ((In Va., N. C.: *white-eye,* strong whisky.))

white-eyed: *adj.* 1. Greatly fatigued, utterly worn out. "I came out just *white-eyed.*" ((Also, reported from upper S. C.)) 2. Severely frightened (descriptive of a Negro). Ala., ((also Va., N. C.)). Popular.

white meat: *n.* Fat salt pork, the best of "sow belly." Ala. Negro and white. Up to standard use. LA.

you-all, ((**y'all, y'all's**)) [jɔᵛl, 'juɔl, ju'ɔl, jɔlz]: *pron.,* sec. per. pl. Colloq. You. When addressed to one person, one or more others of the family or associates are implied. Genitive: *you-all's.* "Did *y'all* put *y'all's* books in *y'all's* desks?" Over most of the South. General. Popular. LA.

B. PRONUNCIATION

a [ʌ] (too stressed for a mere [ə]): Frequent substitution for *an* before vowels: *a egg, a orange, a adjective.* Ala. and elsewhere in the South. Negroes and whites up sometimes to a high popular level. LA.

all right [ɑ: 'raɪt]: Pronunciation in Ala. and Tenn. General equivalent of *yes, very well.*

Baptist ['bæbtɪs(t)]: Pronunciation of most members of the Baptist denomination and of large numbers of others throughout the South.

been [bɛn]: Pronunciation of most of those who substitute [ɪ] for [ɛ]. Ala., Miss. High popular. LA.

chimney ['tʃɪmlɪ] ((in some other sections of the South ['tʃɪmblɪ])): Rabun Co., Ga., in Blue Ridge. Popular. LA.

great [grɛt] (at least when followed by *big*): Ne. Miss. ((Also Va., N. C. Frequent. Also, reported from upper S. C., mid. Tenn.))

help [hɛp]: Evidently the same tendency that dropped the *l* in *calf, half, stalk, walk,* etc., in standard English. Ala., ((also Va., N. C.)). Popular, of a level little above low popular. LA.

hotel ['hotɛl]: Frequent pronunciation of standard speakers, especially in black belt. Ga., Ala. ((Also Va., N. C., S. C., Tenn., La. Less common than formerly.)) LA.

idea ['aɪdɪə]: Frequent pronunciation of many standard speakers, especially in black belt. ((Va.)), N. C., S. C., Ga., Ala. LA.

insurance ['ɪnʃʊrəns]: Frequent pronunciation of many standard speakers, especially in black belt. Ga., Ala. ((also, reported from upper S. C., Tenn., La.)).

Mrs. ['mɪɪz, 'mɪzɪz]: Pronunciations of the title of married women used by many, if not most, Southerners. ['mɪɪz] is more common in Ala., even among standard speakers. ((In s. Va. and n. N. C.: [mɪz] among old persons, ['mɪzɪz] among young persons.)) LA.

theater [θi'etə, -ɚ, 'θi'etə, -ɚ]: Widely used, but usually willingly changed to the standard pronunciation of other American dialects. Ala. ((Second pronunciation common in Va., N. C.)) LA.

umbrella ['ʌmbrɛlə]: Frequent pronunciation of standard speakers, especially in black belt. Ga., Ala., etc. LA. ((Also Va., N. C. low speech [ˌʌmbə'rɪlə].))

yes'm [jɛhm, jæhm]: Ala. Negro; sometimes used by young whites of fairly high speech level. ((Also Va., N. C.; and Negro ['jɛbm̩, 'jæbm̩, jæm].)) LA.

yonder ['jændɚ]: Pronunciation of Civil War generation. Rabun Co., Ga. Reported. LA. ((Va., N. C. ['hjɑndə, 'çɑndə].))

[ɪ] for [ɛ], especially before or after [n]: *general, Wednesday, any, pen, nest* ['dʒɪnɚ], 'wɪnzdɪ, 'mɪ, pɪn, nɪs(t)]. Parts of Ga., Ala., Miss., etc., on into e. Texas, Dallas, Fort Worth areas.

L A. [ju] for [u], in *too, to, do*, etc. Mobile area, Ala.

r before consonants and final: *forty, hunter*, etc. ['fɔrtɪ, 'hʌntɚ]. Sounded in the speech of those native to Rabun Co., Ga., in the Blue Ridge. This is contrary to the much more general Southern dropping of the r in those sections. ((R is generally pronounced in the Southern mountainous sections.))

II. A WORD-LIST FROM THE SOUTHERN HIGHLANDS

JOSIAH COMBS

Texas Christian University

The words and sayings in this list should be examined in the light in which they were written—not for any group of persons primarily interested in the higher study of langugage but for persons interested in the intelligent popular study of language. Dr. Combs has kindly allowed the Editor to select these words and sayings from an unfinished manuscript of his, *The Language of Our Southern Highlanders.*—The Editor

A. GLOSSARY

Adam's-apple: *n.* The Indian turnip or jack-in-the-pulpit, known for its acrid, pungent taste.

ant-bug: *n.* The ant. A survival of the O. E. fondness for compounds.

antic ['æntɪk]: *n.* and *adj.* Given to fun, capers, pranks. "Old Lige is feeble, but he's plum' *antic.*" Cf. Shakespeare, *Hamlet,* I, v, 172: "To put an *antic* disposition on"; *Richard II,* III, ii, 162: " . . . and there the *antic* [clown] sits"; Dryden, Intro. to *Annus Mirabilis:* "*antic* gestures"; *The Medal:* "*antic* sights"; Milton, *Samson Agonistes:* "Juglers and Dancers, *Antics,* Mummers, Mimics."

antigodlin, antigoglin, antisigodlin ['æntɪˌgɑdlɪn, -gɑg-, -saɪ-]: *adj.* Out of plumb or square, slanting. ((See Missouri list.))

aporn ['epǝn]: *n.* Metathesized form of *apron.* Sanctioned by ((Thomas)) Cooper, along with *childern, hunderd, Kathern,* etc.

atwixt: *prep.* and *adv.* Between. Cf. Chaucer, *Romance of the Rose:* "Great love was *atwixt* hem two"; Spenser, *Faerie Queene:* "With dreadful thunder and lightning *atwixt.*"

ben-hicky-my-funker: *n.* A term of disparagement. "He's a pyore *ben-hicky-my-funker.*" Also *hicky-my-funker.*

bereft: *adj.* Crazy, "touched." "Air ye plum' *bereft,* ye fool!"

bilin' ['baɪlɪn]: *n.* Crowd; "the whole *bilin'.*" ((Cf. *the whole kit and bilin',* and *the whole kit and boodle.* Common in the South.)) LA.

17

-bird : part of comp. *n.* Redundantly used after the names of birds : *spar'-bird*, *wren-bird*, etc.

bread-jerker : *n.* The projection formed by the thyroid cartilage in the neck ; the "Adam's apple."

brickle : *adj.* Brittle. Cf. Spenser, *Faerie Queene*: "But being faire and *brickle*, likest glasse seeme."

brouse [brauz]: *vb.* To cohabit.

bunkum-back : *n.* Hog, pig. Heard in the old riddle :

> "I went over to the world of Whickum-Whack,
> And there I saw a *bunkum-back*;
> I took Tom-Tickum-Tack [his dog]
> And run *bunkum-back*
> Out of the world of Whickum-Whack."

bussy ['bʌsɪ]: *n.* Sweetheart. Evidently derived from *buss.* LA.

call, to hev (have) **a :** *phr.* To intend, to have a mind to. "I *hev a call* to go to town today."

chitlins : *n.* The hands.

clark [klɑrk]: *n.* and *vb.* A clerk ; to clerk.

cock : *n.* ((Pudenda muliebra.)) Always a vulgar term among the highlanders, no matter what it is used for. In the vulgar sense, it is always applied to females, never to males, as in England. ((Cf. *cock*, §20, OED = penis.))

cuckol ['kʌkəl]: *vb.* To deceive or prove unfaithful to (in marital relations). It is used only of women. "Well, I hear Samp's wife has *cuckoled* him." Unknown as a noun. (Earlier French form is *coucuol.*)

cud [kʊd]: *n.* ((Same pronunciation in Guilford Co. and a few other counties in N. C.))

cumoldiction [kɪumɑl'dɪk ʃən]: *n.* A curiosity, something unusual.

cumoldictious [kɪumɑl'dɪk ʃəs]: *adj.* Curious, unusual.

darnful : *adj.* Gloomy, mournful, lugubrious.

dew-claws : *n.* Claws, feet. "Jud rared [reared] back on his *dew-claws* and struck at Lonzo."

diamont ['daɪmənt]: *n.* This pronunciation occurs in Jonson's *The Magnetic Lady*: "Yes, here's a *Diamont* of some threescore pound." ((Cf. also Chaucer, *R. of R.*, 4385: "Have herte as hard as *diamaunt*."))

draft: *n.*   A brook or small stream.

drinlin: *adj.*   Puny, ailing.

duck butter: *n.*   Smegma.   ((In s. Va.: *gnat-bread.*))

dulcimore ['dʌlsɪˌmor]: *n.*   Variant of *dulcimer*, a native harp of the highlands; it has nothing in common with the classic dulcimer, resembling rather an ancient, oriental psaltery.

ferro ['fɛro]: *n.*   The locust.   Variant of *Pharaoh?*

gism ['dʒɪzəm]: *n.*   Semen.   ((Also Va., N. C., upper S. C.))

give-out: *n.*   An announcement.   "I hyerd no *give-out* about it."   ((Also, reported from upper S. C.))

gritted bread: *n.*   Grated bread, made from the ears of corn half-hardened.

gritter ['grɪtɚ]: *n.*   Grater for grating corn.

hamestring, to bust a: *phr.*   To make a supreme effort.   Cf. Fr. "Après un bon coup de collier."

hand-goin': *adv.*   One after another.   Same as *hand-runnin'*. "Mace's Jim sot up with [courted] Nance's Liz two nights hand-goin'."

iron and deft: *n.*   Pots, pans, and dishes.

jape [dʒep]: *vb.*   To cohabit, copulate.   Related to M. E. *jape*, "to jest, mock, cheat, ((play))"?   ((*Jazz* reported from e. N. C. and upper S. C. as having same meaning.))

joggle: *vb.*   To walk along slowly and aimlessly.   Variant of *jog.*

joree-bird ['dʒori-]: *n.*   The chewink, of the towhee or sparrow family.

kiljackums ['kɪldʒækəmz]: *n.*   Slang for sorghum molasses.

Kukluck ['kɪuklʌk]: *n.* and *vb.*   An organization originating from the Kuklux Klan of post Civil War days.   Its purpose is to flog husbands who are unfaithful to their wives.

meal's victuals: *n.*   A meal, repast.   Also *meal o'victuals.*   Cf. *Piers Plowman:* "*meales* mete."

methought: *vb.*   I thought.   This old form is rare, but is still heard here and there.   *Methinks* is not heard.

mimic: *vb.*   To resemble in appearance.   "He *mimics* his cousin a sight."   LA.

mountain oysters: *n.*   Testicles of the boar, the bull, ((or the sheep)), whenever the highland gourmet partakes of these delicacies at the table.   Heard also in Texas, ((Va., N. C., S. C., Tenn.)).

of: *prep.*   1. With. "What's the matter *of* that child?"   Cf.:
> "She was most fair and handsome,
> Blue eyes and curly hair;
> There ain't no one in this wide world
> *Of* her I can compare."
>   —Old Folk Song

2. Used redundantly with transitive verbs. Cf.:
> "I will not go to old Jo Clark's,
> I'll tell you the reason why,
> I will not go to old Jo Clark's,
> A-stealing *of* his rye."
>   —*Old Jo Clark*

Cf. also Henry VII's private account book, Aug. 9, 1497: "To John Vandelf for garnyshing *of* a salett."   In Roger Ascham one plays *of* an instrument.   Cf. Fr. "jouer *du* piano."

Old Christmas: *n.*   January 6.   Still observed here and there in spite of the changes which took place with the introduction of the Gregorian calendar.   On the eve of Old Christmas, at midnight, the elder is said to blossom, cows to kneel in prayer, and the cock to crow all night.   ((Still observed in some parts of e. N. C.))

one o'clock (etc.): A euphemistic hint that one's trousers are unbuttoned one (etc.) button(s).   "Hit's *one o'clock*, Rafe."

oxen: *n.*   Ox. The plural is *oxens*. *Ox* is not common. ((Also Guilford Co., N. C.))   LA.

pepper: *n.*   To beat, strike.   Cf. Shakespeare, *I Henry IV*, II, iv: "I have *peppered* two of them."

pernady [pɚˈnedɪ]: *n.*   A dish prepared with bread crumbs and sorghum, and placed in the oven to heat or brown.

pindling [ˈpɪndlɪŋ]: *adj.*   Ailing, weak; said of children.

plumgranny [ˈplʌmgrænɪ]: *n.*   Pomegranate.   ((Also, reported from upper S. C., Tenn.))

poppy doll: *n.*   (From Fr. *poupée*, "doll.")   A home-made rag doll.   Also *poppet doll.*

possum: *vb.*   To pout, sulk; from sulking of the opossum.

prick: *n.*   Vulgarism for *penis.*   ((Formerly standard; cf. OED, §17.   Also Va., N. C., S. C., upper Tenn., Ala., La., etc.))

pursue: *vb.*   To go on, run away.   "Keep on *pursuin'*, and they won't git ye."

race: *n.*   (From O. Fr. *rais*, "root.")   A small quantity, or root (of ginger). "Can I borry a *race* o' ginger?" It is heard now only in *race*-ginger, that is, ginger in the root, not ground.

red'nin'-comb, redd-comb: *n.* (From Scot. *red,* "to rid.") The ordinary long comb for combing women's hair. *Red'nin'* for *redding,* or *ridding* (of lice), originally, for which the fine-comb or "gray-back" chaser is now used.

rumpityfetida ['rʌmpɪtɪ,fɪtɪdɪ]: *n.* Asafetida—and a more polite word than the latter!

shag [ʃæɪg]: *vb.* To copulate. ((Also, reported from upper S. C.))

soojet ['suədʒɛt]: *n.* A sack, pouch.

squinty: *vb.* To squint, as in *squinty-eyed.* Cf. Shakespeare, *King Lear,* IV, vi, 140: "I remember thine eyes well enough. Dost thou *squiny* at me?"

start: *adv.* Entirely, completely. "Look yander, that youngun is *start* necked!" The word is not a variant of *stark;* cf. E. E. "*steort* nakit."

strut-fart: *n.* One who struts around, highly conscious of his own importance. Cf. the French "Il *pète* plus haut qu'il n'a le derrière" ("He tries to fart louder than his 'bum' permits him").

suddent(ly): With excrescent *t,* for *sudden(ly).*

talk to: *vb.* To woo, court. Regan, in *King Lear,* uses the expression in a similar way.

tetchified: *adj.* Choleric, fretful. Also *tetchious.* ((Also Va., N. C., S. C.))

this: *adv.* Used intensively for *jist* (*just*). "I *this* know it's so." ((Is this an example of faulty substitution in restressing, the unstressed form of *this* and *jis*(*t*) being *'is* [ɪs]?))

tidolodeum [tɪdo'lodjəm]: *n.* Anything infinitesimal in size; for example, "one of those little things that gets on a chigger's hind foot and bites it!"

twitchet: *n.* Pudenda muliebria.

ujinctum [ju'dʒɪŋktəm]: *n.* Hell (used with the definite article). "You ought to be in the *ujinctum!*"

use: *vb.* To frequent (for food, forage, etc., of animals). "Squirrels are *usin'* in that tree." Cf. Fletcher:

> "I will give thee for food
> No fish that *useth* in the mud";

Ben Jonson, *Every Man in His Humor*: "Hee *useth* every day to the Merchant's house."

usen: *n.* and *vb.*   Use; to use.

vasty: *adj.* Vast.   Cf. Shakespeare, *I Henry IV*, III, i, 52: "I can call spirits from the *vasty* deep."

we-eruses: *pron.*   We.

wher [hwɜ]: *conj.*   Whether.   Cf. Ben Jonson, *The New Inn*: "I know not *wher* I am, or no, or speake."

wolves: *pl. n.*   Bots or warbles in the backs of cows ((or rabbits and squirrels)), caused supposedly by sprinkling salt on the cows' backs.

wound [waʊnd]: *n.*   Wound.   ((Also, reported from upper S. C., mid. Tenn.   Mainly old people.))   LA.

yagger ['jægɚ]: *vb.*   To cavil.   "Oh, I wouldn't *yagger* about a little thing like that."

B. FIGURES AND IDIOMS

Self-brag is half scandal.

Gi' down and show your saddle.   ((In Va.: "Light and look at your saddle."))

She was born in the middle of the week, a-looking both ways for Sunday.   (She is cross-eyed.)

Drat that brat!   He's athwart of everything he runs afoul of. (He meddles with everything.)

I'll give you the next dime I find rollin' up the hill.

You can have the first nickel I find in a sheep's track.

It's as crooked as a dog's hind legs.

He batted his eyes like a toad in a hailstorm.

She was at him like a bitin' sow.

The devil's apron-string broke loose in that field.   (It is very rocky there.)

The old woman's a-pickin' her geese.   (It is snowing.)

That's the tune the old cow died on.   (Any quick, short tune or "quick-and-devilish" air; or any tune badly played.   The figure seems also to have been known among the Elizabethans, and derived from an old song of the time.)   ((The Editor has heard in s. Va. and n. N. C. the same saying but with *of* instead of the earlier form *on*.))

He don't know B from bull's foot.   ((He is ignorant.))

We'll just put the big pot in the little one.   (That is, we will look around and find something to eat, or "snack" on.)   ((In Va., upper S. C.: To provide a very big and good meal for visitors, usually those unexpected.))

He's mean enough to steal a dime from a dead man's eye. (It was once customary in the highlands to place a dime on each eye of a dead person, when he was "laid out," to hold the lids closed.) ((In s. Va.: " . . . offn a dead Nigger's eye."))

They planted the corn before they built the fence. (They had a child soon after they were married.) ((In s. Va.: "They ate before they said grace."))

I'm as gaily as a buck. ((Feeling in excellent spirits.))

I aim fer to give ye a piece of my mind! (The Bishop of London writes to Lord Burleigh, in 1572: "Thus am I bolde to unfolde a peece of my mynde on the sudden.") ((Common in a number of Southern states.))

Jace laid the revenue officer on the coolin'-board. (He killed the officer.)

He tuk his foot in his hand and lit out fer home.

She ain't got sense enough to grease a gimlet.

He lit a shuck through the woods. (He ran fast.)

Melissy is now in the rise of her bloom. (That is, she has arrived at womanhood.)

He come outn the leetle eend o' the horn. (He was unsuccessful in a deal or trade.)

Maggie's been called to straw. (That is, she is pregnant, in her "lying-in" period.)

III. A WORD-LIST FROM BUNCOMBE COUNTY, NORTH CAROLINA

HUGH C. LAUGHLIN

New York City

In 1918–22 my family was living in Asheville ((Buncombe County)), North Carolina; and I spent each summer there. While reading Horace Kephart's *Our Southern Highlanders*, I was struck by the large number of dialect expressions recorded by Kephart which were also current in the community of my boyhood, Logan and Hardin counties, Ohio. Naturally, my knowledge of mountain speech is relatively limited, and I have not the least doubt that there are many more words and phrases common to the two localities than those I have sent in. ((Mr. Laughlin sent in a large number of interesting words, but the more common words and those having no particular point have been omitted in this list.))

I have a theory as to this parallelism of dialect; I give it for what it is worth. Mr. Kephart and some other writers hold that most mountaineers are descendants of Scotch and Irish settlers who were compelled to locate in the mountains while on their migration westward. The great majority of the residents of my native locality were of the same stock. I recall offhand the following names in Ohio: McLain, McPherson, McCartney, McClure, McClurg, McKinnon, McNeil, Sloan, Henry, Clark, Wilson, Aiken, Milligan, Wallace, Ramsey, Nelson, Lynch, Stewart, Anderson, Wylie, Morton, Jeffers—and Laughlin. These families dominated the religious, political, and social spheres of the community. There were no fewer than three Presbyterian churches in our village of 750, one "straight," one "United," and one "Reformed" ("Covenanter"); and in a hamlet of one hundred or less, three miles away, there were two Reformed Presbyterian churches.

A. DIALECT WORDS COMMON TO LOGAN COUNTY, OHIO, AND BUNCOMBE COUNTY, NORTH CAROLINA

act up: *vb.* To misbehave. "Why did she *act up* when the preacher was here?"

amen corner: *n.* That part of the church where seekers kneel at a revival.

bare-naked: *adj.* Naked.

bobble: *n.* A mistake, especially a slight mistake.

24

broom-stick, to jump over the: *phr.* To get married. (In some sections: common-law marriage.))

caigy ['kedʒɪ]: *adj.* Cautious. In Ohio: inflamed with sexual desire.

chunk of a boy: *n.* A "right good-sized boy."

coon: *vb.* To pilfer; not applied to serious thefts. "Let's go and *coon* some watermelons."

dauncy ['dɔnsɪ]: *adj.* In Ohio: qualmish, slightly unwell; in N. C.: squeamish, fastidious.

dingus: *n.* A small article.

dog-pelter: *n.* A term of contempt; an officer of extremest inconsequence. My father used to say: "I wouldn't vote for a Democrat for a *dog-pelter*." ((Maristan?)) Chapman heard a mountaineer say: "Sech a unhuman man couldn't get my vote for a *dog-pelter*."

fasset ['fæsɛt]: *n.* A faucet.

fer why: *adv.* Why. "He went down town, I don't know *fer why*." ((Cf. Browning, *The Ring and the Book*, VII, 1059: "Who made and sang the rimes about me once! *For why?*"))

ferninst: *prep.* Opposite to; against.

gramp [græmp]: *n.* Grandfather.

hindside first: *adv.* Backwards. "You've put that neck-yoke *hindside first*."

job [dʒɑb]: *vb.* To jab.

lunk-head: *n.* A dolt.

mollygrubs, to have: *phr.* To be slightly unwell or upset; to have the blues. In N. C.: *mullygrubs*.

morfadite ['mɔrfɪˌdaɪt]: *n.* A hermaphrodite.

neighbor: *vb.* To exchange labor with, as in harvest time.

nose out of joint, to have (one's): *phr.* To be in a bad humor. "John Cable's sulkin' 'round with his *nose out of joint*." ((In some parts of the South has reference to a child who is ill-pleased because a brother or sister has just been born, who may secure the attention the child has enjoyed.))

patchin', not a patchin' to: *n.* No comparison with. "Your dog *ain't a patchin' ter* mine."

play-party: *n.* A party where dancing games are played to the singing of the participants. This is to get around the church's ban on dancing. The devil was seemingly in the fiddle. "Weevilly Wheat" was a song common to both sections.

pollyfox: *vb.* To dilly-dally; to waste time.

set up with: *vb.* To court. "Where you says 'makin' a call' on a gal, we says 'settin' up with.' "—John Fox, Jr. ((Used in some parts of the South to mean sitting at a wake. See Williams's list.))

skiff: *n.* A light snow-fall. In N. C.: *skift.*

slam: *adv.* Directly and violently. "He hit *slam* against that tree."

slap-bang: *adv.* Same as *slam.*

slow-poke: *n.* A dilatory person.

smack-dab: *adv.* Squarely, exactly. "I hit him *smack-dab* in the face."

snaps: *n.* String beans.

sooky ['sʊkɪ]: *n.* In N. C.: a cow; in Ohio: a term used in calling cows.

steady by jerks: *adj.* and *adv. phr.* In an uneven manner.

step off: *vb.* To get married. In N. C.: *to step off the carpet.*

stout: *adj.* In good health.

troft [trɔft]: A *trough.*

wait on: *vb.* To court. "I hear that Jim Nelson is *waiting on* Florence."

B. ADDITIONAL DIALECT WORDS COMMON TO LOGAN COUNTY, OHIO, AND BUNCOMBE COUNTY, NORTH CAROLINA, LISTED IN ONE OR MORE DICTIONARIES

beal [bil]: *vb.* To suppurate.

bee-gum: *n.* A sawed-off portion of the hollow trunk of a tree ((frequently the gum)) used as a beehive. ((Cf. *rabbit-gum.*))

being: *conj.* Since, because. "*Being* I can't go with him, I won't wait."

belly-button: *n.* The navel.

bread: *vb.* To provide bread for. "I raised jest enough wheat *to bread* my family."

church: *vb.* To expel from membership in a church. "They *churched* Bill fer fornication."

daylights: *n.* The eyes. "I'll beat the *daylights* out of him." ((In some parts of Va.: the lungs.))

dead'nin': *n.* A clearing made in a forest by girdling the trees.

do-less: *adj.* Shiftless.

doty ['dotɪ]: *adj.* Doted; applied to timber ((or persons whose mind is "tetched")).

flummixed: *adj.* Excited, bewildered.

> **hickory shirt:** *n.* A calico or gingham ((work)) shirt.

holt: *n.* A hold. "I got a good *holt* of him."

hopping mad: *adj.* Very angry.

infare ['mfær,-ə]: *n.* A reception at the bridegroom's house after the marriage.

light down: *vb.* To alight. "*Light down* and take grub." ((In s. Va.: "*Light* and look at your saddle."))

piece: *n.* A minx. "Sal is surely a *piece*."

rambunctious: *adj.* Full of energy. ((In s. Va.: sexual.))

redd up: *vb.* To put in order, as a room.

rip: *n.* An evil-minded woman.

No! a shirt made of 'hickory shirting,' a heavy cotton material having even blue and white stripes —

IV. A WORD-LIST FROM THE MOUNTAINS OF KENTUCKY AND NORTH CAROLINA

CRATIS D. WILLIAMS

Appalachian State Teachers College

booger ['bʊgɚ]: *n.* A demon with which to frighten children; not to be confused with the devil or Satan. Big Sandy Valley, Ky. Common. ((Also, reported from N. C., S. C., Tenn., La. Reported from some parts of N. C.: *n.* and *vb.* The act of sodomy, to commit sodomy.))

bring [breŋ]: *tr. vb.* Usual meaning. Illustrates a pronunciation of *i* in many monosyllabic words ending in *-ing.* Other examples are: *ring, sing, thing, wing.* E. Ky., w. N. C. Rural. Common.

buryin' ['bʌrɪən, 'bærɪən]: *n.* Burial. "Air you goin' to the *buryin'*?" Common. LA.

care [kjɪr]: *n.* and *vb.* Usual meaning. Wautauga Co., N. C. Common. [kjɛr]: E. Ky. Common. LA.

chair [tʃɪr]: *n.* Usual meaning. Wautauga Co., N. C. Common. [tʃer]: E. Ky. Common. LA.

character [ˌkæˈrɛktɚ] ((in some other sections of the South [ˌkjæˈræktə])): *n.* Usual meaning. E. Ky.; Wautauga Co., N. C. Children of rural areas. Common.

clart [klɑrt]: *n.* and *vb.* Feces; to defecate. E. Ky. Rare.

clever: *adj.* Hospitable, polite. "He's the *cleverest* man about his house at all." E. Ky.; Wautauga Co., N. C. Common. LA.

conversation ['kɑnfɚˌseʃən]: *n.* Usual meaning. Wautauga Co., N. C. School children. Rare.

cow [kjɛə]: *n.* Usual meaning. "I haf to melk the *keow.*" ((Note *haf* and *melk.*)) E. Ky.; Wautauga Co., N. C. Common. LA.

coward [kærd]: *n.* Usual meaning. E. Ky.; Wautauga Co., N. C. Common. [kjɑrd]: E. Ky. Rare.

desire [dɪˈzɑr]: *n.* Usual meaning. Wautauga Co., N. C. Heard at Masonic meeting. Common.

diamond ['dɑɪmənt]: *n.* Usual meaning. Wautauga Co., N. C. Rare. E. Ky. Rural. Common.

dido, to cut a: *phr.* To have a fit of anger or drunkenness, or to show any uncommon behavior. "Your pa'll *cut a dido* when he finds out about this." ((Also: *to cut up didoes*. Both expressions occur in a number of Southern states.))

ding-dong: *tr. vb.* To annoy. "He jist *ding-dongs* his pa till he gits whatever he wants out of him." E. Ky. Common. ((In some parts of Va. and N. C.: the penis.))

djuke [dʒuk]: *tr. vb.* To incline or duck. "He *djuked* his head and looked right at the ground." E. Ky. Common.

drotted, dratted, drattet ['drɑtəd, 'drætəd, 'drætət]: *n.* Diminutive oath for "God rotted." E. Ky. Common.

dubious ['dʒubɚəs]: *adj.* Dubious. E. Ky.; Wautauga Co., N. C. Common.

. **dudab, dudad** ['du'dæb, 'du'dæd]: *n.* A frill; a fussy ornament; a "monkey-shine." "What's that little *dudab* for?" "What's that little *dudab* that hangs down at the back of the mouth?" Ky. Common. ((Also, reported from S. C.))

eedient ['idɪənt]: *n.* Idiot. E. Ky. Rural. Common.

fire [fɑr]: *n.* and *vb.* Usual meaning. E. Ky.; Wautauga Co., N. C. Common. ((Elsewhere in South. Uneducated. Common. Cf. also other monosyllables or stressed syllables having [ɑɪ] or [aɪ] before *r: desire, hire, liar, mire, retire, tire*.))

flitter ['flɪtɚ]: *n.* Pudenda muliebria. E. Ky. Rural. Common.

flour, flower [flær]: *n.* Usual meanings. Wautauga Co., N. C. Common. LA.

guy: *tr. vb.* To tease. Wautauga Co., N. C. ((Also other Southern states.)) Common.

hayshant ['he:ʃənt]: *n.* A rascal; an annoying child. "Get out of this kitchen and leave them pies alone, you little *hayshant*." E. Ky. Rare. (Perhaps derived from *Hessian*, since most of the people of e. Ky. are descended from Revolutionary War soldiers who "settled" on land grants. ((For further information on *Hessian*, see Paul G. Brewster's "A Note on the Epithet 'Hessian,'" *American Speech*, XVIII, 72-3; and E[lliott] V. K. D[obbie]'s "A Further Note on 'Hessian,'" *ibid.*, 310.))

heard [hjɪrd, hjɛrd]: pret. and p. p. of *heard*. Usual meaning. E. Ky.; Boone, N. C. Children. Common. LA.

hootentrankis ['hutən'træŋkəs]: *n.* A queer little fixture of some kind. "What's this little *hootentrankis* down on the steering wheel for?" E. Ky. Rare.

jig: *n.* Pudenda muliebria. E. Ky. Common.

lairs [lɑrz]: *n.* Plenty. "They wuz *lairs* of poplar timber in these here woods when I wuz a boy." E. Ky. Rare.

lay a corpse: *phr.* Idiom used to describe the wake for the dead body. "All the fam'bly gethered in when he *lay a corpse.*" E. Ky. Common. ((Also, reported from upper S. C.))

lookin' to die: *phr.* To be dangerously ill; to be on the point of death. "We are a-goin' to set up with Aint Hanner. She is *a-lookin' to die.*" E. Ky.

milk [mjɪək, mɛlk]: *n.* Usual meaning. Wautauga Co., N. C.; e. Ky. Common.

mullygrubs ['mʌlɪ'grʌbz]: *n.* Despondency. "He's in the *mullygrubs* this morning." E. Ky. Common.

obstacle [ɑb'stækəl] ((in s. Va.: ['ɑbstɪk(ə)l])): *n.* Usual meaning. E. Ky.; Wautauga Co., N. C. Common.

quile [kwɑɪl]: *n.* and *vb.* Coil; to coil. "My still worm is puore copper and has twenty *quile* in it." Ky. mountains. Common. ((Also, reported from Tenn.))

quirl [kwɜl]: *vb.* To curl. "Does hit *quirl* like a pig's tail?" Ky. mountains. Common.

sanctum suly ['sæŋktəm 'sulɪ]: *n.* Good whisky. Used by a Ky. moonshiner in describing his product. Perhaps derived from Latin. The mountaineer, however, was illiterate.

set up with: *phr.* To keep a wake for a corpse. W. N C. Common. ((Also, reported from S. C. See Laughlin's list.))

shur [ʃʌr]: *n.* and *vb.* Share; to share. E. Ky.; Wautauga Co., N. C. Common.

sonker ['sɑŋkɚ]: *n.* A fruit cobbler. Perhaps related to an old Manx word meaning "heavy." E. Ky. rare.

speculate ['spɛkəleɪt]: *intr. vb.* Usual meaning. E. Ky.; Wautauga Co., N. C. Somewhat rare.

strack [stræk]: *vb.* To strike. Wautagua Co., N. C. Common. E. Ky. Somewhat rare.

sturp [stʌrp]: *n.* Stirrup. E. Ky. Common.

tad, tat [tæd, tæt]: *n.* A very small boy. "He was just a *tad* of a boy when I saw him last." E. Ky. Common. ((Also, reported from S. C.))

taught [tɑt]: pret. of *teach.* Usual meaning. Boone, N. C. Used in a Masonic lecture by a man who has a doctorate.

this a-way and that a-way: *adv.* ((In all directions.)) Wautauga Co., N. C. ((Also, reported from Va., elsewhere in N. C., upper S. C.))

torn-down: *adj.* Mischievous. "What can a body do with a gang of torn-down younguns under her feet?" E. Ky. Common. ((Also, reported from upper S. C. Also in superlative form: *torn-downdest.*))

towel [tæl]: *n.* Usual meaning. Wautauga Co., N. C. All classes. Common.

towardge, twardge [tə'wɑrdʒ, twɑrdʒ]: *prep.* Toward(s). Wautauga Co., N. C. Children. Common.

umberel ['ʌmbərɛl]: *n.* Umbrella. E. Ky. Rare. Wautauga Co., N. C. Common.

whusky ['hwʊskɪ]: *n.* Whisky. E. Ky. Common.

wudn't ['wʌdənt]: *intr. vb.* + negative. Wasn't. "It *wudn't* what I thought at first." E. Ky.; Wautauga Co., N. C. Careless speakers. Common. ((For the presence of [ə] cf. *haven't* ['hævənt], *couldn't* ['kudənt], *didn't* ['dɪdənt], *wasn't* ['wɑzənt].

V. A WORD-LIST FROM NORTH CAROLINA

FRANCIS C. HAYES

Guilford College

-a, -e: Southern uneducated persons of the lowest class tend to change the pronunciation of a final ((unstressed)) syllable in *-a* or *-e* to [ɪ]. The class just above the lowest mocks at the pronunciation of the lowest, and by over-correction avoids the [ɪ] where it is correct to pronounce it: thus "Miam*i*" is carefully changed to "Miam*a*," "Cincinnat*i*" to "Cincinnat*a*," etc.

a-losin', etc.: Rural people often prefix the preposition *a* to the gerund. N. C. mountains.

backset: *n.* Setback. ((Also, reported from Va., upper S. C., mid. Tenn.)) Common.

big laurel (when white): *n.* The rhododendron. W. N. C. Reported.

birding: *n.* and *vb.* Singing a part in a song such as "Oh come, come, come, come ... " which accompanies the lead tune in "The Church in the Wildwood." A. C. Morris, Florida folklorist, informant. Rare.

bitty, little (etc.): *adj.* Small. *Bitty* is always preceded by a synonymous word, usually *little*. General in the South; usage probably restricted somewhat to women and children. Cf. also: "a *small little bitty* dog" and "a *big large fleshy* woman." W. N. C. Uneducated. Common.

bless, to bless (some one) **out:** *phr.* To scold. ((Very common in many parts of the South.)) Reported.

blow-snow: *n.* A combination of wind and snow. W. N. C.

bobtail: *vb.* To discharge dishonorably from the army. Common.

boogey-man [ˈbʊgɪˌmæn]: *n.* The devil. N. C. mountains. Common. ((Also Va., upper S. C.))

buhr, burr: *n.* A millstone, the buhrstone. Buncombe Co., N. C.; village merchant, 73.

cash-money: *n.* Ready money. W. N. C.

cheat: *n.* "Grows in a wheat field—looks like wheat, but ain't; it's said to be poison." Guilford Co., N. C.; farmer's wife, 70. Rare. ((Also s. Va. Common.))

check: *tr. vb.* To sow corn in squares so that one may plow the cornfield lengthwise or crosswise. Guilford Co., N. C. Common. ((Also Va.))

class, on: *phr.* In class. Some parts of N. C. All classes of people. Common. ((Unknown in some other parts of N. C. The Editor has never heard it in any other state.))

clever: *adj.* Amicable, friendly. "He's the *cleverest* neighbor I ever had." Rural and small towns. Common.

corrupted: *adj.* Ruptured. "I done been *corrupted* several year." Guilford Co., N. C. Negro.

corruption: *n.* Rupture. "I'se turned down by the draft board on account of *corruption.*" Guilford Co., N. C. Negro.

cow-cousins: *n.* Cousins weaned on the milk of the same cow. Banner Elk, N. C.

crawly: *adj.* Infested with bugs. "This time o' year [September] all meal's *crawly.*" Guilford Co., N. C. Common.

crystal ['krɪstɪəl]: Common pronunciation among the semieducated. W. and cent. N. C.

does [duz]: *vb.* Present tense of *do* ((generally singular but may be plural)). Negroes in most of the South.

dozens, to shoot: *phr.* To curse. "Don't come *shooting* no *dozens* at me." N. C. Negro.

Easter bush: *n.* Forsythia. W. N. C. Reported.

eye: *n.* The hole in the center of a millstone. Buncombe, Co., N. C.

facing bench: *n.* The bench placed at the front of the Quaker church overlooking the assembly. The occupants of the *facing bench* face the audience. Guilford Co., N. C.

fair off: *vb.* To become clear; said of the weather. "Hit's been rainin' three days, but I think hit's goin' to *fair off* now." ((Perhaps in most Southern states.))

family decoration: *n.* The annual decoration of graves in the family burying plot. Each family has a different Sunday during the summer or fall for decoration. The ceremony consists of placing flowers on the graves, singing without accompaniment, and listening to sermons and prayers by three ministers. The service may last hours. Yancey Co., N. C. Reported.

favor: *tr. vb.* To rest, as part of the body. "I hurt my left side and could not work for two years. Finally I got to where I could work some by *favoring* my left side." Guilford Co., N. C. ((Also other parts of N. C. and some parts of Va.))

fin, on the: *phr.* Fish are sold *on the fin* (in Shallowford, N. C.) —i. e., caught fresh for you on the spot.

fish [fεʃ]: *n.* Common pronunciaion among Negroes and uneducated whites in some parts of the South.

fodder: *vb.* To pull fodder. "When it gets through weathering, I'll finish *foddering*." W. N. C.

foot-pie: *n.* An apple turnover (pastry). Montgomery Co., N. C.

forebay ['forbe]: *n.* The end of the sluice where the water meets the mill wheel. Buncombe Co., N. C.

goochy ['gutʃɪ]: *adj.* Goosey, ticklish. W. N. C. Common.

half, the biggest: *n.* The majority, most. "The *biggest half* of the people does it." Buncombe Co., N. C.; village woman, 30. ((Also, reported from Va., upper S. C., Tenn.))

hardness: *n.* Breach of concord. "There ought not to be no *hardness* between neighbors." Guilford Co., N. C. ((Also s. Va.))

Harry, Old: *prop. n.* The devil, the Old Scratch. Common. ((Also Va.))

head, to put over (one's): *fig. lang.* "The worst day and night I ever *put over my head*" (heavy rain and high wind). W. N. C.

head of water: *n.* See *forebay*.

hearn [hjɜn]: *vb.* Preterit and past participle of *hear*. N. C. ((Va., S. C., and perhaps all Southern states)). Rural.

high sign, to give the: *phr.* To signal a message with gestures. N. C. and other Southern states. Common.

hope, to hope luck out of (a venture): *phr.* "I *hope you luck out of* it." Guilford Co., N. C.

hoppin' John: *n.* A dish composed of peas and hog-jowl, eaten on New Year's Day for good luck. N. C. and some other Southern states. Uneducated.

it: *expl.* There. "*It* is a book in the French room that might be yours." Guilford Co., N. C. Reported. ((Also some other Southern states. See Wilson's list.))

ivy: *n.* Mountain laurel. W. N. C. Reported.

jit: *n.* A nickel. W. N. C.

John Henry: *n.* A dude, a rustic Beau Brummel. W. N. C. Common. Reported. ((In s. Va. and upper S. C.: the penis.))

lazy-gal, lazy-wife: *n.* A bucket operated by ropes passing through pulleys, used to bring water from a distant spring. W. N. C.

letter-mail: *n.* A letter. W. N. C.

liquorhead: *n.* A habitual inebriate. N. C. Common. ((Also Va., S. C., Tenn.))

March flower: *n.* The daffodil. W. N. C. Reported.

mother-baby: *n.* A boy or a man who is unhappy away from his home. W. N. C. Common.

mule-horse: *n.* A horse with the intelligence of a mule. The term was frequently used by horse-traders. Guilford Co., N. C. Obsolescent.

(negatives): "Have you seen any squirrels today?" "No, hit's so foggy *nobody cain't hardly* see *nothing nohow.*" W. N. C.

oi [aɪ]: Common rural pronunciation occurring in *oil, boil, hoist,* etc. W. N. C.

over: *vb.* To get over, be shocked at, forget. "I can't *over* his marrying that old woman." Ga. Reported.

peach-tree rose: *n.* Flowering almond. The leaves are like those of a peach tree, and the flowers are like tiny roses. Yancey Co., N. C. Reported.

pert [pjɜt]: *adj.* Lively, in good spirits. Sometimes used in this sense: "He got a little too *pert,*" i. e., too sprightly for his good. Buncombe Co., N. C. Rural. Common. ((Also elsewhere in the South.))

pin-hooker: *n.* ((**pin-hook:** *vb.*)) An itinerant trader or broker, as for example, one who buys tobacco from a farmer (who does not know the true worth of his tobacco) and sells it at a profit. ((To buy tobacco, etc., in this manner.)) Montgomery Co., N. C. ((Also s. Va. and other parts of N. C.))

piny rose ['paɪnɪ]: *n.* The peony. One mountaineer explained the name thus: "They smell like pines and look like roses." Yancey Co., N. C. Reported.

pud, to pull the (**his**): [pʊd]: *phr.* To masturbate. W. N. C. ((Also Va. and S. C.)) Boys and men. Common.

quarterly ['kwɔrtlɪ]: *n.* and *adj.* A pronunciation common among all classes in and around Raleigh and Wendell, N. C.

raised up with, to be: *phr.* To grow up with. Buncombe Co., N. C. ((Also Va., S. C., Tenn. Rather common.))

reckon ['rɛkn̩, 'rɛgn̩, 'rɛkɪn, 'rɛkən]: *vb.* To suppose (so). "I *reckon* you are right." N. C. ((Also Va., S. C., Tenn., etc.)) Common.

red laurel (when purple): *n.* Rhododendron. W. N. C. ((In w. N. C. sometimes called *rhododenver.*))

religion, to get: *phr.* To be "converted" to religion, usually after ((preaching and)) hymn-singing pressure at revival meetings. N. C. ((Also Va., S. C., Tenn.)) Common.

rifle-gun: *n.* A rifle. W. N. C.

Scratch, the Old: *prop. n.* The devil, the boogey man. W. N. C. ((Also Va., S. C., Tenn.)) Common.

shtrubbly-headed ['ʃtrʌblɪ'hɛdɪd]: *adj.* Tousled-headed. Bethania (Dutch settlement), N. C. Common.

sister: *n.* A woman. W. N. C. Reported. ((Also reported S. C.)) Common.

skunk, shiftless: *n.* Insulting epithet. W. N. C.

slack: *n.* Overflow of water from a spring, etc.

soft-mouth: *tr. vb.* To pacify and appease. "I caught two Niggers in my barn and ordered 'em out. One of 'em came walking up to me slowly and got to *soft-mouthin'* me, sayin' he wouldn't stay in no barn where he wasn't wanted." Cf. *to sweet-talk.* Guilford Co., N. C.

spell: *n.* A turn, period, "fit." W. N. C. Common.

spell: *vb.* To substitute temporarily (for a person) in a task. N. C.

starvation grass: *n.* A round, thin-stemmed weed which fills my back yard. A neighbor said of it: " 'Tain't no good for nothin', and nothin' won't eat it." Guilford Co., N. C.

sull up [sʌl]: *vb.* To "play 'possum," pretend to be asleep or dead. Applied to persons and opossums. "Did you notice how he *sulled up* when I came in?" W. N. C.

sweet-talk: *tr. vb.* To deceive by flattery. Buncombe Co., N. C. ((Also Va., S. C., Tenn.))

table-muscle: *n.* A large girth, "pot belly." Buncombe Co., N. C.

take off: *vb.* To leave, go somewhere. (("He *took off* down the road in a powerful hurry.")) Reported. ((Also Va., S. C., Tenn.))

taken: *vb.* Preterit of *take.* "I *taken* this picture yesterday afternoon." Heard among the uneducated in the South; used because of "overcorrection." Most users probably say "I *took*" when they are among equals. ((See Dennis's list.))

talk short: *vb.* To speak angrily or contemptuously. N. C. Common.

thumbs, to have green: "She has *green thumbs*" means: everything she plants grows well and flourishes. Montgomery Co., N. C. Rare. ((In Va. and some places in N. C. *a green hand* means the same thing. In Wilson Co., Tenn., *green fingers* means the same thing. Latter reported. Cf. Chaucer's "a *thombe of gold*."))

tickled, to get: *vb.* To be amused. South. Common.

tolerable ['tɑləbḷ]: *adj.* ((A term used in exchanging health greetings. "How are you today?" "Oh, I'm just only *tolerable*.")) W. N. C. ((Also other sections of the South.)) Rural. Common.

toll dish [tol]: *n.* A measure holding one-eighth of a bushel, used at corn mills to measure the miller's share. Buncombe Co., N. C. ((Also s. Va., N. C.)) Rural. Common.

tooth-dentist: *n.* A dentist. N. C. mountains. Common.

tremendous [tri'mɛndɪʌs]: *adj.* Common pronunciation among the "semilearned." Buncombe Co., N. C. and some other sections of the state.

turn-key job, a: *adj.* A finished job on a new house; said of a house when it is ready for occupancy. Guilford Co., N. C.

venereal ['vɛnərəl]: *adj.* Common pronunciation among uneducated. W. N. C.

wait on: *vb.* To wait for. N. C. All classes. Common. ((Also, reported from Va., S. C., Tenn., La., Ala.))

weather: *vb.* To rain, snow, sleet, or blow. ((See *fodder*.)) W. N. C. ((Also elsewhere in the South.))

whaley, to play: *phr.* To bungle. "You *played whaley* and didn't know the tune." Cent. N. C. ((Also s. Va., n. N. C.)) Rural.

what it is?: What is it? Guilford College, N. C.; many other Southern states. Students and uneducated. Common.

whether [hwɝ]: Common pronunciation among the uneducated and some of the educated. Heard frequently on the campus at the University of N. C.

won't be + an infinitive: *vb. phr.* Used as a future negative. "I *won't be to go* to church tonight." Kittrell, N. C. Uneducated.

wouldn't ['wʊənt](((['wʊʔnt]?)): *vb.* + negative. Common pronunciation among all classes around Raleigh and Wendell, N. C. *Shouldn't* and *couldn't* are similarly pronounced.

VI. A WORD-LIST FROM VIRGINIA AND NORTH CAROLINA

GEORGE P. WILSON

Woman's College of the University of North Carolina

The expressions which follow come from my collection of a few thousand dialect words. For the most part, I have not given here the commonplace words. Reference to OED, EDD, etc., means that the word is listed in the work designated in the same sense or nearly the same sense that it has in the Southern dialect. A quotation from a printed work does not mean that this is the source of the word but merely an illustration of the use of the word in print. The source is always an oral one, from the locality or localities indicated. In general, I have avoided giving printed quotations that the reader himself might easily find by means of dictionaries, concordances, and books of quotations. Because of its poetic or literary flavor, I have included an occasional expression that carries a standard meaning—such an expression being unexpected among dialect speakers. By the abbreviation *s. Va.* I refer to Mecklenburg County, Virginia, and the counties adjoining Mecklenburg.

aboon: *adj.* and *adv.* Above; to think oneself superior. "That 'omern's *aboon* her own kinnery." Caldwell Co., N. C. Rare.

abroad: *adj.* and *adv.* Away from home but in the community. "Finny isn't at home just now; she's gone *abroad*." S. Va. Rare.

accoutrements: *pl. n.* Inconsequential things—odds and ends—that collect in one's household. Used in Surry Co., N. C., by a man and his sister, who originally came from sw. Va. Very rare. EDD.

aflower: *vb.* To compliment, to flatter. "I knew he was jest *aflowerin' me*."—Olive Tilford Dargan, *Highland Annals*, 106. W. N. C.

ageful: *adj.* Old, getting old. Guilford Co., N. C. Rare.

aggie forties ['ægɪ 'fɔtɪz]: *n.* (From L. *aqua fortis*.) Anything very strong; generally used in reference to something to drink. S. Va.; Johnston Co., N. C. Rare now. *Ackie fortis* ['ækɪ 'fɔrtɪs]: Swain Co., N. C.

agley [ə'gle]: *adv.* To go wrong morally. "Ef Sally don't watch that gal, she's apt to go *agley*."

alo, alow ['alo]: *interj.* Alas, oh my, ah me. Used in a mildly exclamatory sense by a woman ninety years old, Yancey Co., N. C.: "I said, '*alo*, he's here.'" Cf. Skeat, *Ety. Dict.*, 2nd ed. (1893): "**Halloo, Halloa,** a cry to draw attention. . . . Cf. *halloo*, King Lear, iii. 4. 79, where the folio edd. have *alow*, and the quarto edd. have *a lo* (Schmidt). I suppose it to differ from *Holla*, q. v., and to be nothing else but a modification of the extremely common A. S. interj. *ēalā*, Matt. xxiii. 33,37." Very rare.

alter: *vb.* To castrate. S. Va. LA.

and those: *phr.* This phrase when following a (generally singular) substantive may refer to two or more persons, to one person, or even to no one at all. "Mary *and those* came to see me" may mean that only Mary came. Sections in S. C.; e. N. C.; Forsyth Co., N. C.; sections in Va. Reported. There appears to be in popular French speech a phrase equally as elastic and somewhat similar in its implications—*Messieurs-dames*. Writes Henri Bauche of the French form: "C'est la formule générale, obligatoire, de la salutation à l'arrivée et au départ, à l'entrée et à la sortie. On dit *Messieurs-dames*, tout court, sans nulle addition. Cela signifie 'bonjour,' 'bonsoir,' 'je vous salue,' 'salut,' 'adieu,' 'au revoir,' etc. En principe, évidemment, cette expression ne devrait s'employer que lorsqu'on s'adresse à la fois à des hommes et à des femmes; mais dans le peuple on dit souvent *Messieurs-dames*, lorsqu'il y a en scène seulement des hommes ou seulement des femmes, ou même encore lorsqu'il n'y a qu'un seul homme ou une seule femme. . . . *Messieurs-dames* s'adresse aussi à couple composé d'un seul homme et d'une seule femme."—*Le Langage Populaire* . . . (1920), 172, 248. Compare also the Southern phrase *and all*, which does not necessarily mean anybody or anything in addition to the substantive(s) which pecede(s) the phrase. Cf. Shakespeare, *King Lear*, III, vi, 65–6:

"The little dogs *and all*
Tray, Blanch, and Sweetheart, see, they bark at me." Cf. Tennyson, "Northern Farmer: Old Style": "An' Squoire 'll be sa mad *an' all*."

as: *rel. pron.* That, who, which. "Them *as* thinks they can whup me jest come ahead." W. N. C. Common. LA.

as: *conj.* Than. "I had rather go *as* stay." W. N. C. Common. Also elsewhere in South. Somewhat rare.

back-door-trots: *n.* Diarrhoea. S. Va. Rural. EDD.

banter ['bæntə,-ɚ]: *vb.* To dare, to challenge. Swain Co., N. C.; s. Va. EDD.

bantling: *n.* A child. S. Va., w. N. C. OED.

be: *vb.* Present tense, all persons, singular or plural; generally employed in questions. "You *be* that fellow that's staying at Jink's?" "What *be* your name?" Va., N. C. Rare and obsolescent LA.

bed: *causative* and *intr. vb.* To cause one to go to bed; to lie in bed. "If you fool with me, I'll *bed* you." "He's *bedding* late today." W. N. C.

belch back: *vb.* To rebound, to react unfavorably against, to "boomerang." "If you get a bad architect, his work [house] will *belch back* on you." Guilford Co., N. C. Rare.

belong: *aux. vb.* Should, ought, to be supposed, to be accustomed. "He *belongs* to come to work at eight o'clock." Columbus Co., N. C., and elsewhere in N. C. and Va. Also, reported from Greenville Co., S. C.; Wilson Co., Tenn.; ne. La. Illiterate. EDD.

bench: *n.* Definition by a N. C. mountaineer: "A half-level place on the side of a hill." Swain Co., N. C. OED, EDD.

bes [biz]: *vb.* Present tense of *be*, singular or plural. S. Va. Obsolescent.

blanket, to be born on the right (or **wrong**) **side of the**: *phr.* To be born from a lawful (or unlawful) union. Va., N. C. Somewhat rare. OED, EDD.

blanket, to split the: *phr.* To separate, to get a divorce (and divide the property?). W. N. C.

blinky, blinked: *adj.* Said of milk that is slightly sour. **Blinky-blue**: sour skimmed milk. Cf. *bingy milk*, Rosamond Langbridge, *Charlotte Brontë: A Psychological Study*, 23; and *blinked*, Elizabeth Mary Wright, *Rustic Speech and Folk-Lore*, 212. W. N. C. Common. OED, EDD.

bock [bɑk]: *n.* The string bean. Mountain woman, near Blowing Rock, N. C.: "Do you want some yaller, greasy *bocks*? Had narry a poke [she had brought them out in a paper instead of in a bag]; so jest fotched 'em sich [that is, in this way]." Reported. Probably rare.

bogue around [bog]: *vb.* To wander around aimlessly, restlessly, and nervously. Albemarle Co., Va. Reported.

booger ['bʊgə, -ɚ]: *n.* 1. A haunt, ghost. Cf. Coverdale,

Psalms 90 (91), 5: "Thou shalt not nede to be afrayed for eny *bugges* by night." 2. A louse. 3. The hardened mucous in one's (usually a child's) nose. W. N. C. Also, reported from S. C. in sense 2. LA.

brawtus ['brɔtəs]: *n.* An additional amount given for good measure. S. C. Reported.

breast-baby: *n.* A nursing baby. Cf. *knee-baby, lap-baby,* and *waist-baby.* N. C. Also, reported from S. C., Tenn.

cank: *vb.* To annoy, to fret, to overcome. Cf. *hawk.* Caldwell Co., N. C. OED.

case-knife: *n.* A table knife. S. Va. OED, EDD.

catched [kɛtʃt, kætʃt]: *vb.* Preterit and past participle of *catch.* Some sections of Va. and N. C. Also, reported from upper S. C. Illiterate. Cf. Butler, *Hudibras,* I, i, 163-4:
"As if Divinity *catched*
The itch on purpose to be scratched."
OED, LA.

cattle: *n.* Low, contemptible people. Va., N. C. OED.

caucus: *vb.* To plot, to plan. Cf. Carlyle, *Latter-Day Pamphlets,* I, 24: "Men that sit idly *caucusing* and ballot-boxing on the graves of their heroic ancestors." W. N. C. Common.

cha-cha ['tʃæ'tʃæ]: *n.* An onomatopoeic word. The katydid. Yancey Co., N. C. Rare. (In Va.: *night-shak* ['naɪt'ʃæk].)

civil: *adj.* Respectable; considerate of others. S. Va., w. N. C.

cooberlee ['kubə,li]: *n.* An onomatopoeic word. A bird. S. Ga. Reported.

cooling-board: *n.* A large board used to lay a dead person on before *rigor mortis* sets in. In w. N. C. it is regarded as bad luck to allow a corpse to lie in any position other than straight. To *put* a person *on the cooling-board* means to kill him. The board itself is still in use in some sections of w. N. C. W. N. C. Common. S. Va. Obsolescent.

cooter ['kutə,-ɚ]: *vb.* To travel about aimlessly. Caldwell Co., N. C. LA.

creen [krin]: *vb.* To turn partly around and look, to bend over. "When I walked into the church, she *creened* around and looked at me." Va., N. C. Somewhat rare now.

cucumber: *n.* This word has three pronunciations in Mecklenburg Co., Va.: (1) archaic and obsolescent ['kaʊkəmbə], (2) rural and rather illiterate ['kʌkəmbə], and (3) cultured and current ['kjukəmbə].

cupen ['kʌpɪn]: *n.* Cowpen. S. Va. LA.

cut: *vb.* To castrate. S. Va. LA.

dead, to be dead on (one's) **feet**: *adj. phr.* To be very tired. Va., N. C. Also, reported from S. C.

diddle (with): *vb.* To copulate. S. Va.

diggin's: *n.* Deprecative designation of a locality. S. Va., n. N. C. Also, reported from S. C. OED.

dip: *n.* Sweetened cream to put on pie. Caldwell Co., N. C. Reported. Cf. OED. LA.

dogwood winter: *n.* A cool period that sometimes occurs when the dogwoods are blooming. Caldwell Co., N. C.

drive at: *vb.* To do, to work at. Usually in questions. "Well, John, what are you going to *drive at* today?" S. Va. Old people. Becoming rare.

drunk: *adj.* Said of cake, bread, potatoes, etc., which "fall" or become heavy when cooked. S. Va., w. N. C.

elements: *n.* The sky, air, weather; generally in the plural. S. Va. OED, EDD, Elizabeth Mary Wright, *Rustic Speech and Folk-Lore.*

everwhat: *pron.* Whatever. Catawba Co., N. C.

fair: *n.* Female sweetheart. Mitchell Co., N. C. Reported.

feisty ['faɪstɪ]: *adj.* Vociferously bellicose when safe. "That little fellow is powerful *feisty*—reminds me of a little feist dog in his own backyard, barking and cutting up Jeems Henry when he knows he's safe." S. Va., parts of N. C. (See Missouri list; Horace Kephart, *Our Southern Highlanders*, 94.)

fesper ['fɛspə]: *n.* The evening meal. Forsyth Co., N. C. Rare? Reported.

find: *vb.* To provide for; to furnish a renter with food and other necessities. S. Va., e. N. C. Also, reported from upper S. C. OED.

fornent, fornenst [fə'nent, -'nɪnt, -'nænt; -'nɛnst, -'nɪnst, -'nænst]: *prep.* Against, opposite. W. N. C. Common. Cf. "Bessie Bell and Mary Gray":

> "But they maun lie in Stronach haugh,
> To biek *forenent* the sin [sun]."

(Reported from S. C.: beneath.) OED, EDD.

friz: *n.* The ribbed piece of steel against which the flint of the

flint-lock gun strikes to produce the spark. Yancey and Swain
cos., N. C. Rare. Cf. *frizzle*, OED, EDD.

garden-sass [-sæs]: *n.* Vegetables. S. Va.; Swain Co., N. C.
OED, LA.

gawk, gowk, hunting the: *n.* A sport like "snipe-hunting,"
in which unsuspecting strangers are dupes left to "hold the bag."
Swain Co., N. C.

gear: *n* Property, belongings. "And after the infare at her
father's, they went to their li'l house, where there wa'n't much
gear."—A woman, 96. Yancey Co., N. C. Cf. Margaret Paston,
Paston Letters (1453), I,251: " . . . and whan your *gerr* is remeved
owte of your lytil hous, the dore shall be lokkyd."

gen, gin [gɪn]: *adv.* and *conj.* After, when, if. "*Gin* I work all
the week, I'm jest too tired to dress up uv a Sunday." W. N. C.
Also, reported from upper S. C. OED, EDD, LA.

gnat-bread: *n.* Smegma. S. Va.

go: *vb.* To walk. Cf. Chaucer, *Pardoner's Tale*, 748: "And
God be with you, where ye *go* or ryde!" Shakespeare, *King Lear*,
I, iv, 134: "Ride more than thou *goest*." E. N. C. Rare.

go-devil: *n.* A heavy ax used to split logs. "You won't [stay
at home], less'n it's rainin' *go-devils*."—Olive Tilford Dargan,
Call Home the Heart, 2. Swain Co., N. C.

half-and-half: *n.* and *adj.* A hermaphrodite; hermaphroditic.
"De say he *half-and-half*."—Negro woman, 50. Charlotte Co.,
Va. Also, reported from other parts of Va. Generally used by
Negroes.

half-strainer: *n.* One who puts on airs, tries to associate
with his superiors; a word of decided contempt. S. Va., cent.
N. C. Obsolescent.

handle talk: *phr.* To gossip. "You oughtn't *to handle* no
sich *talk*." Caldwell Co., N. C. Reported.

hand-running: *adv.* Continuously. "I been setting up two
nights *hand-running*." S. Va., w. N. C. Also, reported from
upper S. C., Ga., Tenn., n. La. OED, EDD.

haversack ['hævəsæk]: *n.* A small hand-bag used to carry
clothing, etc., in. S. Va. Also, reported from S. C. OED, EDD.

hawk [hɔk]: *vb.* To exasperate, to chagrin, to "get the best of."
(Cf. *hack* [hæk].) "Hit sho *hawked* ole Rafe when his young
wife run off with that boarder at his house." Va., N. C., some
other Southern states. Rather common.

he-kicking: *adj.* Alive, fresh. "Fish ain't no good unless you put them in the pan *he-kicking.*" E. N. C. Reported.

him: *neut. pron.* It. "I ain't never eat a better apple than *him* [the June pippin]." Swain Co., N. C. Rare. Cf. Tyndale, *Matt.* VIII, 8–9; Rheims trans. *Matt.* VIII, 9. OED, EDD.

his: *neut. pron.* Its. "Each state had *his* burying plot [at Gettysburg]."—A man. 90. W. N. C. Rare.

hit: *pron.* It. Very common in the mountains; many educated persons use this form. More frequent in other Southern sections than generally thought.

hit: *n.* and *vb.* A successful bearing of a vegetable or fruit crop; to bear vegetables or fruit. "My peach trees didn't *hit* this year." Many sections of the South. Rather common. OED, EDD.

hits: *neut. pron.* Its. "That dog done *hits* best to break loose." N. C. mountains. Common.

homely: *adj.* Friendly, familiar; fond of the home; applying onself to matters about the house. W. N. C. OED, EDD. (See Missouri list.)

hone for (after) [hon]: *vb.* To long for, to desire strongly. Cf. William Byrd, *Diary*: "The doctor was much better but *honed after* strong drink." Rural South, especially mountains. Common. OED.

hostel ['hɑstəl]: *n.* A lodging place. Yancey Co., N. C.; a woman, 96. Rare.

hotten: *adj.* Hot. Cent. Tenn. Reported.

hug: *n.* The enclosure made by the arms or the legs or both. "The dog was so scared he set back in my *hug* and whined." Avery and Swain cos., N. C. Also, reported from upper S. C., mid. Tenn.

hunker: *n.* The haunches. W. N. C. OED, EDD, LA.

hunker (up): *vb.* To squat on the haunches; to be humped up or bent over awkwardly. "It was so cold he *hunkered up* in the wagon." W. N. C.

hwa [hwɑ]: *rel. pron.* Who. The interrogative pronoun *who* is pronounced in the current standard way. Mecklenburg Co., Va. Rural. Mainly uneducated.

instrument: *n.* The penis; but the word occasionally refers to the female organ. S. Va. Rare.

it: *expl.* There. "*It*'s a dress-up at my house tonight."

Cf. Thornley's trans. of Longus' *Daphnis and Chloe* (1657), Bk. III, 10: "In the morning *it* was a sharp frost, and the north wind was very biting." Different sections of N. C. Reported. See Hayes's list.

jam(b)-ke-dab ['dʒæmkə,dæb]: *adj.* and *adv.* Close up, completely. "I rid *jamb-ke-dab* up agin that house." Cherokee Co., N. C.; also elsewhere in South.

jape [dʒep]: *vb.* To copulate. S. Va., e. N. C. OED.

jest: *n.* The meaning of this word is not clear to me. Heard only once. "I was as pure of that blockading [making illicit liquor] as the *jest* of God."—A man in Swain Co., N. C., 70. (Not the phrase *jest* [just] *God.* Dr. Kemp Malone thinks that "*jest* of God" may mean the "*just* of God"—that is, the saved, the redeemed.)

keeler ['kilɚ, -ə]: *n.* A wooden tub-like vessel five or six inches deep and eighteen or twenty inches in diameter, used to put milk or other warm liquids into to cool. Yancey and Gaston cos., N. C. Rare. Cf. Shakespeare, *Love's Labor's Lost*: "While greasy Joan doth *keel* the pot." OED. EDD.

kink over: *vb.* To fall over, to faint. "I looked around, and there was father ['fæðɚ] about to *kink over*."—A woman, 90. Yancey Co., N. C. Rare. OED.

knee-baby: *n.* A walking baby—one that stands by one's knee; a second child. "My parents had nineteen children; I'm the *knee-baby*."—A man, 40. N. C.

knob [nɑb]: *n.* A small, round hill. Avery and Burke cos., N. C.; upper S. C. OED, EDD.

knock up: *vb.* To make pregnant, generally in illicit sense. S. Va., N. C., S. C., Tenn., Ala., La.

knuck-bone: *n.* A bone having a rounded end or "ball." "The *knuck-bone* came out of my uncle's hip."—A woman, 90. Yancey Co., N. C. Rare.

la [lɔ, lɒ, lɑ]: *interj.* Oh, ah, lo. (From *Lord?*) Cf. Fielding, *Tom Jones*, Bk. IV, Ch. 14: "*La!* says I, Mr. Jones, what's the matter?" Most Southern states. Common. OED, EDD.

lap-baby: *n.* A baby or child small enough to sit on one's lap. E. N. C.

lavish: *n.* Abundance, a great deal of. "We have a *lavish* of fruit this year." Parts of N. C. OED.

lay-over or **lay-overs to catch meddlers; larus** ['lærəs] . . . ;

la rose ['lɑroz, 'læroz] **catch meddlers; larrows** or **laroes** ... ; **lay rows to catch meddlers; ledlow** ... ; **lay-o's** ... ; etc.: *phr.* A reply given to inquisitive children who ask meddling questions about matters they should be ignorant of. Some form of this expression seems to appear in most Southern states. I have not observed two or more forms in the same community. OED, EDD; *Notes and Queries*, 4th ser., V, 25; *ibid.*, 257; etc.; Apperson, *Eng. Proverbs and Proverbial Phrases*, 354; *Am. Mercury*, VI, 239; *ibid.*, VII, 241; *Am. Speech*, II, 408–9; Mitchell, *Gone with the Wind*, 548; etc. (There is sufficient material on this topic for a substantial paper.)

leak: *vb.* To urinate. Cf. Shakespeare, 1 *Hen. IV*, II, i, 21–2: "Why, they will allow us ne'er a jordan, and then we *leak* in your chimney." Va., N. C. Also, reported from S. C., Tenn., Ala., La., Tex. Common.

link(i)ster, lingster ['lɪŋk(ɪ)stɚ, 'lɪŋstɚ]: *n.* An interpreter. "My grandaddy used to be a *linkister* for the Indians." W. N. C. Rather common. OED, EDD.

listen at: *vb.* To listen to. Common in some sections of the South, even among the educated. One professor of English from S. C. writes: "I use *listen at* regularly. In my dialect (Greenville, S. C.) *listen at* implies less formal attention than *listen to.*"

man-sworn: *adj.* Breaking one's oath, swearing falsely. W. N. C. OED, EDD.

master: *adj.* or part of compound *n.* Skillful, superior, leading. "He was a *master* hand at making chairs." W. N. C. Also, reported from upper S. C., La., Tenn. OED, EDD.

meech, meach [mitʃ]: *vb.* To get around stealthily; to slink; to appear dishonest, shifty. "I seed a fellow *meechin'* round up the cove like he might 'a' been a revenuer." Cf. *mychyn* and note on, *Promptorium Parvulorum*; and Shakespeare, *Hamlet*, III, ii, 147: "Marry, this is *miching* malecho; it means mischief." W. N. C., but sometimes heard elsewhere in the South. OED, EDD.

megs set to go [mɛgz]: *phr.* "He has his *megs set to go*"—that is, he is prepared to go. Halifax Co., Va. Reported.

molewarp, moldwarp: *n.* A senseless person. Caldwell Co., N. C. OED.

moon-calf: *n.* An imagined misshaped animal, a bastard, a simpleton. W. N. C. OED, EDD. One college professor reports: "Sometimes used to describe the actions of adolescent love."

much (up): *vb.* To make much of, to show affection for. "I *muched* the dogs *up*, and they got so they'd follow me." Here and there in N. C. Somewhat rare. OED, EDD.

muckle-dun: *n.* Muddy-brown. W. N. C.

muley, mully ['mjulɪ, 'mʌlɪ]: *n.* A cow that has never had any horns. W. N. C. OED, EDD. In s. Va.: *mully-head.*

musicianer [mju'zɪʃənə, -ɚ]: *n.* A musician. W. N. C. OED, EDD.

musicker ['mjuzɪkə, -ɚ]: *n.* A musician. Less common than *musicianer.* W. N. C. OED, DAE.

morn-gloam: *n.* The first light of morning. Avery and Caldwell cos., N. C. Reported.

nap o'sleep: *n. phr.* A little sleep. S. Va.

napper's house, to go to: *phr.* To go to sleep. S. Va.; Caldwell Co., N. C.

next: *adj.* The one after the nearest (next). "I aim to go to town *next* Saturday [that is, the second Saturday hence]." S. Va., n. N. C. Also, reported from upper S. C.; Charleston, S. C.; Tenn.; La.

no'm [nom, 'nobm̩, nɔm, nɑm]: Contraction of *no* + *ma'm* (madam). S. Va. Uneducated.

oaf [of]: *n.* An insignificant, stupid, irritating person. W. N. C. Rare. OED, EDD, LA.

out: *n.* Ending, failure. "He made a hell of a *out* trying to raise them boys." Here and there in the South. EDD.

outfavor: *vb.* To be better looking than some one else. Remark to a new-born infant: "You do *outfavor* your daddy, don't you?" Guilford Co., N. C. Rare.

pan has [pɑn hɑs]: *n.* Liver-pudding. Caldwell and Catawba cos., N. C. Rare. Reported. LA.

patti-whack ['pætɪˌhwæk]: *n.* Cartilage, the wide white band found in beef; something regarded as tough. Cf. *paxwax,* Skeat's *Etymological Dictionary.*

peep-by-night: *n.* A flower that opens at night, the four-o'clock. Swain Co., N. C.

pensy: *adj.* Reflective, thoughtful. "Jane has *pensy* eyes." W. N. C. OED, EDD.

pewter-eyed: *adj.* Grey-eyed; generally used disparagingly. S. Va.

pieded ['paɪdɪd]: *adj.* Spotted. Swain Co., N. C. Also, reported from mid. Tenn.

pitch a crop: *phr.* To plant a crop. S. Va., w. N. C. OED.

pleasure: *vb.* To please. "Hit'll *pleasure* us to have you eat at our house." W. N. C. and perhaps other Southern sections.

poke along: *vb.* To move slowly and leisurely; used in a derogatory sense. Va., N. C., Tenn., La. OED, EDD.

pole along: *vb.* Same as *poke along.* E. N. C. and parts of Va.

pour up: *vb.* To pour out. Caldwell Co., N. C.

pride: *n.* The ovary of an animal. S. Va. Obsolescent. Also, reported from S. C.

puke: *n.* A low, disgusting person. S. Va. OED, EDD, LA.

puppet, poppet: *n.* A doll. "She's as pretty as a *poppet.*" Halifax and Surry cos., N. C. Also, reported from mountains of N. C.

pure: *adj.* Innocent, guiltless. "I was as *pure* of that blockading [making illicit liquor] as the jest of God."—A man in Swain Co., N. C., 70. Used by Tyndale, Cranmer, etc. OED.

quietus: *n.* The standard literary meaning. "Poor thing [a dying groundhog]; he'll soon have his *quietus.*" Swain Co., N. C.

Richmond, to go to: *phr.* To become pregnant; to be near to giving birth to a child. A localism used mainly by rural Negroes; originating, perhaps, from the fact that many women living in rural sections went to Richmond, Va., to give birth to a baby in a hospital. Mecklenburg Co., Va.

roger: *vb.* To copulate. Cf. William Byrd, *Diary*: Mar. 29, 1711; Mar. 30, 1711; May 16, 1711; etc. OED gives in a quotation as a noun = "A Man's Yard."

roke [rok]: *vb.* Preterit and past participle of *rake.* "Do you want this yard *roke* up?" Guilford Co., N. C.; Spartanburg, S. C. Illiterate. Rare.

rue-bargain: *n.* and *vb.* A bad bargain; to withdraw from a bargain made in good faith. Caldwell Co., N. C. Reported. OED, EDD.

rusty, to cut a: *phr.* To cut a caper. N. C., Tenn., N. J. Reported.

sa, madam ['sɑˌmædəm]: A command to a cow to stand in a better position to be milked; usually accompanied by a push against the hip of the cow. S. Va. Obsolescent. LA.

sad [sæd]: *adj.* Heavy; said of bread, cake, etc. Several Southern states. Older people. OED, EDD.

sanky poke ['sæŋkɪ]: *n.* A traveling bag. Caldwell Co., N. C. Reported.

scringe [skrɪndʒ]: *vb.* To shrink from because of fear or dislike. S. Va. and parts of N. C. OED, EDD.

scritch-owl: *n.* Screech-owl. South. Common. OED, EDD, LA.

scrooch, scrouge, scroonch, scrunch [skrutʃ, skraʊdʒ, skruntʃ, skruntʃ]: *vb.* To crouch, to crowd, to crowd oneself into. S. Va., w. N. C. Also, reported from upper S. C. OED, EDD.

seam-needle, to come to (or **reach**) **the:** *phr.* To reach a good stopping place. Duplin Co., N. C. Rare. Reported.

several: *pron.* and *adj.* A great many. "There are *several* berries this summer." W. N. C. and parts of rural Ind. OED.

shammock: *vb.* To walk in a slouchy, unsteady manner. W. N. C. OED, EDD.

shank of the evening: *n. phr.* Latter part of the afternoon. S. Va. and elsewhere in the South. OED, EDD.

shear corn: *vb.* and object. To cut fresh corn off the ear preparatory to cooking it. Buncombe Co., N. C. Reported.

show out: *vb.* To show off. "They was great folks for *showing out.*" W. N. C. Rare. OED, EDD.

sib: *n.* A companion. E. N. C. Reported.

sib: *adj.* Akin to, having similar tastes, like. "That city fellow is *sib* to us country folks; he likes our mountain ways." Avery Co., N. C. Common. Reported. LA.

skeletum: *n.* Skeleton. Mainly illiterates. Occasional. Cf. Meric Casaubon's trans. of Marcus Aurelius' *Meditations* (1634), Bk. V, 75: "Within a very little while, thou wilt be either ashes, or a *sceletum* . . . "

slip up: *n.* and *vb.* A miscarriage; to miscarry. S. Va., S. C.

smur [smɝ]: *n.* A fog almost as heavy as a rain. Caldwell and Avery cos., N. C. Reported. LA.

so as: *conj.* So that. Cf. *Letters of Elizabeth to James VI (I)*, Let. XXIV: "I hope you shall receaue honorable requital of his amicable embassade, *so as* you shal have no cause to regret his arrival." Rather general in the South. Illiterate. OED.

sodle ['sodl̩]: *vb.* To make no progress. "My fire jes' sets and *sodles*—won't catch up." Randolph Co., N. C. Rare. Reported.

speciment ['spɛsaɪˌmɪnt]: *n.* Specimen. Yancey Co., N. C. OED.

spell: *vb.* To tell, to narrate. Forsyth Co., N. C.

spit cotton: *phr.* 1. An indication that one has drunk some form of alcohol. Cf. Shakespeare, 2 *Henry IV*, I, ii, 236-8: "... if it be a hot day, and I brandish any thing but a bottle, I would I might never *spit white* again." S. Va. 2. To be angry. "But the Negroes understood him. They would whisper to each other, 'You better look out; the Sheriff's *spitting cotton* this morning,' referring to Papa's habit of expectorating freely when he was angry."—Robert B. House, *Miss Sue and the Sheriff*, 68. Also, reported from upper S. C. in sense 2. (See *cotton, to spit*, Missouri list.)

spread-nadder: *n.* Spreading-adder. S. Va.

swingle, swingle-knife: *n.* and *vb.* A wooden knife used to break flax; to beat or break flax with such a knife. Yancey Co., N. C. Rare. Cf. Skeat's *Etymological Dictionary*; and *swengyl, Promptorium Parvulorum.* OED.

take after: *vb.* To have illicit sex relations. "I don't think much of that 'oman; she *takes after*." Mecklenburg Co., Va. Rare. LA.

that: *def. art.* The; used when not demonstrative or emphatic. "Give *that* feed to *that* cow." S. Va.

tickler: *n.* A flat pocket flask, generally used for whisky. S. Va. Older persons.

tohind, t'hind: *prep.* and *adv.* Behind. "Look *t'hind* ye, and ye'll see the snake." W. N. C.

torn-downdest: *adj.* Wildest, most destructive, most full of life. "I was one of the *torn downdest* tomboys you ever heard of." —A woman, 90. Yancey Co., N. C. Also Avery and Caldwell cos., N. C.; upper S. C.

tory: *n.* A person who pillaged or mistreated Southerners during the Civil War and Reconstruction; generally has reference to a Southerner. Yancey Co., N. C. Rare. OED, EDD.

tourer ['turɚ]: *n.* A tourist. Swain Co., N. C.

treadle: *n.* The chalaza of an egg. S. Va. OED, EDD.

trinkle: *vb.* To move around in an annoying manner. "I've cooked a-many a meal's victuals with a gang uv young uns *a-trinklin'* around underfoot."—Maud Minish Sutton. Caldwell Co., N. C.

trim: *vb.* To castrate. S. Va. LA.

tritchet ['trɪtʃɛt]: *n.* Pudenda muliebria. Same as *twitchet.* S. Va. Rare.

trollop: *n.* and *vb.* One who goes about a great deal; to go about a great deal. Swain Co., N. C. (See Missouri list.)

true, to be: *adv. phr.* To be sure. "He is, *to be true,* a very strong man." Used by some freshmen at the Woman's College of the University of North Carolina who came from piedmont and w. N. C.

trunk, a white: *n.* A white flour sack (bag) carried by a beggar or tramp. "I'm getting so danged poor I'll have to get me *a white trunk* and get on the road [and beg]." Swain Co., N. C.

twat [twɑt]: *n.* Pudenda muliebria. S. Va. and parts of N. C. Also, reported from S. C., Texas, La. OED.

twitchet ['twɪtʃɛt]: *n.* Same as *tritchet.* S. Va. and parts of N. C. Also, reported from S. C., Tenn.

two-three: *n.* A few, two or three. "I'll be through with this job in *two-three* jerks of a sheep's tail." Many parts of the South. Educated and illiterate.

t-y-t ['tiwaɪ'ti]: *n.* A lie. Generally used in a euphemistic sense: "Ah, Jane, you've told a *t-y-t.*" S. Va.

unfeed: *vb.* To defecate. W. N. C. Reported.

vagus ['vegəs]: *adj.* Very important, powerful. "Judge Hankle is a *vagus* man."—A Negro woman. Ga. Reported.

vixen: *n.* A bad girl. Avery and Caldwell cos., N. C. Near Mt. Mitchell, N. C., is (or was) a little post office named Vixen.

waist-baby: *n.* A baby tall enough when standing to reach one's waist. S. C.

wa'n't [wont, wɑnt]: *vb.* plus neg. *Was* + *not, were* + *not.* S. Va., e. N. C. Common. Rare in mountains. Also, reported from mid. Tenn., S. C., n. La.

wanton: *n.* Has the usual literary meaning. Caldwell Co., N. C.

wapsy ['wɑpsɪ]: *n.* Debilitation, weakness. A venereal disease: Swain and Yancey cos., N. C. Rare.

wasper: *n.* Wasp. "These ain't no crickets; they's damned *waspers.*"—A woman who put wasps in the bed of a roomer because he would not pay or move away. Swain and Guilford cos., N. C.

welkin: *n.* The sky. S. Va. Old people. Cf. Shakespeare, *Tam. of the Shrew,* Induction, II, 46: "Thy hounds shall make the *welkin* answer them ... " EDD.

what all: *pron.* Everything, all; an emphatic term. Cf.

Chaucer, *T. and C.*, V, 1850: "Lo here, *what alle* hir goddes may availle"; Shakespeare, *Midsummer Night's Dream*, I, i, 229:

"He will not know *what all* but he do know." Many sections of the South. Common. OED, EDD.

whin(d)le ['hwɪn(d)l̩]: *vb.* To whine, to fret. W. N. C. OED, EDD (*whingle*).

whip-stitch, every: *n.* All the time. "I've been working every *whip-stitch* since you left." W. N. C. OED, EDD.

whistle-pig: *n.* A groundhog. W. N. C. Common.

wood's-colt: *n.* A bastard. W. N. C. Also, reported from upper S. C., La. LA.

work on: *vb.* To castrate. S. Va., N. C., S. C.

worration [ˌwʌ'reʃən]: *n.* Worry, annoyance; a blend of *worry* + *botheration*. Guilford Co., N. C.

wrong-side-outwards ['rɔŋsɪˌdəutədz]: *adj.* and *adv.* A self-explanatory term. S. Va. Rare.

yan, yon [jæn, jɑn]: *adj.* and *adv.* That way or direction; a demonstrative word generally accompanied by pointing in the direction meant. W. N. C. LA.

yanside: *prep.* Beyond, farther than. EDD. LA.

yard-child: *n.* A bastard. Miss. Reported. LA.

you all: *pron.* So much can be said about this much discussed pronoun that nothing is being said here. In spite of many clarifying articles on the subject, there is still much misunderstanding. LA.

you uns [juns, juənz]; **you unses** ['juənsɪz]: *pron.* You ones; generally plural. W. N. C. Common.

you uns all ['junsˌɔl]: *pron.* You all; a plural form. Not so common as *you uns*. Cherokee and Swain cos., N. C.

VII. A WORD-LIST FROM MISSOURI

CONSTANCE BEY, LEWIS E. CALLISON, CLARISSA CHILDERS, ELIZABETH EDWARDS, HELEN GETZ, EMMA KRUMSIECK, NELL LATIMER, RUTH LINVILLE, PATRICIA LOCKRIDGE, LOIS McCLANAHAN, GUY OSBORN, SABINA TEDFORD, WILMA WADE AND MARGARET YOUNG

All from Missouri except one, Mr. Callison (Arkansas)

The words listed here were contributed by the persons whose names appear above. All were students in an English language class conducted by Dr. Robert L. Ramsay at the University of Missouri during the summer of 1941. The initials, in parentheses, after an item indicate the person or persons making the contribution.—The Editor

aggie: *n.* A marble ((of agate)). Carroll Co. (M. Y.)

anti-godlin: *adj.* and *adv.* Not parallel to something having well-established lines. My grandfather explained the term by saying it referred to the idea of the "four corners of the earth" as created by God; hence anyone who laid the foundation of a new building should make it "square with the world"; otherwise it would be *anti-godlin*—against the wish or example of God. Greene Co. (W. W.) ((See Combs's list.))

anty-over: *n.* A game played by tossing a ball over the house to one or more players on the other side. Saline Co. (E. K.) ((Also Va., N. C., S. C.))

at, to be at (oneself): *phr.* To exhibit sound judgment. "He was *at himself* when he made that trade." Grundy Co. (L. M.)

baby-beef: *n.* A calf not yet a year old. Pike Co. (N. L.) ((Also Wis.; Wilson Co., Tenn.))

bait: *n.* A large amount; usually refers to food. "He et a big *bait* of fish." Camden Co. (G. O.) ((In most Southern states?))

bammy-gilly-um ['bamɪ'gɪlɪəm]: *n.* Balm-of-Gilead. Douglas Co. (W. W.) ((Also Va.))

bee-gum: *n.* A bee-hive. Livingston Co. Rural. (R. L.) ((Also Va., N. C. Cf. *rabbit-gum* and *ash-gum* in the same states.))

belly-buster: *n.* A dive in which the water is hit "flat" with the abdomen. Nw. Ark. (L. C.) ((Also, reported from Transylvania Co., N. C.; Greenville, S. C.))

belly-rub: *n.* Almost any dance. Nw. Ark. (L. C.) ((Also, reported from Nashville, Tenn.; Durham, N. C.; Charleston, S. C.))

berry-glaumer ['bɛrɪˌglɔməʳ]: *n.* A person who can pick strawberries very rapidly. "A real *berry-glaumer* never eats a berry while picking berries." Greene Co. (W. W.)

biggety ['bɪgətɪ]: *adj.* Haughty, overbearing, vain. Saline Co. Elderly farm women. Rare. (E. K.) ((Also Va., N. C., S. C., Tenn. Rather common.))

bitch-wolf: *n.* Presumably a she-wolf; now used only as a standard for hyperbolic comparison. "He's as hungry as a *bitch-wolf.*" Nw. Ark. (L. C.) "She is as cold as a *bitch-wolf on stilts.*" (Other Missouri students.)

blue-john: *n.* Skimmed milk; generally sour. Perry Co. (C. B.) Polk Co. (G. O.)

bobble ['babl̩]: *n.* A slight mistake or error. "See that *bobble* in my tatting." "I made a *bobble* on the piano." Randolph Co. (S. T.)

boughten [bɔtn̩]: *vb.* Past participle and adjective from *buy*. That which is purchased, ready-made. Nw. Mo. Rural. Becoming rare. (C. C.) ((Also upper S. C., Me.))

bow-dark ['boˌdɑrk]: *n.* (Fr. *bois d'arc*.) A low-growing tree, widely planted in hedges, very strong and durable when used for fence posts; Osage orange. Greene Co. (W. W.)

bush-whacker: *n.* Member of a guerilla band; a term surviving Civil War days. Greene Co. Old people. (W. W.) ((Also, reported from Greenville, Camden, and Laurens cos., S. C.))

busy as a cranberry merchant: *phr.* Very busy. Carroll Co. and elsewhere in Mo. (M. Y.)

call: *vb.* To remember. "I can't *call* his name right now." Carroll Co. (M. Y.) ((Also Va., N. C., S. C.))

canner: *n.* An old cow. Randolph Co. (S. T.)

captain: *n.* A dapper young person who delights people with his suave manners; a young son who appears promising. Grundy Co. (L. M.) ((In Va.: a term applied by workmen or tenants to their boss. Also, reported in the latter sense from Miss., upper S. C.))

channel cat: *n.* A catfish. Nw. Ark. (L. C.) ((Also, reported from S. C., La.))

chick-a-lick-click-click [ˌtʃɪkəˈlɪkˌklɪkˌklɪk]: *interj.* A sound used to call hens. A different sound is used to call roosters (*pata-*

too-ta, q. v.). Saline Co. an old German farmer. Heard only once from this man. (E. K.)

civvy-cat: *n.* A species of skunk. Camden Co. (G. O.)

cloud: *n.* A Negro. Randolph Co. Used mainly by uneducated whites. (S. T.)

combine [kəm'baɪn]: *vb.* To harvest wheat or oats with a "combine." Pike Co. (N. L.)

cotton, to spit: *phr.* To be extremely thirsty. ((This term has other meanings. See *spit cotton*, Wilson's list.)) Holt Co. Common. (H. G.)

cow-grease: *n.* Butter. Gentry Co. Vulgar. Rare. (C. C.) ((Also, reported from Va., N. C., S. C., Tenn.))

crawdad: *n.* A crawfish. Livingston Co. (R. L.)

crawdaddy: *n.* A crawfish. Gentry Co. (C. C.) Nw. Ark. (L. C.)

crow-bait: *n.* A worn-out horse. Randolph Co. (S. T.)

dauncy ['dɔnsɪ]: *adj.* Dizzy, sickly. Gentry Co. (C. C.) Caldwell Co. (E. E.) Andrew Co. (H. G.) Common.

do-hicky ['du₁hɪkɪ]: *n.* A term used as the substitute for the name of something. "What is that *do-hicky* you are making?" Livingston Co. Rural. (R. L.) ((Also Va., N. C., S. C.))

done in: *adj. phr.* Very sick, ((exhausted?)). Caldwell Co. Uneducated. Common. (E. E.)

draw: *n.* A small creek. Caldwell Co. Common. (E. E.)

dreen [drin]: *n. and vb.* A drain; to drain. "The *dreen* is stopped up." "Did you *dreen* the pipes?" Caldwell Co. (E. E.) ((Also Va., N. C., S. C.))

druthers, to have (one's) ['drʌðəz]: *phr.* To have one's desires ((rathers)). "If I had my *druthers*, I'd go fishing." Mo. Ozarks. Common. (P. L.) ((Also Va., N. C.))

duster: *n.* A sandstorm. Randolph Co. (S. T.)

elm ['ɛləm]: *n.* Elm. Caldwell Co. (E. E.) ((Also other Southern states.))

everything an' all: *n. phr.* A phrase expressing completeness, the entire. Randolph Co. (S. T.)

fair up: *vb.* To become clear or less cloudy. Rural. Common. ((In Va.: *to fair off*. Also reported in the latter form from upper S. C.))

feisty ['faɪstɪ]: *adj.* Flirtatious, giddy; used to describe a vivacious girl whose morals the neighborhood is beginning to question. "I'd wear out a razor-strop on any girl of mine that was as *feisty* as them two of Belle Brown's." Greene Co. Common. (W. W.) ((Also, reported from upper S. C. See Wilson's list.))

fire: *vb.* To dry up, as corn during the drought. "Dad says that north field of corn is sure to *fire* if it don't rain soon." Pike Co. Common. (N. L.)

fit to kill: *adv.* Applied to the highly dressed style of a person. "My, she was dressed up *fit to kill.*" Caldwell Co. Common. (E. E.) ((Also Va., N. C. Reported from upper S. C.))

fornet [fər'nɛt]: *adj., adv.,* ((and *prep.*)) Even, along the side of. "We got *fornet* the other car before we knew who was in it." Greene Co. Very rare. (E. K.)

gang-plow: *n.* A plow having wheels and two or more bottoms. Pike Co. Common. (N. L.)

garb out: *vb.* To dress or overdress. "Here he comes all *garbed out* in his best bib and tucker." Several rural sections. (C. C.)

gatherin' ['gæðrən]: *n.* A festering—usually a boil. Camden Co. (G. O.)

gaum [gɔm]: *vb.* To soil or smear. Camden Co. (G. O.) Livingston Co. (R. L.)

gee [dʒi]: *vb.* To agree, to get along well together. Andrew Co. Common. (H. G.) ((Also Va., N. C. Reported from upper S. C.))

get-up: *n.* 1. Clothing; an uncomplimentary term. "She's got on the darndest *get-up* I've ever seen on any mortal." 2. A party. 3. An activity. Caldwell Co. (E. E.)

ghostes ['gostəz]: *n.* Ghosts. Saline Co. Rather common. (E. K.) ((Also Va., N. C., Texas. Uneducated.))

Gilly, by ['dʒɪlɪ]: *interj.* See *Jacks, by.* (W. W.)

give out: *vb.* To become exhausted. Grundy Co. Common. (L. M.) ((Also Va., N. C. Reported from upper S. C.))

gone gosling: *n.* A doomed person, animal, or thing. (L. C.) ((Also Va., N. C.))

gullup ['gʌləp]: *n.* ((The amount of liquid—molasses—that can be poured from a jug or bottle before the container "gets air"? An onomatopoeic word? Cf. a similar word in Paul Green, *In Abraham's Bosom,* 17: "The water can be heard *gluking* over the cataract of their Adam's apples.")) "I used three *gullups* of molasses in this cake." Rare. (H. G.) ((Also, reported from upper S. C.))

gumbo ['gʌmbo]: *n.* A tough, hard clay soil. Saline Co. Common. (E. K.) ((Also, reported from Ga., La., Texas.))

halves, to go: *phr.* To divide equally or to share equally. Livingston Co. Rural. (R. L.) ((Also Va., N. C.))

handle, to fly the: *phr.* To give up quickly. Caldwell Co. Common. (E. E.) ((In Va.: *to fly off the handle*, to become angered easily.))

hatrack: *n.* An old ((emaciated?)) cow. Randolph Co. (S. T.)

headest start: *n.* An advantage. A term commonly used by school children. "It's no fair; you had the *headest start*."

heart, to stick (one's) **heart in** (one's) **pocket**: *phr.* To become indifferent towards a woman whom one has been courting. Caldwell Co. Educated. Common. (E. E.)

hens, to beat hens a-rastlin': *phr.* To be most unusual. Livingston Co. Rural. (R. C.)

hog down corn: *phr.* To turn hogs into a field of corn and allow them to eat it. Middle West. Common. (N. L.)

home-place: *n.* The farm on which one grew up as distinguished from the "place" on which one lives after marriage. "I'm going to help Pa cut wheat over on the *home-place* this evenin'." Greene Co. Farmers. Common. (W.W.) ((Also, reported from upper S. C., mid. Tenn.))

homely, as homely as a mud-fence: *phr.* Ugly. Caldwell Co. Common. (E. E.) ((In Va.: *as homely (ugly) as a mud-fence daubed with toads.* Reported from Greenville, S. C.: *as plain as a mud-fence.* See *homely*, Wilson's list.))

horn, to come out at the big end of the: *phr.* To be successful. Mo. Ozarks. (P. L.) ((Also Va., N. C., S. C. Cf. the opposite: *to come out at the little end of the horn.*))

horse and team: *n. phr.* A team of horses and the wagon. Caldwell Co. Farmers. Common. (E. E.)

ingern ['ɪŋən] ((in Va. and N. C.: ['iŋən])): *n.* Onion. Mo. Ozarks. Popular. (P. L.)

Jacks, by: *interj.* An expression of surprise, seldom heated enough to represent swearing, but occasionally used for *by God.* Douglas Co. Rural. Rare. In the Turn-Back region between Halltown and Chesapeake, Lawrence Co., *by Gilly* is used instead of *by Jacks.* (W. W.)

juice, to juice a cow: *phr.* To milk. Saline Co. Rather common. (E. K.)

kerflip [kəˈflɪp]: *adj.* Fine, stylish, neat. "Your hat is *ker-flip.*" Livingston Co. Rural. (R. L.)

kitchen safe [ˈkɪtʃən]: *n.* A cupboard. Gentry Co. Rural. (C. C.)

laid up: *adj.* Ill, hurt, unable to work. Caldwell Co. Common. (E. E.) ((Also Va., N. C. Reported from S. C., Fla., La., Tenn.))

larapin' [ˈlærəpɪn]: *adj.* Good, pleasing, delicious. "This blackberry pie is *larapin'.*" Mo. Ozarks. Popular. (P. L.)

lawsy mercy [ˈlɔzɪ ˈmɜsɪ]: *interj.* Contraction of *Lord, have mercy.* Mo. Ozarks. Common. (P. L.) ((Also Va., N. C., S. C.))

lay by: *vb.* To plow (corn) the last time. Middle West ((and the South)). Common. (N. L.)

least chap: *n.* The youngest boy ((?)) in a family. Phelps Co. Rural. Common. (H. G.)

loblolly [ˈlɑbˌlɑlɪ]: *n.* A mud-hole. Grundy Co. (L. M.) ((Also Va., N. C.))

long-yearling: *n.* A beef between one and two years old. Pike Co. (N. L.)

make over: *vb.* To show affection for. "Her grandmother *made over* her too much." Mo. General. (C. C.) ((Rather common in a number of Southern states.))

maters [ˈmetəz]: *n.* Tomatoes. Mo. Popular. (P. L.) ((Also Va., N. C., S. C., Tenn.))

mess: *n.* A portion of, enough to make a meal: "a *mess* of greens (or turnips)." Mo. Ozarks. (P. L.) ((Also Va., N. C., S. C., Tenn.))

miller, to drown the: *phr.* To empty the flour bin. "Better go to the mill, Jim. I *drowned the miller* this morning and need some flour." Caldwell Co. (E. E.)

molly-huggin' [ˈmɑlɪˈhʌgən]: *n.* Love-making, "petting." Used by a minister's wife whose family came from Ohio. Saline Co. Rare. (E. K.)

more'n farmers have hay: *fig. phr.* Much, a great deal. "That lawyer has *more* money'n *farmers have hay.*" Rural. (C. C.) ((Cf. Va.: *more than Carter has oats.*))

Mrs., the [ˈmɪzəz]: *n.* The wife. (S. T.)

muckle to it: *phr.* To work hard. ((*Knuckle to it?*)) Mo. Ozarks. (P. L.)

mumblety-peg ['mʌmlti,pɛg]: *n.* A game played by tossing a two-bladed knife into the air and letting it fall on soft wood. Saline Co. Less common than formerly. (E. K.) ((Also Va., N. C., S. C. Obsolescent.))

noodle: *vb.* To catch fish with the hands by reaching into holes along the bank. Camden Co. (G. O.)

overhalls ['ovɚ,hɔlz]: *n.* Overalls. Common. Saline Co. (E. K.) ((Also Va.))

pair of beads: *n. phr.* A string of beads. Mo. Ozarks. (C. C.) Nw. Mo. (L. M.)

pallet ['pælət]: *n.* A bed made by placing bed-clothing on the floor. Grundy Co. Fairly common. (L. M.) ((Also Va., N. C., S. C.))

pata-too-ta [,pɑtə'tutə]: *interj.* A sound used to call roosters. A different sound is used to call hens (*chick-a-lick-click-click, q. v.*) Saline Co. An old German Farmer. Rare; heard only once. (E. K.)

pert [pɝt]: *adj.* Bright, smart, vivacious. "He's a *pert* little fellow." Mo. Ozarks. (P. L.) ((In Va. [pjɝt] means as above; [pɝt] means saucy, "smarty."))

piddle: *vb.* To waste time, to do nothing in particular. Caldwell Co. (E. E.) Livingston Co. (R. L.) ((Also Va., N. C., S. C., Ga., Tenn.))

play-pretty: *n.* A toy, perhaps a home-made toy. Saline Co. (E. K.) ((Also Va., N. C., Tenn.))

poke: *n.* A bag. Grundy Co. Old persons. Obsolescent. (L. M.) ((Also mountains of Va., N. C., W. Va. Common.))

poker, to have hold of the wrong end of the: *phr.* A saying meaning that one is on the losing side, is making a bad bargain. Mo. Ozarks. (P. L.) ((Cf. old saying used by Henry VIII, Jonson, etc.: "to get (have) the *right* (*wrong*) *sow by the ears.*"))

poo-wee, powee ['puwi, 'pʊwi]: *interj.* A sound used to call hogs. Saline Co. Common. (E. K.)

postes ['postəz]: *n.* Posts. Saline Co. Fairly common. (E. K.)

quile [kwaɪl]: *n.* and *vb.* Coil. "Bull snakes are awful sassy; they just *quile* up and blow at a body." "He was so mad I thought he'd die in his *quiles.*" "My least 'un coughed till he couldn't sleep; then I put a greasy rag 'round his neck, and he jist *quiled* down and slept till mornin'." Greene Co. Common. (W. W.)

rambunctious: *adj.* Unmanageable, disagreeable. Saline Co. Common. (E. K.) ((In Va.: lustful.))

refugee: *n.* A person who came into sw. Mo. from Ga. or Va. via Ark. during the last years of or just after the Civil War. Greene Co. Old persons. Obsolescent. (W. W.)

rick up: *vb.* To pile wood in a orderly manner. Andrew Co. Farmers. Common. (H. G.)

roasting-ear ['rosn͵ɛr]: *n.* Corn on the cob. Saline Co. Common. (E. K.) ((Also Va., N. C., S. C., Tenn.))

rot-gut: *n.* Strong or bad liquor. Nw. Ark. (L. C.) ((Also Va., N. C., S. C.))

sanks, to go to [sæŋks]: *phr.* To go to sleep. "Now shut your eyes and *go to sanks*." Livingston Co. Rural. (R. L.)

sashay [sæ'ʃe]: *vb.* To parade, to strut about. "I saw you *sashaying* up the street yesterday." Caldwell Co. Uneducated. (E. E.) ((Also Va., N. C., S. C.))

shank's ponies, to ride: *phr.* To walk instead of ride. Livingston Co. Rural. (R. L.)

shenannigan, to pull a [ʃə'nænɪgən]: *phr.* To "pull" a stunt. Caldwell Co. (E. E.)

shindig: *n.* A dance. Nw. Ark. Lower class. (L. C.) ((Also Va., N. C.))

shivaree ['ʃɪvɚ͵i]: *n.* (Fr. *charivari?*) A boisterous party for newly-weds at which guns are fired into the air, bells are rung, etc., and at which the newly-weds are supposed to serve candy, cigars, and the like to the crowd. Greene and Lawrence cos. (W. W.) ((Heard years ago in Va. Also, reported from Lauderdale Co., Fla.; Texas.))

shocky ['ʃɑkɪ]: *n.* Salt. May be a word coined in the collector's family; a few persons outside the family use it. Livingston Co. (R. L.)

sky-windin': *adv.* A great distance. "The mule kicked the dog *sky-windin'*." Nw. Mo. Rural. (C. C.) ((Also s. Va., n. N. C., upper S. C.))

slat-bonnet: *n.* A sun-bonnet whose "brim," instead of being stiffened by starch, is made of a rectangular cloth folded and stitched in parallel rows about one inch apart to form long pockets into which strips of lightweight cardboard may be thrust. Douglas Co. Common. (W. W.) ((Also Va., N. C.))

slaunchways: *adj.* and *adv.* Diagonal, not level, not straight.

"The road runs *slaunchways* across the field." "Don't hold your cup *slaunchways*; you'll spill your coffee." Gentry Co. Common. (C. C.) Andrew Co. (H. G.) ((Also Va., N. C.))

slick as a ribbon: *adv.* Completely. "I forgot to go as *slick as a ribbon.*" Livingston Co. Rural. (R. L.)

smack: *adv.* At once. "Go *smack* and do it." Foothills of Ozarks. (C. B.) ((Also Va., N. C.))

sop [sɑp]: *n.* A vulgar term for *gravy*. Randolph Co. Uneducated. (S. T.) ((Also Va.))

stand-table: *n.* A small decorative table used in a living-room or bed-room to place books, pictures, or trinkets on. Saline Co. Common. (E. K.) Grundy Co. (L. M.)

stove up: *adj.* Sore and stiff, generally from overwork or exposure. Andrew Co. Common. (H. G.) ((Also Va., N. C., S. C.))

stripper: *n.* A milkcow that is almost dry. Middle West. Common. (N. L.)

sukee, suk ['su:ki, suk]: *interj.* A term (repeated) used in calling cows. Saline Co. Common. (E. K.) ((Also, reported from upper S. C.))

sulky-plow ['sʌlkɪ-]: *n.* A plow that has wheels and one bottom. Pike Co. Common. (N. L.) ((Also Va.))

swig: *n.* and *vb.* A drink; to drink. Mo. Ozarks. (P. L.)

sympathizer: *n.* A person who was suspected of favoring the cause of the Confederacy. Greene Co. Almost obsolete. (W. W.)

tanty-see-bow [ˌtæntɪ'si,bo]: *adj.* and *adv.* ((Fr. *tant et si beau?*)) Now satisfactory after having been otherwise. If a skirt that had been uneven at the bottom was hemmed up until it hung correctly, one would ask, "Does it look *tanty-see-bow* now?" Or a farmer would kick aside a clod that had prevented a taut string from making a straight line by which to mark the row in the garden, squint along the line, and say, "H'm—I guess it's *tanty-see-bow* now."

tie-hacker: *n.* A man who hacks (hews) railroad ties with a broad-ax. Douglas Co. Rural. Common. (W. W.)

toad-strangler: *n.* A heavy rain. Greene Co. Rare. (W. W.) ((Also Va., N. C., S. C.))

T-road ['tirod]: *n.* A three-branch road that forms a *T*. Andrew Co. Common. (H. G.)

trollop ['trɑləp]: *n.*   A tramp or a person given over to idleness. Andrew Co.   Common.   (H. G.)   ((See Wilson's list.))

wash-house ['wɔʃˌhaʊs]: *n.*   A small house in which washing is done.   Caldwell Co.   Rural.   Common.   (E. E.)

weather-breeder: *n.*   An unusually fine day.   Livingston Co. Rural.   (R. L.)   ((Also, reported from upper S. C.))

well-heeled: *adj.*   Prosperous.   Saline Co.   Common.   (E. K.)

whack: *n.*   A bargain, an agreement.   "John and I made a *whack.*"   Foothills of Mo. Ozarks.   Low.   (C. C.)

whack: *n.*   A lie.   Gentry Co.   (C. C)   ((Also Va., N. C.))

whomper-jawed ['hwɑmpɚˌdʒɔd]: *adj.*   Irregular, uneven, lopsided.   "This pattern is *whomper-jawed.*"   "Your barn is a bit *whomper-jawed.*"   Andrew Co.   Common.   (H. G.)   Carroll Co.   (M. Y.)

whopper-jawed ['hwɑpɚˌdʒɔd]: *adj.*   Crooked, uneven. Randolph Co.   (S. T.)   ((Also Va.))

wire: *n.*   Daring, shrewdness, wit.   Caldwell Co.   Common. (E. E.)

wiry: *adj.*   Daring, shrewd, witty.   Caldwell Co.   Common. (E. E.)

VIII. TOBACCO WORDS

L. R. DINGUS

Transylvania College

To the list of Dr. Dingus I have added, in double parentheses, some words. Unless otherwise labeled, my words come from southern Virginia. Neither Dr. Dingus nor I would claim that this composite list is complete. Doubtless there are many more expressions connected with tobacco on the farm. This list, however, will serve as a "starter" and a challenge to others to send in additional tobacco words and to collect words connected with other occupations.

Below is Dr. Dingus's comment on his list.—The Editor

The words given here are taken from tobacco growers and farmers, dealers, in the unmanufactured product, people on the street, newspapers, agricultural publications, books. Each word recorded has been checked later so as to reduce to the minimum errors as to meaning and use. In case of doubt, the word or the use has been discarded. No effort is made to give the general or, much less, the exclusive use of the word. Only the word, the meaning, and the use as applied popularly and widely by those who have to do with the growing of tobacco and the disposal of the unmanufactured product, are here recognized, unless the word and the use have come out of the technical and scientific sphere and have been taken up by the streetman and farmer as an every-day word. This list is, therefore, not intended for the scientific specialist or the manufacturing technician.

The geographical area of this list centers around Lexington, Kentucky, reaches over into southern Ohio, eastern Tennessee and southwestern Virginia—burley—light-tobacco districts, par excellence. It also in some measure extends out into the western part of the state—the "black-belt." However, much of the special usage noted here, I have discovered, reaches over a much wider area—wherever the "weed" is grown. In these farther areas, no effort has been made to be inclusive or to differentiate variations of detail.

age: *intr. vb.* and *tr. vb.* To stay in storage the requisite time for imparting the desired flavor; to bring about the desired flavor by storing.

air-cure: *vb.* To cure in the open air—for use or for storage.

((**ambeer** ['æmbɪə, -jɛə, -ɚ]: (From *amber?*) The yellow spittle made from chewing tobacco.))

barn: *n.* The building in which tobacco is cured. ((In Va., N. C. the barn is made of logs and daubed with clay.))

barn-rot: *n.* and *vb.* The decay of tobacco while in the barn, caused by too much moisture and too little ventilation among the stalks; to decay in such a manner.

bed, tobacco bed: *n.* A spot of ground specially prepared for sowing the seed. ((In Va. also *plant-bed.*))

barn-tender: *n.* A person who takes care of the barn while the tobacco is being cured.

basket: *n.* and *vb.* A large flat container, often made of wicker, used to hold different grades of tobacco for the market; to put tobacco into such a basket.

((**big Oronoco**: *n.* A variety of tobacco similar to *little Oronoco, q. v.*))

black-fire: *n.* and *vb.* A disease due to excess of moisture, turning the leaf dark or black; to have this disease.

black-French: *n.* and *vb.* A virus disease; to have this disease. The word *French* alone is often used; also *white-French.* I have heard a farmer say: "My tobacco is *Frenching* this hot wet weather."

black-leg, black-shank: *n.* A destructive disease attacking the stalk in the plant bed.

black-tobacco, dark-tobacco: *n.* 1. A variety of tobacco grown especially in western Kentucky; it is also grown in other parts of the country. 2. A shade of color of the cured leaf affecting the price on the market. The *black-belt* is a district where the soil and climate are suitable for this type of tobacco. Formerly the term *export-tobacco* was often used. This kind of tobacco has a stronger, more marked flavor which was preferred in certain foreign countries.

blight: *n.* A leaf disease causing the plant to wither and die.

blue-mold: *n.* A disease attacking especially the young plants while in the bed.

((**boots**: *n.* The stipules of tobacco. See *trash.* In N. C.: *crumbs.*))

bright: *adj.* Having the desired shade of color; a variety of tobacco.

broom-rape: *n.*   A leafless parasitic herb, attaching itself to the roots and injuring the plant.

((**bud-worm:** *n.*   A worm, smaller than the *tobacco-worm*, that feeds on the bud and the upper leaves.   S. Va., n. N. C.))

bug-juice: *n.*   A poison, such as Paris green, used to kill insects attacking tobacco (and other plants).   The term is often used facetiously.

bulk: *n.* and *vb.*   A pile of tobacco; to put in a pile after curing so as to retain the proper amount of moisture for later handling and marketing.   Frequently: to *bulk down* or *to bulk up*.

bull-gang or **the bulls:** *n.*   Men who handle (load or unload) the hogsheads as they are taken to the warehouses for storage and aging.

burley: *n.* and *adj.*   A bright and light variety of tobacco suitable for cigarets.

burley-belt: *n.*   A district having the soil and climate suitable for producing burley tobacco.

burn: *vb.*   1. To turn yellow, especially the lower leaves in rainy or dry weather and die.   2. To get too hot from moisture and close packing in the barn; the leaves turn dark, lose quality, and sometimes rot.   ((3. To become dark, limp, and "dead" because of excessive sunshine after being cut or pulled.))

((**button:** *n.* and *vb.*   The tip of the plant just before it blooms; to reach this state of round maturity.))

case, in: *adj. phr.*   In proper condition—cured and having the correct amount of moisture to ensure handling without injury or loss.   ((Same as *in order*.))

club-root: *n.*   A disease in which nodules appear on the roots.

((**coddle:** *vb.*   To wilt from the heat of the sun.))

condition, in: *adj. phr.*   ((Same as *in case*.))

((**crumbs:** *n.*   Same as *boots*.   N. C.))

cud: *n.*   A chew of tobacco.   Same as *quid*.

cure: *vb.*   To remove the moisture for preserving ((and to induce the color and quality desired for the market)).

((**curing:** *n.*   The amount of tobacco being cured in a barn.))

((**cutters:** *n.*   A grade of tobacco better than the tips.))

dark-tobacco: *n.*   Same as *black-tobacco*.

dip: *n.* and *vb.*   The small amount of tobacco snuff into which a wooden "tooth-brush" is dipped before inserting brush and snuff into the mouth; to rub snuff on the gums.   See *snuff*.

dodder ['dɑdə, -ɚ]: *n.* A parisitic vine that attaches itself to the plant and tends to sap its vitality.

drop: *vb.* To distribute plants on the row in the proper places.

dropper: *n.* A person or a machine that drops or places plants at regular intervals.

dry: *vb.* To remove sap or excess moisture in preparation for handling or storage.

((**filler**: *n.* A low-grade tobacco put inside cigars or plug tobacco.))

fire: *intr. vb.* To turn yellow in the field and die either from excessive rain or from excessive dryness and heat.

fire: *tr. vb.* To cure or dry out tobacco by means of a fire in the barn.

fire-cure: *vb.* To use artificial heat in the barn for curing tobacco.

((**firing**: *n.* The act of keeping a fire in the barn for curing tobacco.))

((**flea-bite**: *n.* Very small holes in the tobacco leaf caused by flea-bugs.))

((**flea-bug**: *n.* A small flea-like insect that eats holes in the leaf; the flea-beetle.))

((**flue**: *n.* The stone, brick, or tin conduit used to circulate heat in the barn while curing tobacco.))

((**flue-barn**: *n.* A barn having flues as distinguished from an "open-air" barn, the latter being used to cure tobacco by the "open-air" process.))

flue-cure: *vb.* To cure by artificial heat passing through flues.

flyings: *n.* The lowest leaves, generally poor in quality but marketable.

Frenchman; *pl.* **Frenchmen**: *n.* Stalk(s) with short, erect small leaves and worthless as to quality. E. Va.

frog-eye: *n.* and *vb.* A spot-disease whose appearance on the leaf suggests the term; to spot thus.

((**grade**: *n.* and *vb.* 1. A general term applied to the quality of tobacco while it is "on the hill" (in the field). 2. A term applied to the quality of tobacco after it has been cured—lugs, tips, fillers, wrappers, etc. 3. To sort tobacco, as in 2, above.))

((**green**: *adj.* State of tobacco in the field before it becomes "ripe"; uncured tobacco, whether in the field or in the barn.))

gross up: *vb.* 1. To pile up. 2. To run up the price.

hand: *n.* A bunch of ten to twenty leaves of the same grade tied together by a leaf (the "tier").

((**hand-plant:** *n.* "Each planter takes a 'hand-plant' to start with. . . . [After embedding the plant in the first hill,] he then picks up the plant on the hill as he moves forward, and by the time he reaches the next hill has adjusted the plant in his hand to insert into the hole in the next hill. Thus the 'hand-plant.' "— F. P. Love, *The Art of Curing Fancy Yellow Tobacco* (Danville, Va., 1884), 15.))

hang: *vb.* To suspend the leaves of tobacco or the stalks on a stick.

hogshead: *n.* A large barrel made of wooden staves, head, and hoops (usually) in which the cured and dried tobacco is stored and aged.

((**horn-worm:** *n.* Same as *tobacco-worm.* S. Va., n. N. C.))

house-burn: *n.* and *vb.* The darkening of the leaves induced by too much moisture and too little ventilation; to bring about this condition.

((**kill, to kill out:** *vb.* To dry out the remaining portion of sap in the leaves by a temperature of 180–200 degrees, to complete the process of curing by high artificial heat. Dr. Dingus thinks the spelling should be *kiln.* He may be correct, but I have seen only *kill.*))

leaf-scald: *n.* Rotting of the leaf due to excessive moisture and lack of ventilation.

leaf-spot: *n.* A leaf disease showing small yellow spots.

((**little Oronoco:** A variety of tobacco having small, narrow leaves, close together on the stalk.))

loaded-stick: *n.* A tobacco stick holding as many stalks ((or bundles of leaves)) as it should hold.

long-green: *n.* 1. A poor quality of tobacco. 2. Freshly cured tobacco being used directly for chewing or smoking before it has aged properly.

long-red: *n.* The (small) upper leaves of high marketable quality.

lugs [lʌgȝ]: The lower leaves ((not the best quality of tobacco)).

makings (singular not heard): *n.* Scraps of leaves dropped in handling tobacco but now gathered and sold at a low price.

miller, tobacco miller: *n.* A moth (sometimes as large as a humming bird) which feeds on the nectar in the "Jimson" weed and deposits on the green tobacco its eggs, which hatch into tobacco worms.

mosaic, leaf-mosaic: *n.* A disease appearing on the leaf and making it spotted.

mosaic-burn: *vb.* To develop mosaic on the leaves.

nesting: *n.* Placing cured tobacco in baskets by grade, usually with the better "hands" outside.

one-sucker tobacco: *n.* 1. Tobacco from which the suckers have been removed only one time before cutting ((or pulling)). 2. Tobacco on which the top sucker or the blooming branch has been left until just before cutting.

((**order:** *tr. vb.* To induce pliableness in tobacco by hanging it in damp air or by hanging it in an "ordering-house."))

((**order, to be** (or **get**) **in:** *phr.* To be in a state of pliancy because of moisture. Tobacco must be "in order" before it can be stripped or otherwise handled. Same as *in case.*))

((**ordering-house:** *n.* A small tight house, generally daubed, in which tobacco is hung and steam applied to induce pliancy.))

((**ordering-pit:** *n.* A large hole, or cellar, dug under a pack-house (or some other house) in which tobacco is hung to get it "in order" by means of the moisture from the earth.))

pack: *vb.* ((1.)) To place for storage in piles, in hogsheads, etc. ((2. To store tobacco in a pack-house in bulk after it has been cured, either before or after stripping.))

packer: *n.* One who packs tobacco.

((**pack-house, packing-house:** *n.* A house in which tobacco is stored after it is cured.))

pin-hook: *vb.* To buy privately, usually small crops and at bargain prices, tobacco in the barn or at the warehouse ((and sometimes in the field)).

pin-hooker: *n.* A dealer who pin-hooks. The dealer and his method are generally frowned upon.

((**plant-bed:** *n.* The small plot of ground upon which logs are piled and burned, and tobacco seed are sowed. Also called *tobacco-bed.*))

((**plant-cloth:** *n.* The cheese-cloth placed over a plant-bed to protect the tender plants from wind, frost, and insects. Also called *plant-bed cloth.*))

((**planter:** *n.* 1. A person who plants tobacco by hand. 2. A machine used in planting tobacco. It is drawn by horses and carries a man (or boy) on each side who inserts a plant in the opening in the row made by a metal blade. Water is loosed at proper intervals.))

((**planting-peg**: *n.* A "peg made of wood [usually a 'fat' pine knot], 5 inches long, one and a quarter inches in diameter at large end, and tapering to a point."—F. P. Love, *The Art of Curing Fancy Yellow Tobacco* (Danville, Va., 1884), 15.))

plug: *n.* A flat oblong hand-pressed piece of tobacco, especially for chewing.

press: *n.* and *vb.* A machine for exerting pressure on tobacco that is being placed in a hogshead for storage or aging; to exert this pressure.

prime: *vb.* To pluck the lower dead or worthless leaves. ((In Va., N. C.: also to pluck the good leaves for curing. Same as to *pull.* Current.))

primer: *n.* One who primes tobacco.

primings: *n.* The lower leaves, formerly waste, now one of the grades on the market.

prize: *vb.* 1. To estimate the value of. 2. To raise the price of by bidding higher. 3. To put in hogsheads for aging and press down hard with machinery.

pull: *vb.* To strip leaves from the stalk.

puller: *n.* One who pulls leaves.

put down: *vb.* To place in piles so as to hold moisture for later handling. Cf. *to bulk.*

quid: *n.* A cud, or chew, of tobacco.

((**raise**: *vb.* To increase the temperature while curing tobacco.))

re-dry: *vb.* To put "in case," to impart the right amount of moisture for aging.

re-drier: *n.* A machine or equipment for re-drying.

((**red-tobacco**: *n.* 1. Air-cured tobacco. 2. Flue-cured tobacco having a reddish color.))

re-set: *vb.* To set, or plant, a second time.

ring-spot: *n.* A disease that at first appears as a small ring in the leaf but later becomes a hole.

((**ripe**: *adj.* In the stage ready to be pulled or cut for curing.))

ripen: *vb.* To mature, to age ((in the field)).

root-rot: A disease which turns the roots black and causes the plant to die.

((**run red**: *vb.* Same as *to house-burn.* N. C.))

rust: *n.* A disease affecting the leaves. ((It begins near the stem and turns the leaf pale-brown before the tobacco gets ripe. Occurs mostly in late tobacco)).

scab: *n.* A leaf disease.

scaffle ['skæfḷ]: *n.* Scaffold. Framework for holding or hanging tobacco while curing.

((**scald:** *vb.* To "raise" on tobacco too rapidly and cause it to become limp and darkened.))

((**scrape down:** *vb.* To pull away with a hoe the surface dirt on the tobacco hill.))

season: *n.* Proper amount of moisture in the air to put tobacco in condition to handle without crumbling.

seed-bed: *n.* Specially prepared ground for tobacco seed. ((Same as *plant-bed*.))

set: *vb.* To plant or transplant the young plants taken from the bed, in rows in the field.

setter: *n.* 1. A person who sets plants. 2. A machine used in setting. ((A tin cylinder having a funnel-shaped lower end that opens and closes. Into this cylinder are dropped the plants, which are "set" when the lower end is inserted into the soft earth and opens.))

((**shingle:** *vb.* To lay green tobacco in close rows after it has been placed on sticks, with the "tails" next to the ground and the "heads" (stems) exposed to the sun. This protects against "coddling" and burning.))

short-red: *n.* The smaller leaves next above the "long-red" on the stalk.

size: *vb.* To grade, to classify.

((**smokers:** *n.* A grade of tobacco used to make cigarets; it is lighter in quality than "fillers."))

snuff: *vb.* 1. To inhale snuff through the nose. 2. To take snuff into the mouth and rub it on the gums with a small wooden "toothbrush."

snuff-dipper: *n.* One who uses snuff by dipping the brush into the snuffbox and inserting the snuff into the mouth.

snuff-pincher: *n.* One who takes a pinch of snuff between his forefinger and thumb and with a delicate gesture lifts the snuff to his nose and "snuffs" it up. Since this form of using snuff is disappearing, the term is now rare.

snuff-user: *n.* A person who uses snuff in any form.

sore-shin: *n.* A disease appearing on the surface of the stalk.

((**sort**: *vb.* Same as *to grade*.))

spads [spɑdz]: *n.* The lower leaves (marketable).

spear: *n.* and *vb.* A round sharp-pointed instrument for piercing a hole in the stalk in preparation for curing; to make a hole with such an instrument.

spot: *n.* A disease making the leaf spotted.

stalk-rot: *n.* A deep-seated disease of the stalk.

stem: *vb.* To remove the stem from the leaf.

stemmer: *n.* A person or a machine that removes the stem.

stemmery: *n.* Machinery for stemming. ((A place where tobacco is stemmed. Va., N. C.))

stick: *n.* and *vb.* A small (usually) flat piece of timber ((four feet and four inches long)) on which the freshly pulled or cut tobacco is hung before being cured ((and packed away)); to arrange tobacco on such a stick; to punch a hole horizontally through the stalk before hanging.

sticker: *n.* The person who pierces—"sticks"—the stalk.

streak: *n.* and *vb.* A mark from bruising or mishandling; to cause such a mark.

strip: *vb.* To pull leaves ((of the cured tobacco)) from the stalk and arrange by grades.

stripper: *n.* A person who strips.

((**strip(ping)-house**: *n* A small house in which tobacco is stripped and graded.))

sucker: *n.*, and *intr. vb.* and *tr. vb.* A shoot growing from the stalk just above the leaf; to form suckers; to strip off suckers.

sun-cure: To cure in the open air, as opposed to *fire-curing*, *flue-curing*, *house-curing*, and *barn-curing*.

sweat: *n.* and *vb.* The moisture appearing on leaves while curing, especially during wet weather and because of poor ventilation; to form such moisture.

sweepings: *n.* The leaves or parts of leaves that crumble during handling, gathered up and marketed; formerly used as fertilizer.

((**tie**: *vb.* 1. To wrap twine around the stems in bundles, or "hands," of green tobacco before curing it. 2. To wrap a leaf around the stems of bundles, or "hands," of cured tobacco after it has been graded.))

tier [tɪə, -ɚ]: *n.* A row or layer of green or cured tobacco.

((**tier** ['taɪə, -ɚ], **tie-leaf**: *n*. A smooth tough leaf used to wrap the head of a bundle, or "hand."))

((**tierce** [tɪəs]: *n*. A cask smaller than a hogshead, used for shipping tobacco. The bottom is smaller than the top. N. N. C.))

tier-pole, tier-stick: *n*. One of several wooden beams upon which the smaller "loaded" sticks of tobacco are hung.

tips: *n*. The upper, smaller leaves, a grade having a light delicate flavor.

((**tobacco-fly**: *n*. Same as *miller*.))

((**tobacco-gum, gum**: *n*. The dark, bitter, sticky gum on the surface of tobacco.))

((**tobacco-wax**: *n*. Same as *tobacco-gum*.))

((**tobacco-worm**: *n*. A large green worm that feeds on green tobacco. Same as *horn-worm*.))

top: *n*. and *vb*. The uppermost part of the stalk; to pluck off this part to prevent the bloom and seed from forming.

((**trash**: *n*. Inferior leaves, broken leaves, "boots," and other waste parts of the leaf, collected, especially in hard times, and sold. Generally made into snuff, or used in making extracts for insecticides.))

twist: *n*. Leaves twisted into a roll for chewing.

vent: *n*. An air-hole in the side or roof or gable of a barn to induce ventilation; it is usually provided with shutters for the control of moisture and temperature.

((**warehouse**: *n*. A large building where tobacco is sold at auction to bidders of different tobacco companies.))

wire-worm: *n*. Larva that feeds on the root of tobacco.

worm: *n*. and *vb*. Same as *tobacco-worm*; to pull worms off by hand and destroy them.

((**wrap**: *vb*. Same as *to tie*. S. Va., n. N. C.))

((**wrapper**: *n*. The best grade of tobacco, used as the outside cover ("wrap") for cigars.))

((**yellow**: *vb*. 1. To assume a yellow color because of ripening in the field. 2. To become yellow after being put in the barn and after the heat has been raised to 90–100 degrees; to cause this process of yellowing to come about by raising the heat.))

((**yellow Oronoco**: *n*. A medium-size Oronoco that cures bright.))

THE AMERICAN DIALECT SOCIETY

PUBLICATION OF THE AMERICAN DIALECT SOCIETY

Number 3

Published by the
AMERICAN DIALECT SOCIETY
May, 1945

Obtainable from the Secretary of the Society
Woman's College of the
University of North Carolina
Greensboro, North Carolina

Continued on Cover 3

PUBLICATION OF THE AMERICAN DIALECT SOCIETY

Number 3

———————

———————

Published by the
AMERICAN DIALECT SOCIETY
May, 1945

Obtainable from the Secretary of the Society
Woman's College of the
University of North Carolina
Greensboro, North Carolina

Number 4

Published by the
AMERICAN DIALECT SOCIETY
... May, 1945

In relationship with the Secretary of the Society
and in a collection of the
University of North Carolina
Chapel Hill, North Carolina

I. THE SECRETARY'S REPORT

The annual meeting of the Society was held in New York City at the Hotel Pennsylvania, December 28, 1944, from 4 to 6 P.M. The meeting was an interesting and full one, papers and discussions running beyond the two hours allotted. Some sixty-five persons attended, more than were able to find seats in the small room where the meeting was in session.

The following papers were read and discussed:

"Some Combining Forms in Current English," I. Willis Russell, University of Alabama.

"Notes on Dialect in Early American Writers," Harry R. Warfel, Department of State.

"Some Characteristics of the English of the Middle Atlantic Seaboard," Major Henry Lee Smith, Jr., Language Section, Information and Education Division, Army Service Forces.

It was regrettable that, because of travel restrictions, Dr. Josiah Combs, Texas Christian University, was unable to be present and read his paper, "Lincoln's Gettysburg Address in the Vernacular of the Kentucky Mountaineers."

Reports were given by the Secretary, the Auditing Committee, and the President.

All the officers of 1944 were re-elected for another year. The revised constitution was adopted. It follows this report. (For the old constitution, see *Dialect Notes*, II, 278–9.)

The next meeting, war conditions permitting, will be held at or near Chicago, in conjunction with the Modern Language Association of America.

B. SOME MATTERS REPORTED ON AT THE MEETING

1. *Publishing.* Finding a capable printer who would print our journal at a reasonable price was a discouraging labor. Finally after corresponding with or interviewing fifteen printers, the Secretary secured a satisfactory printer, the Waverly Press, of Baltimore. Two numbers of our organ, the *Publication of the American Dialect Society*, were issued for 1944: Number 1, *Instructions to Collectors of Dialect*, and Number 2, *Word-Lists from the South*.

2. *Membership.* In an effort to secure more members, the Secretary sent out several hundred letters to persons and libraries

that had been members or that he thought might become members. The following are some figures concerning membership:

Life members..	19
Paid-up members.....................................	166
Unpaid but probably "good" members................	37
Paid-up libraries.....................................	80
Total actual members............................	302
Former members not responsive by word or money.....	56
Former library members that have not rejoined.........	55
Potential members..................................	111
Total actual and potential members..............	413

3. *Financial report.* This report is as of December 13, 1944.

Receipts

Received from Mr. A. W. Read:

Feb. 19 one check from MLA...................	$100.	
Feb. 19 one check from E. L. Thorndike for new new words..	50.	
Sept. 2 one cashier's check for the Society's money....................................	374.45	
Sept. 2 43 checks, mainly for dues.............	97.60	
Total.....................................		$622.05
Less 2 "bad" checks...........................	4.00	
Actual total...............................		$618.05
Sept. 11 from Edgar Kurt for PADS No. 1..........	.25	
Dues from members.............................	170.00	
Dues from libraries.............................	148.00	
Grand total receipts.........................		$936.30

Disbursements

For envelopes.....................................	$9.19	
" express...	1.91	
" miscellaneous...................................	21.48	
" paper..	16.84	
" postals and stamps.............................	48.14	
" printing 1200 PADS No. 1......................	87.82	
" typing...	1.25	
" stencils..	1.20	
" telegrams.......................................	1.64	
Total disbursements...........................		$189.97
Balance on hand.............................		$746.33

Disbursements yet to be made

Cost of 600 copies of PADS No. 2

   "   of express on same

   "   of mailing same

II. REVISED CONSTITUTION OF THE AMERICAN DIALECT SOCIETY

I. NAME AND OBJECT

1. The name of this Society shall be the "American Dialect Society."

2. The object of the Society is the study of the English language in North America, together with other languages influencing it or influenced by it.

II. OFFICERS

1. The principal officers of the Society shall be a president, a vice-president, and a secretary-treasurer. These shall be elected at the annual meeting and shall enter upon their duties on the first of January following and shall serve for one year, or until their successors are elected.

2. Four members of the Society shall be elected who, together with the president, the vice-president, and the secretary-treasurer, shall constitute the executive council. These four members shall be elected for a term of four years, one post falling vacant each year.

3. The executive council shall have power to fill any vacancy in their number by appointment until new officers are chosen.

4. The executive council shall control all expenditures, determine the selection and distribution of the publications of the Society, and administer the other affairs of the Society.

5. The executive council may appoint district secretaries, who shall care for the interests of the Society in their respective districts. Local groups may become affiliated with the Society on conditions determined by the executive council.

III. MEMBERSHIP

1. Any person interested in the object of the Society may become a member by paying the dues set by the executive council and by filing his name and address with the secretary-treasurer, and he may continue his membership by paying the annual dues.

2. A person may become a life member by paying a sum set by the executive council and thenceforth be exempt from annual dues.

IV. MEETINGS

1. An annual meeting for the presentation of a report by the secretary-treasurer, for the election of officers, and for other purposes as determined by the executive council, shall be held at a time and place to be determined by the executive council.

2. Timely notice of this meeting shall be sent by the secretary-treasurer to all members.

3. Special meetings may be called at any time by the executive council.

4. A quorum shall be ten members in good standing.

V. AMENDMENTS

Amendments to this constitution may be made at the annual meeting by a two-thirds vote of the members present, provided at least ten members have expressed their approval of them, in writing, to the secretary-treasurer sixty days before the annual meeting.

III. COMMENTS ON *WORD-LISTS FROM THE SOUTH, PUBLICATION OF THE AMERICAN DIALECT SOCIETY,* NUMBER 2

Although the Editor and the contributors to the *Word-Lists* are highly pleased with the laudatory comments from scores of scholars in this country and abroad, only those comments which suggest some improvement in methods of collecting or presenting material or which bring additional information are given here. Editorial comments are placed in double parentheses.

GENERAL SUGGESTIONS

Identification of natural objects.

One general suggestion which, as a naturalist, I feel impelled to make concerns the lack of definite identification of terms applied to natural objects. Surely in the colleges where most collectors of dialect have headquarters there are botanists, entomologists, and other scientists who could assist by providing technical names of the objects involved. This would give the terms definite standing and make them available for use by others.—W. L. McAtee.

Indecent words.

The lexicographers and other scholars of the English language have not treated adequately or frankly the large group of words classed as indecent. During the two years before the First World War I was a student in Europe, mainly in Germany. I early noticed that Europeans are much more matter-of-fact, less squeamish than we about such words, without in the least descending into the vulgar. I also noticed that certain terms of this type in German showed linguistic kinship with English. As a university student, I had ready access to standard and scholarly reference books. And what I at first merely suspected began to show positive evidence: I discovered that neither Webster, the Century, Funk and Wagnalls, nor the Oxford treats these words candidly, and often not at all. Wright's *English Dialect Dictionary* is fuller but not adequate. The biologists have gone ahead with their studies, dismissing or ignoring inhibitions. The Freudians are now reveling in this hitherto forbidden psychological area of the inner or hidden life. Only the linguists hold aloof and are turned aside by squeamishness and social taboo. The time is about ripe for linguists frankly and scientifically to undertake this task from

7

a language point of view. I believe that they would produce positive results worth the effort.—L. R. Dingus

The English seem to be squeamish on "unconventional" speech, and prevent the printing in full of certain indecent words. (See Eric Partridge's remark under *c*nt*, in his *Dictionary of Slang and Unconventional English*.) The French are sensibly liberal in this respect, and in their researches do not hesitate to print expressions which they would not, of course, bandy about in public. —Josiah Combs

A suggestion on "Instructions to Collectors of Dialect."

Although the *Instructions* are very complete and should be very useful, I think that there certainly should be provision for at least approximate dating of the usage(s).—W. F. Bryan.

COMMENTS ON SPECIFIC EXPRESSIONS

The comments below have to do with different meanings, different pronunciations, different parts of speech, and different locales where the expressions are found.

The comments are arranged alphabetically for this number of the *Publication*. The page reference is given. The commentator's initials follow his comment. Here are the chief persons offering information: *W. F. B.*—Dr. William F. Bryan, retired head of English at Northwestern University (now living at Tryon, N. C.): born in eastern N. C.; lived 20 years in eastern N. C.; 5 years at Chapel Hill, N. C.; 7 years at Asheville, N. C.; 35 years in and around Chicago; and 17 summers in northern Vt. *B. Q. M.*— Dr. B. Q. Morgan, professor of German, Stanford University: born in Mass., 1883; lived in Conn. till 1904; Madison, Wis., 1907– 34; Stanford, 1934 to date. *M. C. P.*—Miss Mary Celestia Parler, department of English, Bethel College, Ky.: born in Wedgefield, Sumter Co., S. C.; father a physician, mother a college graduate; has lived in S. C., Wis., N. C., R. I., and Georgia; unless otherwise indicated, her comments refer to usages in or around Wedgefield, S. C. *R. A. W.*—Miss Rosemary A. White, department of English, Nazareth College, Rochester, N. Y.: has always lived in Rochester except for three years in England and one year in Cambridge, Mass.; ancestors for three generations lived in Rochester; unless otherwise indicated, her comments refer to usages in or around Rochester, N. Y.

((**alo, alow,** 39: Pronunciation a misprint; should be ['elo].))

and those, 39: I am interested in your item *and those*, and the comments thereupon. I have heard *Messieurs-'dames* often in French, in a similar sense. Bauche might have extended his comments even further, in popular speech; among the folk in France, it is nearly always *M'sieurs-'dames* or *'Dames-'sieures.*— Josiah Combs

antigodlin, etc., 17: [æntɪ'gazlɪn] is the form heard here.— M. C. P.

back-door-trots, 39: *To have the trots* familiar in Conn.—B. Q. M. *Trots* the only form I have heard here; common.—M. C. P.

be, 40: One of my farmer friends in n. Vt. uses "I *be*" in statements, possibly more emphatic than "I *am.*"—W. F. B.

belly-button, 26: Commonly known here.—R. A. W.

belly-buster, 53: *Belly-flopper* in Conn.; I think also *belly-whopper.*—B. Q. M.

bitty, little, 32: Generally known here; mainly used by children or by adults to children.—R. A. W.

booger, 40: Used in all three senses by all classes.—M. C. P.

catched, 41: Heard in Conn. in my youth; always [ketʃt].— B. Q. M.

Christmas Eve, 7: Also *New Year's Eve*; used by all classes.— M. C. P. Used here; we make distinctions: "the morning of Christmas Eve," "Christmas Eve about four o'clock."—R. A. W.

church, 26: *To church*, as I have known the term, means to call before local church authorities for some offense. The penalty is not necessarily expulsion but may be censure or some form of penance—or even acquittal.—W. F. B.

cock, 18: Also **cunt** [kʌnt]. Cf. the Wife of Bath's use of *queynte.*—W. F. B. ((Cf. the Miller's use also. The Editor had *cunt* in his manuscript, but one reader advised against including the term, on the ground that it was common throughout the country in the same sense. But the word was reported to me from Alberta, Canada, as meaning penis. The etymology of the word is also interesting.))

cuckol, 18: In the Kentucky mountains *cuckol'* is used mainly as a verb. Used literally, it means that one man makes a *cuckol'* of another by having carnal knowledge of the latter's wife: "Hank *cuckol'ed* John seven year." Sometimes the verb may refer to the conduct of the wife who has been unfaithful to her husband.

Used figuratively, it means to reach the wrong conclusion through faulty reason or prejudice. As a noun, the word means the husband who has been abused as above.—Cratis D. Williams.

dido, to cut a, 28: Used in my family. It was not always accompanied by *cut*: "I'll have none of your *didoes*."—R. A. W.

dingus, 25: Familiar to me in Conn.—B. Q. M.

do-hicky, 55: Used here.—R. A. W.

dratted, etc., 29: Really a past participle. I am familiar with *drat it* as a mild imprecation.—W. F. B.

dumb chill, 8: A chill *un*accompanied by shaking.—M. C. P.

fasset, 25: Common in my youth in Conn.—B. Q. M. Commonly used by workmen who repair faucets.—R. A. W.

((**fornent,** 42: [fɚ'nent] should be [fɚ'nɛnt].))

gism, 19: Common among boys in Conn. in my childhood.—B. Q. M.

go-devil, 43: I have heard this word used recently ((in the sense given)) in Polk Co., N. C.—W. F. B. A farm implement used in cultivating very young corn in a field that has been listed (deeply furrowed). It resembles a high sled with a seat on it. At the back of the sled is a disk on each side which throws a little dirt in to the corn. The verb means "to cultivate with this implement." Holt Co., Mo. Common.—Allen B. Kellogg.

handle, to fly (off) the, 57: Commonly used here to mean "to become angered."—R. A. W.

Harry, Old, 34, and **Scratch, the Old,** 36: Used in my family.— R. A. W. ((Recently reported from Atlanta: *Old Hairy-* (or *Harry-*) *toe*, meaning Satan.))

hotten, 44: Not an adjective here but a verb meaning "to make hot."—M. C. P.

knee-baby, 45: I have heard this kind of expression here: "She's got one *lap-chile*, one *po'ch chile*, and three *ya'd chillen*." —M. C. P.

knock up, 45: Familiar to me from my youth in Conn.—B. Q. M.

lay-over ... to catch meddlers, 45: Heard here as "Lay-overs to catch meddlers, and it'll catch you first one."—M. C. P.

leak, 46: I also know the expression "to take a *leak*." I am not sure of having heard this in Conn., but know it was used in Wis. and Cal.—B. Q. M. *Leak* is not heard as a verb here, but "to take a *leak*" is heard.—M. C. P. ((When the Editor recorded *leak* as a verb, he perhaps had his eye too much on Shakespeare;

otherwise he would have recorded *to leak* and *to take a leak*. Both occur in Va. and N. C.))

master (hand), 46: Familiar to me from Conn. Also applied to women: "She's a *master hand* at making pies."—B. Q. M.

meech, 46: I know this expression in "Don't look so *meechin'* " in the sense of needless humility, without the suggestion of dishonesty.—B. Q. M.

nose out of joint, 25: Used here in the sense of the ill-pleased child; not common.—R. A. W.

one o'clock, 20: Familiar to me from boyhood in Conn.— B. Q. M.

overhalls, 59: Common here some years ago among workmen. —R. A. W.

piece, 11: From earliest childhood I have been familiar with this expression.—R. A. W.

rambunctious, 60: Used occasionally here in the sense of unmanageable or disagreeable.—R. A. W.

roasting-ear, 12: Is never heard; everyone says *mutton corn*.— M. C. P.

rumpityfetida, 21: A marvelous bowdlerizing euphemism! I envy Combs's having picked that up.—W. F. B.

sashay, 60: I have always known this but do not remember having heard it recently.—R. A. W. Since *sashay* is connected with the dance step the chassé, readers of PADS may wish to examine these two words in lexicographical works: *NED*, s. v. *chassé*, st. and v. (the *NED* lists *sashy*, *sas(s)hay* as "U.S. vulgar"!); *DAE*, s.v. *sash(a)y*, v.; Wentworth, *ADD*, p. 530. An excellent quotation comes from Herman Melville, *Mardi*, Ch. I: "In good time making the desired longitude upon the equator, a few leagues west of the Gallipagos, we spent several weeks *chassezing* across the Line, to and fro, in unavailing search for our prey."—Elliott V. K. Dobbie.

so as, 49: Familiar to me in the sense "so that" in my youth in Conn.—B. Q. M.

spell, *vb*., 36: Webster calls this obsolete, but I think not. It is quite active in my vocabulary; familiar to me from childhood. —B. Q. M.

spit cotton, 50, 55: I know in the sense of being so dry-mouthed that saliva does not flow freely but can be ejected only in aerated white flecks.—W. F. B.

step off, 26: Generally known here, though less common than formerly.—R. A. W.

the, sick in the bed, 13: We never say *sick in bed.*—M. C. P.

wait on, 37: Not common here; but my Scottish housekeeper, who, despite a thirty-year residence in Rochester, clings to her native idiom, uses it.—R. A. W.

wa'n't, 51: Common in N. E. in my youth. The *a* as in *father.*— B. Q. M.

washwoman, 14: In my family this was the usual and I think the only synonym for *laundress.* When I first heard the more usual *washerwoman,* it sounded strange.—R. A. W.

whack, 62: Familiar to me in the sense of "a lie."—M. C. P.

IV. NOTES ON THE SOUNDS AND VOCABULARY OF GULLAH[1]

LORENZO D. TURNER

Fisk University

For the article which follows Dr. Turner has drawn upon the wealth of his forthcoming book, *Africanisms in the Gullah Dialect*. This study will probably be published by the Linguistic Society of America. It will discuss Africanisms in the vocabulary, sounds, syntax, morphology, and intonation of the dialect; and it will point out similarities between the Gullah and the African languages in the methods employed to form words. Each of these aspects will cover a chapter. The opening chapter will be devoted to the backgrounds of Gullah. One chapter will contain texts in phonetic notation. The chapter on African words in Gullah will contain between 4000 and 5000 such words with the pronunciation and the meaning they have in Gullah and in the West African languages, between twenty-five and thirty of these languages being represented.

Dr. Turner has been engaged in the study of Gullah since 1930.—The Editor

THE GULLAH AREA

The dialect known as Gullah or Geechee[2] is spoken by a large number of ex-slaves and their descendants who live in the coastal region of South Carolina and Georgia, both on the Sea Islands and on the mainland nearby. The present writer's field work on

[1] The writer's study of the Gullah dialect was made possible by grants from the American Council of Learned Societies.

[2] There are two theories regarding the origin of the word "Gullah," pronounced ['gʌlə] and, by many of the ex-slaves, ['gula]. One is that it is derived from "Gola," a tribe and language of Liberia. The name of this tribe and language is pronounced in different ways by the different neighboring tribes. Among these varying pronunciations are the following: [gola, gula, gura, gɔla, and gɔra]. See F. W. H. Migeod, *The Languages of West Africa* (1913) 2. 345. The other theory is that the word "Gullah" is derived from "Ngola" [ŋgɔla], the name of a tribe in the Hamba Basin of Angola.

The word "Geechee" ("Geejee") usually pronounced by the Gullahs ['ɟⱶ‑ic ‑łi] (['ɟⱶɨɟ ‑łi]), is very probably derived from the name of another tribe and language of Liberia, among the different pronunciations of which are the following: [gitʃi], [gidʒi], [gitsi], [gisi], etc.

13

this dialect covered the area extending southward along the Atlantic coast from Georgetown, S. C. to the northern boundary of Florida, a territory approximately two hundred and fifty miles in length.　The communities in South Carolina that furnished the most distinctive specimens of the dialect were Waccamaw (a peninsula near Georgetown) and James, Johns, Wadmalaw, Edisto, St. Helena, and Hilton Head Islands.　Those in Georgia were Darien, Harris Neck (a peninsula near Darien), Sapeloe Island, St. Simon Island, and St. Marys.　On the mainland of both South Carolina and Georgia many of the communities in which specimens of the dialect were recorded are situated twenty miles or further from the coast.

METHOD OF COLLECTING MATERIAL

In each community where the dialect was studied, at least three informants were selected.　These three persons, two of whom were above sixty years of age, were born in their respective communities[3] and had had a minimum of contact elsewhere. Their parents were also born there.　In studying the vocabulary of Gullah, however, the writer consulted a great many additional informants in each of the several communities.

Specimens of the dialect were gathered by means of interviews with informants during which work-sheets were used similar to those prepared by the staff of the Linguistic Atlas of the United States and Canada, but made suitable for use among the Gullahs. In addition, phonograph recordings were made of many varieties of Gullah material, including autobiographical sketches of informants, narratives of religious experience, prayers, sermons, religious and secular songs, folk tales, proverbs, superstitions, descriptions of living conditions on the Sea Islands, recollections of slavery, methods of planting and harvesting crops, methods of cooking, systems of counting, etc.

AFRICAN BACKGROUND OF THE GULLAHS

The Gullahs are descendants of slaves brought to South Carolina and Georgia, prior to the Civil War, principally from the West Coast of Africa.　Those sections of West Africa supplying the largest numbers were Senegal, Gambia, Sierra Leone, Liberia, the

[3] See footnote 6.

Gold Coast, Togo, Dahomey, Nigeria, and Angola. A conservative estimate of the number of Africans brought to South Carolina and Georgia direct from the West Coast of Africa during the one hundred years prior to 1808, when the Slave Trade Act prohibiting further importation of slaves to the United States became operative, would be at least 100,000.[4] Between 1808 and 1860 this traffic, though less active, continued nevertheless.[5] Records revealing the number of these slaves who remained in coastal South Carolina and Georgia and of those who were taken there from other places are not available; but the large number of Africanisms still surviving among the Gullahs would seem to indicate that a large percentage of these "new" slaves (i.e. those who were coming direct from Africa to Charleston and other places nearby until almost the beginning of the Civil War, and who on arriving in the United States presumably had little or no acquaintance with the English language) were occupying the Gullah region, and thus were augmenting the Africanisms of the Gullahs already there and strengthening their African speech habits. Moreover, isolated as the slaves were on the Sea Islands, they found it much easier to retain elements of their native culture than those slaves living in less isolated areas. Africanisms are still numerous in Gullah. They are found in the sounds, vocabulary, syntax, morphology, and intonation of the dialect, and there are many similarities between Gullah and the African languages in the methods used to form words.

THE SOUNDS OF GULLAH

This treatment of Gullah sounds is based upon a study of the pronunciation of twenty-one Gullah informants. The following letters and numerals will be used when reference is made to these informants:

Edisto Island, S. C.:
Diana Brown................................. E1
Anne Crosby................................. E2
Hester Milligan............................. E3

[4] See Elizabeth Donnan, *Documents Illustrative of the History of the Slave Trade to America* (1935) 4. 278–587.
[5] See W. E. Burghardt DuBois, *The Suppression of the African Slave Trade to the United States of America* (1896) 108–50. See also Frederic Bancroft, *Slave-Trading in the Old South* (1931) 359–60.

Wadmalaw Island, S. C.:

Saki Sweetwine.. W1

Prince Smith... W2

Sarah Ross... W3

Johns Island, S. C.:

Lucy Capers.. J1

Sanko Singleton.. J2

Susan Quall.. J3

St. Helena Island, S. C.:

Samuel Polite.. H1

Anne Scott... H2

Paris Capers... H3

Sapeloe Island, Ga.:

Katie Brown.. S1

Shad Hall.. S2

Balaam Walker.. S3

St. Simon Island, Ga.:

Wallace Quarterman[6].................................. SS1

David White.. SS2

Belle Murray... SS3

Harris Neck and Brewer's Neck, Ga.:

James Rogers... HN1

Bristow McIntosh....................................... HN2

Scotia Washington...................................... BN1

The following are the sounds of Gullah together with a few of the words in which they were observed:

VOWELS AND DIPHTHONGS

[i]—feel; hair; James, ra*i*sin; give, itch, whicker

[ɪ] ([ɨ])—hill; weave, screech; creek; g*e*neral, deaf; c*a*labash, January; such, put; t*o*mbstone; cask*e*t, J*e*nkins; Mar*y*; Sat*u*rday

[e]—day; air, bear; clear, beard; bed, egg

[ɛ]—edge; make, take; br*o*ther, shut, touch, etc.

[a] ([aˑ, ã])—at, back; after, half, aunt; barn, marsh; calm, palm, father; can't

---

[6] Wallace Quarterman was born in Liberty County, Georgia, and when quite young moved to St. Simon Island, where, until his death recently, he lived more than seventy years.

[ɒ] ([ɒ·])—body; borrow; corn, cork; coffee, office; dog, hog; wash; daughter; all; August; bundle, color

[ʌ]—bucket, month; bird, burn

[o]—boat, post; door; oven

[u]—cool, goose, do; Luke, Matthew

[ʊ]—bull, look; coop, hoop, room, etc.

[ə] ([ə̄])—about; daughter, Martha

[ɪu]—duty, Tuesday

[ɒɪ] ([ɐɪ])—boy, join, boil; by, die, while; bite, nice, like, right

[ɒʊ] ([ɐʊ])—cow, plow; house, about

These sounds require further explanation:

[i]. [i] in Gullah is practically Cardinal No. 1.[7]

[ɪ]. In addition to the principal member of the [ɪ]—phoneme, there is a considerably retracted variety, the central vowel [ɨ], which is heard occasionally when there is an adjacent k, g, l, or r. A shorter variety of the central vowel [ɨ] occurs in the final open syllable of a word. A still shorter and less retracted variety of [ɨ] occurs in words and phrases of more than two syllables: ['satɨde] "Saturday," [ɸə̄ tɨ'mɒrə̄]" for tomorrow," etc.

[e]. Gullah [e] is slightly higher than Cardinal No. 2. It is never diphthongized. W1 uses a slightly lower [e] in all positions than any of the other informants.

[ɛ]. [ɛ] is practically Cardinal No. 3. A few of the informants used a more open variety of [ɛ] before nasals—a pronunciation quite common also among Negroes in Charleston, S. C. HN1 used a very open variety of [ɛ] in all positions.

[a]. [a] is practically Cardinal No. 4. It is used regularly in positions where in General American [æ] and long [ɑ] are usually heard. Before and after palatal plosives, E2, J2, W1, and W2 used a variety of [a] that was slightly above cardinal. W1 and J2 used a slightly retracted variety of [a] after [h]. A nasalized variety of the phoneme occurs in the word [cḁ̃] "can't."

[ɒ]. In the pronunciation of Gullah [ɒ], the tongue is held very low and almost fully back. The lips are usually somewhat rounded. In the speech of HN1, HN3, E3, and J2, the lips are quite rounded, and in that of SS1 the sound is fully back and has less lip-rounding after [k] and [t] than elsewhere. In Gullah, [ɒ] is regularly used in positions where in GA [ɑ] and [ɔ] occur. In

---

[7] For a description of the cardinal vowels see Daniel Jones, *An Outline of English Phonetics* (1932) 31–36.

many words it occurs where [ʌ] and [aʊ] or [ɑʊ] would be used in cultivated American speech.

[ʌ]. In the pronunciation of Gullah [ʌ], the tongue is slightly lower than for Cardinal [ɔ] and somewhat more advanced.

[o]. [o] is slightly above cardinal and is never diphthongized. The lips are fully rounded.

[u]. The principal member of the [u]-phoneme in Gullah is practically Cardinal No. 8. An advanced variety occurs after alveolar consonants.

[ʊ]. The position of the tongue in the pronunciation of Gullah [ʊ] is slightly higher than half-close and is considerably advanced from the position required for [u].

[ə]. The [ə]-phoneme comprises two varieties: (1) a short one with a tongue position somewhat higher than half-open, and (2) a fairly long one with a more retracted tongue position and approximately half-open but more advanced and higher than that required for [ʌ]. The former is indicated by the notation [ə̆], and the latter by [ə̄]. [ə̆] is used always in unstressed positions, as in the first syllable of "about." [ə̄] occurs in final syllables and is used in the newer type of speech to replace [ʌ] by persons who try to distinguish stress.

[ɒɨ]. In the pronunciation of the principal member of the [ɒɨ]-phoneme, the tongue begins at a low and almost fully back position, frequently with lip-rounding, and moves in the direction of [ɨ]. When adjacent to [l] (which in Gullah is clear in all positions), [c], [ɟ], or [ʃ], the first element of the diphthong is usually advanced, sometimes to [a]. The first element is considerably advanced and raised to [ɐ] when the diphthong is followed by a voiceless consonant and frequently also when preceded by fricative r.

[ɒʊ]. Before a voiceless consonant, the first element of [ɒʊ] is regularly advanced and raised to [ɐ].

CONSONANTS

[p] ([p']) — pen, stopper, swamp

[b] ([b̥]) — baby; tube; coop

[t] ([t'], [ṭ], [t], [ɾ]) — take, Tuesday, cut; month, think; butter; little

[d] ([ɾ]) — dog; this, with, teethe; brother, puddle

[ç] ([ç ʰ]) — chew, March; fence

[ɟ̧] — Jack, edge; measure; reins; zigzag; rubbish

[k] ([k'], [k⊣], [c⊦])—cool; case, careful, cat

[kp]—['kpākpā] "to pound" (from Mende [kpākpā])

[g] ([g⊣], [ɟ⊦])—gutter; egg; gable, garden

[gb]—[gbla] "near" (from Mende [gbla])

[m]—March, former, bottom

[mb]—[m'bila] a personal name (from Kongo [mbila] "a call")

[mp]—[m'puku] "rat" (from Kongo [mpuku])

[n]—turn; palm, mushroo*m*

[nd]—[n'dɔmbe] a personal name (from Kongo [ndɔmbe] "black-
ness")

[nt]—[n'tama] a personal name (from Twi [n₁tã₁mã₃][8] "a dress")

[ɲ]—[boɲ] "tooth" (from Wolof [boɲ] "tooth"); new, young,
united

[ŋ]—long; round, pound, down; [ŋ'di] a personal name (from
Ewe [ŋ₁di₃] "morning"; [ŋ'gaŋga] a personal name (from
Kongo [ŋgaŋga] a "doctor")

[8] Tones are given for words from the following West African languages:
Twi, Fante, Ewe, Ibo, Efik, Ibibio, Vai, and Yoruba. The low, mid, and
high level tones will be indicated, respectively, by the inferior numerals
1, 2, and 3 placed after the syllables whose tones they represent. Glides
from one tone level to another will be indicated as follows:

3-1 = a tone falling from high to low
3-2 = a tone falling from high to mid
2-1 = a tone falling from mid to low
1-3 = a tone rising from low to high
1-2 = a tone rising from low to mid
2-3 = a tone rising from mid to high

The accentuation of Gullah words of more than one syllable is indicated
by the mark (') placed before the syllable for the main stress and (ˌ) placed
before the syllable for the secondary stress, when it is thought necessary to
indicate the secondary stress. Wholly unstressed syllables are not marked.
The accentuation and intonation of Gullah words vary somewhat with
individual speakers. A word is given the pronunciation used by the particular speaker from whom it was obtained. In the case of many Gullah
words the syllables differed not so much in stress as in tone. These differ-
ences are indicated by inferior numerals placed after the syllables. Where-
as Gullah does not have significant tone in the sense in which the West
African tone languages do, it does have a characteristic intonation and
rhythm. In the case of words from non-tone African languages the accentuation is given only when there was an opportunity to obtain it from native
speakers of the language.

Other diacritics are as follows: ' glottalization; ʰ aspiration; ~ nasaliza-
tion; ₒ unvoicing; ⊣ fronting; ⊦ backing; the sign : when placed after vowel or
consonant indicates that the sound is relatively long; the sign · indicates
intermediate length.

[l]—sale, long; Brewer, proud, fritter; Mary, bureau; war
[φ]—fall, staff
[β] ([ϑ])—river, very; we, weary; white, while
[ʃ] ([ʃ'])—dish, shine; ashes, rushes, cedar, sister, shoes, soda, etc.
[s]—seven; shrimp, shrink
[z] ([ẕ])—rose; examine; mouse
[j]—yonder; ear, hear
[r]—right, bright, tree; Sarah
[h]—hand, hard, heap; ashes, altar

[p]. [p] is generally unaspirated in Gullah. Before long vowels in very emphatic speech, however, it is often followed by slight aspiration. Some informants used the ejective (glottalized) *p* [p'] at the beginning of a stressed syllable. Here the glottal stop was weak and occurred just after the mouth closure was released. These variants of *p* are not distinctive in Gullah.

[b] Some informants used an unvoiced variety of *b* in such words as [bŏ'nanō] "banana," [kʊḇ] "coop," [cꟸ uḇ] "tube," etc.

[t]. [t] appears regularly in all positions where in G A the voiceless inter-dental fricative [θ] is used. Several varieties of *t* were observed. Between vowels the alveolar tap is the usual sound in Gullah. J2 used the voiced *t* between vowels and between a vowel and *l;* W1 used the post-alveolar *t* before front and back vowels; HN1 regularly used the dental *t* in initial position; E3 frequently used the retroflex *t* in medial position, as in [bɪ'φoʈɒɪm] "formerly." As in the case of *p*, a weakly glottalized *t* [t'] was sometimes heard at the beginning of a stressed syllable.

[d]. [d] occurs regularly in all positions where in G A the voiced inter-dental fricative [ð] is used. The retroflex flap [ɽ] occurs between vowels and medially before *l* as a substitute for the G A alveolar [d] and [ð]. HN2 used the retroflex *d* in these positions. SS1 and HN1 used the dental *d* in all positions. E2 and E3 used an unvoiced *d* in final position.

[cꟸ]. The voiceless palatal plosive usually occurs in those positions where in G A the voiceless palato-alveolar affricate [tʃ] would appear. In emphatic speech [cꟸ] is sometimes slightly aspirated.

[ɟꟸ]. The voiced palatal plosive usually occurs in those positions where in G A the voiced palato-alveolar affricate [dʒ] and the voiced palato-alveolar fricative [ʒ] would be used. Occasionally it is heard where [z] or [ʃ] would be found in G A. A voiceless variety of [ɟꟸ] frequently appears in final position.

[k].   Before front vowels (including [a]), a very advanced variety of the [k]-phoneme occurs.   Several informants used the voiceless palatal plosive [cǀ] here, making it difficult for the listener to distinguish such a word as "chat" from "cat" or "chase" from "case."   As in the case of [p] and [t], a few informants used a weakly glottalized *k* [k'] as a non-distinctive variant of *k* at the beginning of a stressed syllable.

[g].   Before front vowels (including [a]), a very advanced variety of the [g]-phoneme occurs.   Several informants used here the voiced palatal plosive [ɟǀ].   An unvoiced variety of *g* is frequently heard in final position.

[n].   [n] is replaced by [m] when a bilabial sound precedes, as in ['kɒɸm] "coffin," ['hɛβm] "heaven," ['opm] "open."   It is replaced by the palatal nasal [ɲ] when [c] or [ɟ] follows: [ɸɛɲcǀ] "fence," [reɲɟǀ] "reins."   [n] regularly replaces G A final [ŋ] in words of more than one syllable.

[ɲ].   [ɲ] is heard in Gullah in many positions where [n] or [j] occurs in G A.

[l].   [l] in Gullah is generally clear not only before vowels but finally and before consonants.   Two informants (J2 and W3) occasionally used a dark *l* finally and before a consonant.   SS1 used only dental *l's*, all of which were very clear.   In many words *l* replaces G A *r*.   Some informants used *l* and *r* interchangeably, especially between vowels.   On Edisto Island, S. C., G A initial *l* was occasionally replaced by *n*: [nʌl] "lull," etc.

[ɸ].   The voiceless bilabial fricative in Gullah is used regularly in positions where in G A the voiceless labio-dental fricative [f] occurs.   W3 and SS1 frequently articulated the sound with slight lip-rounding.

[β].   The voiced bilabial fricative in Gullah generally replaces G A [w], [hw], and [v].   E2, E3, H3, and HN1 used the frictionless continuant [ϑ] in positions where the other informants used [β]: [ϑɪʃ] "wish," [ɸɒɪϑ] "five," etc.

[ʃ].   [ʃ] frequently replaces G A [s] and [z].   In some words [ʃ] was rather weakly glottalized by H3, W3, and SS1: [ʃ'eβ] "shave," [ʃ'ɑɪn] "shine," etc.

[s].   With some informants, [s] was fronted a great deal more than with others.   This fronting appeared to be more marked on the Sea Islands of Georgia than on those of South Carolina.   In the speech of H2 and H3, [s] was post-alveolar.   [s] replaces [ʃ] in [sβɪmp] "shrimp" and [sβɪŋk] "shrink."

[z]. A voiceless variety of the [z]-phoneme is frequently heard in final position. [z] was palatalized by H3 in several words: [ɸʌʐ] "furs," ['tʌʐde] "Thursday," etc.

[j]. [j] was inserted by many informants in the following words and phrases: ['mʌsmɨljən] "muskmelon," [pɒɪ'jazə] "piazza," [ɟɬjem] "give them," ['mɒɪjont] "my own." S3 substituted [j] for [r] in ['jabɪt] "rabbit" and a few other words.

[r]. In Gullah, r never occurs finally nor before consonants, but only before vowels. With many informants it is used interchangeably with l, especially between vowels. HN1 used an alveolar r with slight uvular articulation in the word [rʁɐɪt] "right." Examples of the intrusive r appear in ['stʌdə̀rɪn] "studying," [tə̀rə̀m] "to them," etc.

[h]. Initial [h] is heard in many words which in G A begin with a vowel sound: ['hambrɐɪlə] "umbrella," ['haɾɪcɬok] "artichoke," ['hɛmptɪ] "empty," etc.

NASAL + PLOSIVE

The combination of initial nasal plus a plosive consonant is frequently heard in the Gullah speaker's pronunciation of African words containing such combinations. With the exception of [ŋd] each of these combinations observed in Gullah consisted of homorganic nasal plus plosive.

LABIO-VELAR PLOSIVES

[gb] and [kp], each articulated as one sound, are sometimes heard in the Gullah speaker's pronunciation of African words containing these sounds.

OTHER CONSONANT COMBINATIONS

The Gullah speaker usually avoids most consonant clusters familiar to speakers of General American English. He does so either by dropping one of the consonants or by using a vowel to separate them.

VOCABULARY

The most distinctive feature of the Gullah vocabulary is to be found in the large number of African words which it contains.

These words have come from several of those West African languages spoken by the slaves who were being brought to South
Carolina and Georgia direct from Africa until almost the beginning
of the Civil War. Among these languages are Wolof (Senegal
and Gambia), Bambara and Malinke (French West Africa),
Mende (Sierra Leone), Mandinka (Gambia), Fula (West Africa),
Vai (Liberia and Sierra Leone), Temne (Sierra Leone), Twi, Fante,
and Gã (Gold Coast), Ewe (Togo and Dahomey), Jeji (Dahomey),
Hausa (Northern Nigeria), Yoruba, Ibo, Efik, and Ibibio (Southern Nigeria), Kongo, Kimbundu, and Umbundu (Angola), and
Tshiluba (Belgian Congo).

The writer has collected between five and six thousand African
words in the Gullah region of coastal South Carolina and Georgia.
Approximately four-fifths of these are now used only as personal
names. Most of the remainder are used daily in conversation.
There are also many African words which one hears only in songs
and stories. Only a few examples of each of these three groups of
African words can be given here.

Gullah personal names

A. SOME PERSONAL NAMES

In addition to the English names which the Gullahs give their
children, they frequently use an African word or group of words
describing some circumstance connected with the child at the
time of its birth or later. Very often they use English words for
the same purpose. The practice is well known among the various
African tribes of whom the Gullahs are descendants. The following Gullah personal names will illustrate the nature of this practice:

1. Time of birth
    [alan'saro] "three-o'clock prayer time" (Mandinka, [alan-
        saro])
    [a'me] name used in greeting persons born on Saturday
        (Ewe, [a₁me₃])
    [aŋ'ku] name given a boy born on Wednesday (Ewe, [a₁ŋku₃])
    ['asigbe] "market day" (Ewe, [a₁si₁gbe₁])
    [ba'φata] "high tide" (Mandinka, [ba fata])
    ['bimbi] "five-thirty in the morning" (Fula, [bimbi])
    [φi'tiro] "six o'clock prayer" (Mandinka, [fitiro])
    [ɲu'nala] "early" (Mandinka, [dʒunala])

[mpi'aza] the season when the grass is burned—from July to October (Kongo, [mpiaza])

[ŋ'di] "morning" (Ewe, [ŋ₁di₃])

[o'ruŋɟan] "Night is reproaching him" (Yoruba, [o₂ruₐ-ŋ₃gã₁ː])

['oʃumi] "my month" (Yoruba, [o₂ʃu₁ mi₂])

['pɛgba] the Mende month corresponding to January (Mende, [pɛgba])

['pɪndɨ] "night" (Mende, [kpɪndɪ])

[suŋ'gila] "to visit at night" (Kimbundu, [suŋgila])

['zãzɒzɒ] "walking about at night" (Ewe, [zã₃zɔ₁zɔ₁])

2. Physical condition or appearance of the child

[adi'ti] a deaf person (Yoruba, [a₂di₂ti₃])

[a'ɲika] "She is very beautiful" (Vai, [a₁ɲi₁ka₃])

[a'rupɛ] a short person (Yoruba, [a₁ru₃kpɛ₁])

[ban'duka] "to be disfigured" (Kongo, [banduka])

['doɟi] "to speak loudly" (Jeji, [doɟi])

['gɒɪgɒɨ] "sluggishly" (Yoruba, [gɔ₁igɔi₁])

['hudidi] "bleeding" (Jeji, [hũdidi])

[ka'male] "vigorous, active" (Bambara, [kamale])

[la'ɸija] "to be well" (Jeji, [lafija])

[laku'muna] "to move the tongue" (Kongo, [lakumuna])

[ma'bibi] "faintness, fatigue" (Kongo, [mabibi])

[si'nola] "sleeping" (Mandinka, [sinola])

['βande] "filthy" (Ewe, [βa₁nde₁ː])

['zaŋga] "to soil, to defecate"—used in reference to babies only (Kongo, [zaŋga])

3. Temperament, character, and mental capacity of the child

['abeʃe] a worthless person (Yoruba, [a₂be₁ʃe₂])

[a'diβe] "to be industrious" (Ewe, [a₁di₁ve₃])

[a'dodo] "to be obstinate, quarrelsome" (Ewe, [a₁do₁do₁])

[a'ɲani] "to beg habitually" (Wolof, [aɲani])

['bede] "to be intelligent" (Yoruba, [gbe₃de₁])

[bet'siβi] a mischievous person (Ewe, [gbe₁tsi₁vi₃])

[bum'bulu] a fool (Kongo, [bumbulu])

[go'jito] "haughty, proud" (Jeji, [gojito])

['momo] "to pry into" (Bambara, [momo])

[ji'nisa] "to make dissatisfied" (Kongo, [jinisa])

4. Religion, magic, and charms

['bambali] "immortal" (Bambara, [bambali])

[e'salu] the bundle of charms of the witch doctor (Kongo, [esalu])

['ɸuka] the formalities which have to be observed in approaching a great chief or in the worship of God (Kongo, [fuka])

[ɟone'g˧ɛni] an amulet (Bambara, [ɟonɛgɛni])

['kuɟ˧i] "sudden death" (Ewe, [ku₃ɟ˧i₁₋₃])

['puka] a string of beads (Twi, [pu₃ka₃])

['sambi] a worshipper (Kongo, [nsambi])

['sɛbɛ] an amulet made of leather (Twi, [sɛ₃bɛ₂])

[ꞵi'luki] a penitent (Kongo, [mviluki])

5. Greetings, commands, and exclamations

[a'gali] "Welcome!" (Wolof, [agali!])

[da'jije] "Sleep well" (Twi, [da₁ji₃je₂])

[o'gũɸɛtimi] "Ogũ [the god of war] likes mine" (Yoruba, [o₁gũ₃fɛ₃ti₂mi₂])

[o'kõɲe] "Oh, my friend!" (Ewe, [o₃₋₁ xõ₃ɲe₁])

['tiɟu-'iku] "Be ashamed to die" (Yoruba, [ti₂ɟu₃-i₂ku₃])

['tiꞵɒni] "It is thine" (Yoruba, [ti₂wɔ₂ ni₂])

6. Place of birth

[ala'ꞵaɲo] name of a place in the Ewe country (Ewe, [a₁la₁va₁ɲo₁])

[a'mamɸo] a decayed dwelling or habitation (Gã and Twi, [a₁ma₁mfõ₃])

[ba'male] a platform (Bambara, [bamale])

['daji] on the ground (Jeji, [daji])

[ɸɒ'kɒmba] a valley (Kongo, [fɔkɔmba])

['lɑɪnde] a forest (Fula, [lainde])

['mɒŋgɒ] a hill (Kongo, [mɔŋgɔ])

['ɲaba] a swamp (Kongo, [ɲaba])

[ɒbo'daŋ] a cave (Twi, [ɔ₁bo₁da₃ŋ])

['randa] a thicket (Wolof, [randa])

[tɒk'pɒmbu] "under the palm tree" (Mende, [tɔkpɒmbu])

[tili'buŋko] a man from Tilibo, a country to the east of the Gambia (Mandinka, [tilibuŋko])

B. SOME OTHER WORDS USED IN CONVERSATION

['anduɲu] "I was not with you" (Wolof, [anduɲu])

[ban!] "It is done" (Vai, [ban₁] "to be finished"; [a₃ ban₁] "It is finished"; Bambara, [ban] "to be finished"; "the end") ['bidi'bidi] a small bird (Kongo, [bidibidi])

['bɒbɒbɒ] "woodpecker" (Kongo, [mbɔbɔbɔ])

['bɒma] a large snake (Kongo, [mbɔma] the black python)

[boɲ] "tooth" (Wolof, [boɲ])

['bʌkrə̄] [(bʌ₁krʌ₃)] "white man" (Efik and Ibibio, [m₁ba₁ka₂ra₂])

['daøa] "fat" (Vai, [da₃fa₁])

['dede] "correct" (Yoruba, [de₃:de₃:])

[dɛt] a hard rain (Wolof, [dɛt])

['dɪndɪ̄] a small child (Vai, [dɪn₃ dɪn₁])

[dɔ̌] "to, towards" (Ewe [dəɜ])

[dɔ̌] "to be" (Ibo, [de₁])

[do] "child" (Mende, [ndo])

[enu'ɸole] "to be pregnant" (Ewe, [ɸo₁ le₁ e₃nu₁] "She is with
    child")

[ɸa] "to take" (Twi and Fante, [fa₁])

['ɸuɸu] "dust" (Ewe, [fu₃fu₁₋₃])

['ɸuɸu] "mush"; flour made into a thin batter and cooked (Mende
    [fufu] food made of cassava, grated and fermented; Ewe,
    [fu₁fu₁] yam or cassava boiled and pounded; Jeji, [fufu] food
    made from maize, fish, and palm oil; Hausa, [fu:fu:] a food
    made from cassava)

[ˌɸula'ɸaɸa] "woodpecker" (Mende, [fulafafa])

['gʌmbo] "okra" (Tshiluba, [tʃiŋgɔmbɔ]; Umbundu, [otʃiŋgɔmbo])

['guba] "peanut" (Kimbundu, [ŋguba]; Umbundu, [oluŋgupa];
    Kongo, [ŋguba])

['gulu] "pig" (Kongo, [ŋgulu])

['ɟamba] "elephant" (Umbundu, [ond₃amba])

['ɟambi] a red sweet potato (Vai, [d₃a₁mbi₃])

['ɟiboli] a large fly (Vai, [d₃i₃bo₁li₁] any insect or animal that is
    afraid of water)

['ɟiga] a species of flea (Ewe, [ɟi₁ga₃] "sand-flea"; Yoruba, [ɟi₁ga₃];
    Wolof, [ɟiga]; Mandinka, [d₃iga]; Hausa, [d₃iga])

['ɟɒgal] "to rise" (Wolof, [ɟɒgal])

['ɟoso] "witchcraft" (Mende, [nd₃oso] fabulous spirits dwelling in
    the woods)

[ɟuk] ([ɟug]) "disorderly" (Wolof, [ɟug "to be disorderly";
    Bambara, [ɟugu] "wicked")

[kiŋ'kβaβi] "partridge" (Kongo, [kiŋkwavi])

['kunu] "boat" (Bambara, [kunu])

['kutə̄] "tortoise" (Bambara and Malinke, [kuta])

[ma'laβu] ([ma'laϑu]) any alcoholic beverage (Kongo, [malavu])

['muŋgβa] "salt" (Kongo, [muŋgwa])

[na] "and" (Twi [na₁]; Ibo, [na₁])

['nanse] ([a'nanse]) "spider" (Twi and Fante, [a₁na₁nse₁])

['ɲinɪ] (['ɲmɪ]) "female breast" (Mende, [ɲinɪ])

['poɹo] "heron" (Vai, [po₃dʒo₃])

['sɒ ɛ a 'dufe] "Put wood on the fire" (Vai, [sɔ₃₋₁: ɛ₁ a₁ du₁fe₁] "The wood has been consumed")

[so! so!] a call to horses (Vai, [so₂] "horse"; Mende and Jeji, [so] "horse")

['sβaŋgɒ] "proud" (Mende, [suaŋgɒ])

[tot] (['totə̄m]) "to carry" (Kikongo, ['tota] "to pick up"; Kongo, [tɔta] "to pick up"; Kimbundu and Umbundu, [tuta] "to carry." Cf. Mende, [tomɒ] "one who carries a message")

['tutu] "excrement" (Hausa, [tu:tu])

['unə̄] "you"; "your" (Ibo, [u₃nu₁])

['βaŋga] "witchcraft" (Umbundu, [ɔwaŋga]; Kimbundu, [ɔwaŋga])

['βudu] "witchcraft" (Ewe, [vo₁du₃] a tutelary diety or demon; Jeji, [vodū] a fetish)

[βulisā'kpākpā] "woodpecker" (Mende, [wulisākpākpā])

C. SOME WORDS, PHRASES, AND SENTENCES HEARD ONLY IN SONGS AND STORIES

[a'βɒkɒ]. Mende, [a wɒkɒ], ([a gbɒkɒ]) "in the evening"

[baka'leŋga]. Mende, [mbakaleŋga] a group of musicians playing their instruments

[ɸa'lani]. Vai, [fa₁la₃₋₁:n₁] "He died long ago"

[gbla]. Mende, [gbla] "near"

[ha]. Mende, [ha] "to die"; "death"

[hola'tɪtɪtɪ]. Mende, [hoʊ la tɪtɪtɪ] "Hold the door tightly"

['hūma]. Mende, [hūma] "to steal"

['ɹamba]. Mende, (dʒamba] "to give a present to"

['kamba]. Mende, [kamba] a grave; Vai, [ka₃mba₃]

['kara'bara]. Vai, [ka₁ra₁gba₃ra₁] "Rise with the beads"

[kasɪ'tɛ]. Vai, [ka₁sɪ₃tɛ₃₋₂:] "surrounded by rust"

['komɛ]. Mende, [komɛ] "to assemble"

['kpaŋga]. Mende, [kpaŋga] a field burned before clearing; that which remains

[ku'hā]. Mende, [kuhā] "distant"; "from afar"

['mɒnɛ]. Mende, [mɔnɛ] "affliction"; "to suffer"

[na]. Vai, [na₁] "to come"
[nu]. Vai, [nu₃:] "there"
[ŋ'go]. Mende, [ŋgo] "word, voice"
[pi]. Vai, [pi₁:] "grass"
[pon]. Vai, [po₃n] "far away"
['sihã]. Mende, [sihã] "to borrow, to steal"
[tu]. Vai, [tu₁:] "to beat"
[βa]. Mende, [wa] "to come"
['βoŋga]. Mende, [woŋga] "family, relatives"
[ji]. Mende, [ji] "to sleep"

Continued from Cover 2

CENTRAL SOUTH Charles S. Pendleton, George Peabody
College for Teachers
SOUTHWEST Josiah Combs, Texas Christian University
MIDDLE WEST Frederic G. Cassidy, University of Wisconsin
ROCKY MOUNTAINS Levette J. Davidson, University of Denver
PACIFIC COAST Harold B. Allen, San Diego State College
CANADA Henry Alexander, Queen's University

THE AMERICAN DIALECT SOCIETY

Membership in the Society is conferred upon any person interested in the activities of the Society. Dues are $2.00 a year for persons or institutions. Members receive free all publications. The price of any issue when purchased separately will depend upon the production cost of the issue.

The *Publication of the American Dialect Society* is issued at intervals during the year.

PUBLICATION OF THE AMERICAN DIALECT SOCIETY

Number 4

PROVERBS
AND HOW TO COLLECT THEM

By

MARGARET M. BRYANT

Published by the

AMERICAN DIALECT SOCIETY

November, 1945

Obtainable from the Secretary of the Society
Woman's College of the
University of North Carolina
Greensboro, North Carolina

OFFICERS

OF

THE AMERICAN DIALECT SOCIETY

Continued on Cover 3

PUBLICATION OF THE AMERICAN DIALECT SOCIETY

Number 4

PROVERBS
AND HOW TO COLLECT THEM

By

MARGARET M. BRYANT

Published by the

AMERICAN DIALECT SOCIETY

November, 1945

Obtainable from the Secretary of the Society

Woman's College of the

University of North Carolina

Greensboro, North Carolina

PROVERBS AND HOW TO COLLECT THEM

During recent years the American Dialect Society has been sponsoring the collection and organization of proverbial material, a work being carried out by a committee, of which the present writer is chairman. The purpose of this paper is to encourage and assist the efforts of those who would like to collect proverbs, but who may feel that they have too little information about proverbs themselves, as well as about the best ways of collecting them. The paper is divided into two parts, the first of which deals with the theoretical and historical aspects of the study of proverbs, and the second with the practical problems of collection.

PART I

PROVERBS

A. THE NATURE OF THE PROVERB

The word *proverb* suggests to the average person a short, pithy, epigrammatic statement setting forth a well-known elementary truth; in other words, a wise saying. The word itself has come to us through the Old French *proverbe* from the Latin *proverbium*, *pro*, "for," + *verbum*, "word," signifying the use of a figurative expression for the plain word. The Greek equivalent is παροιμία, παρα, "alongside" + οἶμος, "way," "road," or "alongside the way," denoting a trite roadside saying, one which comes from the folk. These names bring out two qualities of proverbs: popularity and figurativeness. Only the first of these is essential; every proverb must have been adopted by the people but not every one contains a figure of speech. For example, "Haste makes waste" is a direct assertion. Proverbs, however, differ from ordinary speech in that they usually contain a touch of fancy in the phrasing, a touch that gives them their pungency or "salt" (a term used by James Howell in his definition in 1659).

Many persons have endeavored to give a formal definition of a proverb, but no attempt, from Aristotle's on, has met with universal approval. Simple though it may seem at first, it is difficult to find a significant distinguishing trait which will not include or eliminate too much. As yet, after centuries of study and endeavor no one has found the magic formula, the phrase, the sentence, or the group of sentences which will classify every proverb. The

3

chief difficulty is that there are three separate groups: true proverbs, proverbial phrases (which may have many divisions), and sententious sayings. There is, however, general agreement as to the principal characteristics of proverbial sayings, and few people have trouble in recognizing a proverb.

Aristotle in writing on proverbs in his *Rhetoric* pointed out that they were remnants saved from the "wrecks and ruins of ancient philosophy" by reason of their conciseness and cleverness, thereby showing that he felt that brevity, sense, and piquancy, or "salt," were intrinsic in them.   Again, in discussing metaphors, Aristotle speaks of proverbs as "metaphors from species to species,"[1] which seems to suggest their figurative application.   For example,   "A tree is known by its fruit" is based on actual observation of fact in nature, but as a proverb it can be applied to many other things. So with the seaman's "A drowning man will catch at a straw," "to be in the same boat with someone," "to go on the rocks," "to put in an oar," and innumerable other metaphors.   Although Aristotle recognized that proverbs could be figurative, he was cognizant of the fact that not all proverbs were, for he said, "Some proverbs . . . are also maxims."[2]   He likewise knew that a proverb was of the people if we can assume from the preceding quotation that a maxim can be a proverb as well as the other way round, for he wrote: "Even trite and common maxims should be used, if they can serve; since, just because they are common, they seem right, on the supposition that all the world is agreed upon them."[3] From the observations of Aristotle on proverbs in his *Rhetoric*, Professor B. J. Whiting in his excellent essay "The Nature of the Proverb" concluded that the Greek philosopher held a proverb to be "a short saying of a philosophic nature, of great antiquity, the product of the masses rather than of the classes, constantly applicable, and appealing because it bears a semblance of universal truth."[4]

The first English definition is "an old said saw," the earliest recorded instance of which, according to Professor Whiting's research,[5] was in Sir Thomas More's *The Dialogue Concerning*

---

[1] *Rhetoric*, III, xi, 14; translated by Sir Richard C. Jebb and edited by John E. Sandys (Cambridge: Harvard University Press, 1909), p. 176.

[2] *Ibid.*, II, xxi, 12; Jebb, p. 115.

[3] *Ibid.*, II, xxi, 11; Jebb, pp. 114–115.

[4] *Harvard Studies and Notes in Philology and Literature*, XIV (1932), 278.

[5] *Ibid.*, p. 291.

Tyndale (1528).[6] In the same year William Tyndale, More's adversary, wrote the first general discussion of the nature of a proverb which is to be found in English.[7]

No other definition need be noted until 1614, when William Camden, including a collection of proverbs in his *Remains Concerning Britaine*, defined them as "concise, witty, and wise Speeches grounded vpon long experience, conteining for the most part good caueats, and therefore both profitable and delightfull."[8]

James Howell in the preface to his ΠΑΡΟΙΜΙΟΓΡΑΦΙΑ, *Proverbs, or, Old Sayed Sawes & Adages* (1659) stated that the chief ingredients that go to make a true proverb are "sense, shortnesse and salt,"[9] an oft-quoted phrase. Although here he left out the most essential, and generally recognized characteristic of a proverb, that is, popularity, he went on to say: "Proverbs may not improperly be called the Philosophy of the Common Peeple, or, according to Aristotle, the truest Reliques of old Philosophy, whereunto he adds another remarkable Saying, That as no man is so rich who might be able to spend equally with the Peeple, so none is so wise as the Peeple in generall."[10] In an introductory poem Howell wrote:

> "The Peeples voice, the Voice of *God* we call,
> And what are *Proverbs* but the peeples voice?
> Coin'd first, and current made by common choice,
> Then sure they must have *Weight* and *Truth* withall."[11]

He was fully conscious of the necessity of acceptance by the people, for he called proverbs "the truest Franklins or Freeholders of a country."

Howell in this collection, even though he realized that proverbs must be the *vox populi*, incorporated five hundred witty sayings which he invented. His coinages did not bear the public stamp

[6] *The English Works of Sir Thomas More*, edited by W. E. Campbell with an Introduction and Philological Notes by A. W. Reed (London: Eyre and Spottiswoode, Ltd., 1927), II, [105]. This definition, which is incomplete to the extent that it makes only two requirements of the proverb, antiquity and currency, was repeated in Thomas Cooper's *Thesaurus Linguae Romanae et Britannicae* (1565).

[7] Whiting, *op. cit.*, p. 292.

[8] P. 301.

[9] "To the Knowingest Kind of Philologers," sig. a4r.

[10] *Ibid.*

[11] *Ibid.*, sig. a1v.

and have therefore remained within the covers of his book.   His
knowledge was greater than he realized, for a proverb is in a sense
autochthonous among the people who father it.   It grows naturally
and without effort, being passed from person to person and from
generation to generation and often from nation to nation.   Howell
was one of the first to stress the fact that proverbs belong to the
people and carry with them the evidence of their origin.   That
they may arise in any walk of life, in various forms, and under
varying circumstances, is attested by some verses in the eighteenth
century periodical *The British Apollo:*

> "Proverbs deduce their Origine
> From sev'ral Causes, thus in fine:
> Some *Local* are and from the site
> Of Places, Simile's Invite:
> From Accidents some, and Mishape,
> From odd Events, and after-claps;
> From Thoughts some, stretch'd upon the Tenters;
> And some from Comical Adventures;
> And some arise from Circumstances,
> As Whimsical, as in *Romances*;
> But most (and often they the best,
> As with sound Sense, and Reason drest)
> From Casual Sayings of the Wise,
> And none but Fools, their Force despise."[12]

An important book of the nineteenth century devoted to proverbs is Archbishop Richard C. Trench's *On the Lessons in Proverbs*
(later entitled *Proverbs and Their Lessons*), first given as lectures
to various young men's associations.   In this book are many
keen observations and much valuable material on the nature of
the proverb.   He writes: "The fact that they please the people,
and have pleased them for ages—that they possess so vigorous a
principle of life, as to have maintained their ground, ever new and
ever young, through all the centuries of a nation's existence—nay,
that many of them have pleased not one nation only, but many;
so that they have made themselves a home in the most different
lands—and further, that they have, not a few of them, come down
to us from remotest antiquity, . . . all this . . . may well make us
pause."[13]   He continues: "And then . . . some of the greatest
poets, the profoundest philosophers, and the most learned scholars,

[12] III, No. 1 (1710), sig. a25.
[13] New York, 1855, p. 10.

the most genial writers in every kind, have delighted in them, have made large and frequent use of them, have bestowed infinite labor on the gathering and elucidating of them."[14]

Proverbs are still being studied. One may quote the definition of Professor Whiting as an instance: "A proverb is an expression, which, owing its birth to the people, testifies to its origin in form and phrase. It expresses what is apparently a fundamental truth,—that is, a truism,—in homely language, often adorned, however, with alliteration and rhyme; it is usually true, but need not be. Some proverbs have both a literal and figurative meaning, either of which makes perfect sense, but more often they have but one of the two."[15] Finally, one should not omit the definition in the *NED*, which is: "A short pithy saying in common and recognized use; a concise sentence, often metaphorical or alliterative in form, which is held to express some truth ascertained by experience or observation and familiar to all; on adage, a wise saw."

All the attempts through the centuries at defining and describing the nature of the proverb testify at least to the fact that proverbs are the people's possessions. They are an index to what the people regard as true.

B. HISTORY OF THE PROVERB

Hebrew literature is rich in proverbs, and many of the wise sayings ascribed to King Solomon and others in the Old Testament have become a part of the living lore of the many peoples who have inherited a share of Hebrew culture. Jesus, in his teachings, made frequent and effective use of popular sayings, some taken over from earlier Jewish literature, some borrowed from the speech of the people about him, and some, apparently, coined, or at least recast, by himself.

From the earliest times proverbs also held a significant place among the Greeks, as may be evidenced by their constant use by Homer, Pindar, and the great tragedians, the comic poets, and Plato, and by the effort Aristotle devoted to collecting and writing about them. The interest of the Romans was no less great than that of the Greeks, since the grammarians and rhetoricians almost always included the proverb in their discussions, and the great

---

[14] *Ibid.*, p. 11.
[15] *Op. cit.*, p. 302.

writers—among them Plautus, Terence, Cicero, Horace, Juvenal—
sprinkled their works with "the jewels of the multitude."[16]   Patris-
tic writers, both Greek and Latin, and the later theologians made
liberal use of proverbs, probably to give a sense of homely realism
to what could be highly abstruse propositions, and it is both significant and amusing to find the first recorded instance of "Love
me love my dog" in St. Benard of Clairvaux.[17]

Many proverbs have come down to us from the Middle Ages
through the Latin translations which spread from one country
to another by means of the church and were later retranslated
into the vernacular.[18]   Authors like Chaucer, Gower, and Lydgate
dotted their pages with proverbs and proverbial phrases. Some
idea of the importance of proverbs at that time may be gained
from looking into such works as W. W. Skeat's *Early English
Proverbs* (1910), George L. Apperson's *English Proverbs and Proverbial Phrases* . . . (1929), and Professor Whiting's *Chaucer's Use
of the Proverb* (1934).   The late Dr. Samuel Singer of Switzerland
left almost finished a manuscript of voluminous proportions,
bringing together the entire body of medieval and early vernacular proverbs of Western Europe,[19] which we hope will be published in the not-too-distant future.

The next outstanding scholar after Aristotle to turn his attention
to the proverb was Erasmus, who by his epoch-making *Collectanea
Adagiorum*, first published in 1500, aroused such enthusiasm for
proverbs that for two centuries they were discussed, assembled
into large collections, and translated from one language to another.[20]

The Renaissance evidenced great interest in proverbial sayings,
as may be borne out by the fact that in the days of Queen Elizabeth
a short speech composed wholly of proverbial saying was delivered

[16] See James Gilchrist Lawson, *The World's Best Proverbs and Maxims*
(New York: George H. Doran and Co., 1926), Introduction, p. v.

[17] Apperson, *English Proverbs and Proverbial Phrases*: *A Historical
Dictionary* (London: J. M. Dent and Sons, 1929), pp. 386–387.

[18] Friedrich Seiler, *Deutsche Sprichwörterkunde* (München: C. H.
Beck'sche Verlagsbuchhandlung, 1922), pp. 80ff. See also Arpad Steiner,
"The Vernacular Proverb in Mediaeval Latin Prose," *American Journal
of Philology*, LXV (1944), 37–69.

[19] Richard Jente, "A Review of Proverb Literature since 1920," *Corona*
(Durham, N. C.: Duke University Press, 1941), p. 44.

[20] This work of Erasmus did much to encourage popular as well as scholarly interest in proverbs.

by a member of the House of Commons on an act against double payment of debts.[21]　Shakespeare not only scattered proverbs throughout his plays but even used them for titles, as in *All's Well That Ends Well.*　Notice how aptly he employs them when he has Coriolanus show scorn for the people by scorning their proverbs:

> "Hang 'em!
> They said they were an hungry; sigh'd forth proverbs,
> That *hunger broke stone walls, that dogs must eat,*
> That *meat was made for mouths,* that *the gods sent not
> Corn for the rich men only;* with these shreds
> They vented their complainings."[22]

Rabelais and Montaigne studded their pages with wayside sayings, and Cervantes crowded them into the mouth of Don Quixote's squire, Sancho Panza.　In fact, the Renaissance period was the golden age of the proverb.　The use of the proverb was so common that there are many authors who cannot be thoroughly understood and enjoyed without a knowledge of the proverbs of the time.　Although the later seventeenth and eighteenth centuries were less tolerant of proverbs and inclined to regard them as "low," more recent writers who have wished to characterize the folk or to appeal to the ordinary man have constantly employed them, as did Scott and Dickens in England and Mark Twain in America.

During the Renaissance, along with the employment of proverbial sayings in speech and writing, came the desire to preserve them, a desire which has continued to the present.　There were numerous collections, often giving Latin and vernacular versions of the same proverbs side by side.　One of the first printed compilations in English was Richard Taverner's *Proverbs or Adagias,* based on Erasmus's work.　In 1546 John Heywood published his *Dialogue Conteining Proverbes,* the first printed collection of purely English proverbs, which went through six editions from 1546 to 1598[23] and was one of the best known books of the day.　William Camden's popular compilation appeared in 1614, and two years later the collection of Thomas Draxe was published, containing

[21] Janet E. Heseltine, *The Oxford Dictionary of English Proverbs,* compiled by W. G. Smith (Oxford: Clarendon Press, 1935), Introduction, pp. xiv–xv.

[22] I, i, 218–223.　(Italics are the present writer's.)

[23] Heseltine, *op. cit.,* p. xlv.

2541 English entries along with Greek and Latin proverbs. John Clarke's compilation of 1639 was very much like that of Draxe. In the following year appeared a collection bearing the initials G. H., the second edition of which came out in 1651 with the title *Jacula Prudentum* and was attributed to George Herbert.[24] In 1641 was printed the first alphabetical compilation, by David Fergusson. In 1659 James Howell brought out his collection which he added to his *Lexicon Tetraglotton* the next year. The best collection up to that time was John Ray's, which appeared in 1670, being practically a summary of those that had gone before; the edition of 1678 added new material. This book has been reprinted many times and is still one of the most usable collections. H. G. Bohn's oft-reprinted *Handbook of Proverbs* (1855) includes all of Ray's 1813 edition. W. C. Hazlitt (1st ed., 1869, and 3rd ed., 1907) also uses Ray as a basis, adding a few of his own findings, but still employing the alphabetical order by initial letter, as does W. G. Smith in *The Oxford Dictionary of English Proverbs* (1935). Apperson's *English Proverbs and Proverbial Phrases*...(1929, on the other hand, uses an arrangement according to the important word in the proverb.

A number of standard books of quotations have been issued, revised and reissued time after time, drawing upon older collections of proverbs, but increasing the material or information slightly. The best known are: J. K. Hoyt, *Hoyt's New Cyclopedia of Practical Quotations*..., revised by K. L. Roberts (1927); *Putnam's Complete Book of Quotations* (1927); the American edition of W. G. Benham, *Benham's Book of Quotations, Proverbs and Household Words*... (revised ed., 1936); B. Stevenson, *The Home Book of Quotations, Classical and Modern* (1935); J. K. Moorhead and C. Lee, *A Dictionary of Quotations, an Alphabet of Proverbs* (c. 1935) in the Everyman's Libary, edited by Ernest Rhys; John Bartlett, *Familiar Quotations, a Collection of Passages, Phrases and Proverbs Traced to Their Sources*... (11th ed. by Christopher Morley, 1937).

These are the most important collections dealing with the proverb in English. Other less important collections have appeared from time to time and have gone through many printings, for the

---

[24] See *The Works of George Herbert* (New York: John B. Alden, 1883), p. 437, footnote. (There is still some question concerning the ascription to George Herbert.)

public does not forsake the sayings to which it has helped to give birth.

In addition to the general compilations that have been made, a few American scholars of the twentieth century have recognized the importance of the proverb and have turned their attention to studies of particular authors. Among them are M. P. Tilley, *Elizabethan Proverb Lore in Lyly's "Euphues" and Pettie's "Petite Pallace" with Parallels from Shakespeare* (*University of Michigan Publications in Language and Literature*, Vol. II, 1926); Richard Jente, *The Proverbs of Shakespeare with Early and Contemporary Parallels* (Reprinted from *Washington University Studies*, Humanistic Series, Vol. XIII, 1926); and B. J. Whiting, *Proverbs in the Earlier English Drama* (Harvard University Press, 1938). Whiting, one of the most active workers in proverbs, has produced a number of articles on various phases of the proverb (e.g., "The Origin of the Proverb" in *Harvard Studies and Notes in Philology and Literature*, Vol. XIII, 1931) as well as his two excellent books (the one just mentioned and the one on Chaucer), and is now preparing a study of the American proverb as found in several hundred novels published between 1928 and 1938. In the year 1926 Thomas H. Russell brought together *The Sayings of Poor Richard: Wit, Wisdom and Humor of Benjamin Franklin in the Prefaces, Proverbs and Maxims of Poor Richard's Almanacke for 1733 to 1758.*

Special collections have likewise been made of definite localities, such as Emma Louise Snapp's *Proverbial Lore in Nebraska* (*University of Nebraska Studies*, No. 13, 1933), F. W. Bradley's "South Carolina Proverbs" (*Southern Forklore Quarterly*, Vol. I, No. 1, March, 1937), Harold W. Thompson's collection of New York State proverbs presented in Chapter XIX of *Body, Boots and Britches* (J. B. Lippincott Company, Philadelphia, 1940), and Ramon F. Adams' *Cowboy Lingo* (Houghton Mifflin Company, Boston, 1936). The *Frank C. Brown Collection of North Carolina Folklore*, now being prepared for publication under the general editorship of N. I. White, will contain a selection of North Carolina proverbial material.

Another type of special collection is that of proverbs pertaining to one subject, such as William Jackson Humphrey's *Weather Proverbs and Paradoxes* (Williams & Wilkins Company, Baltimore, 1923).

The basic handbook, however, for anyone interested in the field is *The Proverb* (Harvard University Press, 1931; with an *Index* issued as No. 113 of the FF Communications, Helsinki, 1934) by Archer Taylor, who has also issued numerous monographs and articles on the subject, two of which supplement his book: "An Introductory Bibliography for the Study of Proverbs" (*Modern Philology*, Vol. XXX, No. 2, 1932) and "Problems in the Study of Proverbs" (*Journal of American Folk-Lore*, Vol. XLVII, No. 183, 1934). For a more complete bibliography see Richard Jente's "A Review of Proverb Literature since 1920," *Corona* (Duke University Press, Durham, North Carolina, 1941). A bibliography of Latin American proverbs may be found in Ralph Steele Boggs's *Bibliography of Latin American Folklore* (H. W. Wilson Company, New York, 1940), and also in his "Folklore Bibliography for 1942 [etc.]," *Southern Folklore Quarterly*.

C. ORIGIN OF THE PROVERB

That the proverb is an index to what the people regard as true, something growing out of their ideals of life and conduct, has been clearly shown by anthropologists. In the introduction to *Jamaica Proverbs*, Martha Warren Beckwith says that proverbial sayings give a truer picture of the mental life of the Negro in Jamaica than even song or story reveals, for in them he expresses "his justification of the vicissitudes of life."[25] She also shows how borrowed sayings undergo a process of remolding under the influence of native conditions and are interpreted to meet the circumstances of native life,[26] as "No ebery ting wha' got sugar a sweet," improvised from the European "All is not gold that glitters"; or "Darg hab liberty fe watch gubnor," a reinterpretation of "A cat may look at a king."[27] New sayings are also framed upon old patterns, as in "Big words break nobody's skin" or "Big word naber break man jawbone" from "Hard words break no bones."[28]

The eminent sociologist Edvard A. Westermarck has also shown how the native proverbs of Morocco have grown out of the life and

[25] *Publications of the Folk-Lore Foundation* (Poughkeepsie, N. Y.: Vassar College, 1925), No. 6, p. 5.
[26] *Ibid.*
[27] Izett Anderson and Frank Cundall, *Jamaica Negro Proverbs and Sayings* (Kingston, Jamaica: The Institute of Jamaica, 1910), Introduction, pp. v–vi.
[28] *Ibid.*

thoughts of the people and are significant documents for revealing their character, temperament, opinions, feelings, manners, and customs.[29]   According to Westermarck, a large number of Moroccans carry on robbery as a regular trade and thus have many proverbs in connection with it, as "Selling and buying is better than robbery."[30]   The robber when caught excuses himself with: "Lack of work is a misfortune"[31] or "The cold teaches one to steal charcoal."[32]   When the authorities want to catch somebody, no matter whom, and seize an innocent person, the Moors say, "The minaret fell down, hang the barber."[33]   The same kind of evidence can be found in Raymond Firth's "Proverbs in Native Life with Special Reference to Those of the Maori, I and II,"[34] in George Herzog's *Jabo Proverbs from Liberia*,[35] and in any number of studies of proverbs among native tribes.   The value of proverbs as evidence of popular opinion may be questioned on discovering not infrequently two that contradict each other, as "Look before you leap" and "He who hesitates is lost," or "It is never too late to learn (mend)" and "You can't teach an old dog new tricks." The simplification of proverbial maxims is undoubtedly due to necessary brevity, and the one-sidedness has to be corrected by other proverbs.   One should not suppose that a nation's proverbs on a particular subject tell the entire truth about their feelings concerning it.

Firth begins his essay "Proverbs in Native Life, with Special Reference to Those of the Maori" with the words: "The proverb is the rough diamond of folklore . . . a homely, rugged, and outspoken piece of wisdom. Brief almost to curtness, cryptic at times . . . still a jewel of truth embedded in a quaint linguistic matrix . . ."[36]   He continues by saying, "It is by nature not a literary product; it is a saying of the people, forged by a happy

---

[29] *Wit and Wisdom in Morocco: A Study of Native Proverbs* (London: George Routledge & Sons, Ltd., 1930).

[30] "The Study of Popular Sayings" in *The Frazer Lectures, 1922-32*, edited by Warren R. Dawson (London: Macmillan and Co., Ltd., 1932), p. 199.

[31] *Ibid.*, p. 200.

[32] *Ibid.*

[33] *Ibid.*, p. 201.

[34] *Folklore*, XXXVII (1926), 134-153, 245-270.

[35] Published for the International Institute of African Languages and Cultures by the Oxford University Press, London, 1936.

[36] *Op. cit.*, I, 134.

thought, tempered by everyday use in the intimacy of the home or the contact of work or play."[37]

Even though we accept the validity of Firth's descriptions, we still do not know how these sayings originated. Every one of them must have had an author, an author "who did but clothe in happier form what others had already uttered," to use the words of Archbishop Trench.[38] At some moment of emotional stress, a particular individual utters a remark, an apt or picturesque phrase, that appeals to the community and lingers in its memory. Churchill's "Blood, sweat and tears," uttered in a moment of stress and strife and understood by millions of people as it was said, may continue to be used and become proverbial.

Each saying struggles into recognition, and each person who aids in the uttering and reuttering may claim a share in its production as it is used over and over again under circumstances which, either literally or figuratively, resemble those of the original occurrence. So it has been with all the proverbs of the centuries. In this sense only is a proverb without an author. Many sayings expressed with sense and felicity fail to pass into general circulation and cannot be called proverbs. They must stand the test of time and gain the confidence and sanction of the many. It is the approval of the multitude, the endorsement of the crowd, that creates proverbial sayings. They must also be adaptable to changing circumstances and environments, or else they will become obsolete and die.

What has been said applies to the popular proverbial saying, which uttered at first spontaneously by an unknown person in connection with some occurrence or set of circumstances, struck the imagination and finally gained universal acceptance. Then there are literary proverbs or sententious sayings of the learned, the authors of which can usually be traced. These polished sayings of wisdom, such as Dryden's "Sweet is pleasure after pain," Pope's "A little learning is a dangerous thing," Gray's "Where ignorance is bliss, 'tis folly to be wise," have become a part of the language and are quoted by many who have no idea of the literary inventors of the expressions.

Occasionally the origin of a popular saying is known, as Frank-

[37] *Ibid.*

[38] *Op. cit.*, p. 25; or the definition as ascribed to Lord John Russell (1792–1878): "A proverb is the wisdom of many and the wit of one."

lin's "Three removes are worse than a fire" and James J. Corbett's "The bigger they come, the harder they fall." The tracing of these bits of wit or wisdom to their sources, however, is rare. Most of them are foundlings, knowing nothing of their parents, and have made their place in the world on their own merits.

Many probably originated in families, then spread to the community and from the community to other communities, and finally became full-fledged proverbs. Just as these sayings pass from the family to the nation, so they pass from nation to nation, true cosmopolites. In fact, the purely national proverbs form only a portion of the stock of any language, and for this reason it is practically impossible to trace the source of the most common proverbs, those that seem to be the heritage of the world. But behind each is a history inviting the lover of the lore to dig more deeply into the mines of antiquity where with perseverance there is gold to be found, unknown history of past ages, if not the original source of each saying.

D. FORM OF THE PROVERB

In order to live proverbs must be used, and in order to be used they must fix themselves in the memory of their users. One of the essential characteristics in the struggle for survival is form, for upon that the initial acceptance of the proverb and its continued popularity largely depend. There is no one form which belongs to the proverb, for it is a unique turn of phrase, an unusual use of a word, an alliteration or perhaps a specific rhythm that gives the individual expression its appeal. Epigrammatic statements, such as "Children and fools speak the truth," "A penny saved is a penny earned," "Time and tide wait for no man" constitute a large number of proverbs.

Often, however, there is a rhythmical balance in phraseology and many times a contrast in meaning accompanying the balance. For example, "Waste not, want not," "Like father, like son," "Nothing ventured, nothing won" illustrate parallelism of structure, the two phrases of each one being similar in grammatical form, rhythmically balanced, and showing a certain antithesis in their meaning.

All proverbs differ in form in some way from ordinary speech. There may be pithy, epigrammatic statement, antithesis, paradox, parallelism, metaphor, simile, rhythm, rhyme, hyperbole, personification, alliteration, or some other imaginative touch in phraseology. Tennyson's remark "It is not what you say, but how you say it" is applicable to the proverb, for in many cases it is the form that gives the proverb its point and emphasis.

Of the numerous devices employed in giving a proverb currency, the most significant is rhyme. The Chinese, for instance, express a great many proverbs in couplet form. All of us are familiar with such rhymes as:

> "Early to bed, early to rise
> Makes a man healthy, wealthy, and wise."
> "Little strokes fell great oaks."
> "No pains, no gains."

Even a false rhyme, such as we often find in nursery rhymes and in the widely current "A stitch in time saves nine" is at times effectively employed for fixing the proverb in the memory.

Rhyme accompanied by brevity and alliteration, a close ally of rhyme, is doubly effective, as in "Birds of a feather flock together." Alliteration is common in proverbs, as in: "Speech is silver; silence is golden," "Spare the rod and spoil the child," "Money makes the man," "Manners make the man," "Live and learn."

Two figures of speech that one occasionally finds in proverbs are paradox, as in "The tongue breaks bone though itself has none" and "No news is good news"; and hyperbole, as in "Her tongue is loose at both ends and tied in the middle" and "Not to have the chance of a snowball in hell."

Three of the most common figures of speech, however, are personification: "Hunger is the best cook," "Truth will out," "Love is blind," "Walls have ears"; metaphor: "Brag is a good dog, but Hold-fast is better," "Necessity is the mother of invention," "Sorrow is laughter's daughter"; and simile, the most numerous of all, especially in the proverbial phrases: "If March comes in like a lamb, it will go out like a lion," "None so deaf as he who will not hear," "None so blind as he who will not see." Examples of the thousands of proverbial phrases using the simile are "as busy as a bee," "as proud as a peacock," "to screech like an owl," "to sing like a lark," "to drink like a fish."

By means of these formal aids, proverbs succeed in impressing themselves upon the people's memory. For the classification of proverbs see pages 22–23, Part II.

E. CONTENT OF THE PROVERB

To a large extent, proverbs employ the concrete. Sayings like "Don't cross the bridge before you come to it" and "Don't put all your eggs in one basket" have become current because they convey an image with which every one is familiar. The effectiveness of "Great oaks from little acorns grow" is due to the fact that the hearer immediately gets a picture of a very large tree and is able to compare with it the tiny acorn, since both are objects of the world that he knows. Thus proverbs are born from life and life's experiences, and they often in their subtle observations, show a great knowledge of the human heart.

The appeal, however, comes from the novel use of a familiar image as applied to the happenings of life. Metaphorical application gives to simple words an added semantic value. The seaman's "A small leak will sink a great ship" no one will dispute, but when applied in other fields, it gains in meaning.

In proverbs and proverbial sayings we find the people's customs and tastes: as "to back the wrong horse," from horse racing; "to hit below the belt," from boxing; "to have an ace up one's sleeve," from card playing; "to bark up the wrong tree," from hunting; "to get to first base," from baseball. Among those that show superstitions are:

> "Sing before breakfast, cry before night."
> "See a pin, pick it up;
> All the day you'll have good luck."

Then there are legal and medical sayings. The legal maxims, the basis of common law, are accepted by man as good rules by which to live. Examples of legal sayings are:

> "Two wrongs don't make a right."
> "Those who will not work shall not eat."
> "Silence gives consent."
> "First come, first served."

Among the medical sayings are:

> "An apple a day keeps the doctor away."
> "After dinner rest a while;
> After supper walk a mile."
> "You're the doctor."

Many professions and trades have added to the stock of proverbial lore, as may be seen from a few: "a baker's dozen," "Stick to your last," "as fresh as paint," "to change one's tune," "to peddle one's wares," "to pass muster," "to hit the nail on the head," "to be out of the picture," "any port in a storm," "Politics makes strange bedfellows."

There are numerous weather proverbs, such as "It never rains but it pours," "Lightning never strikes twice in the same place," "April showers bring May flowers," "It's an ill wind that blows nobody good," "Rain before seven, fair before eleven."

Other phases of life have also made their contributions, and we find proverbs which have to do with nature, animal life, love, marriage, money, home, clothing, punishment, books, stories, tools, instruments, friends, relatives, and dozens of other topics. Lastly, many pertain to virtue and wisdom, vice and folly, and still others have come down to us from the Bible, so that there is always a proverb for admonition, reprobation, or command.

F. FUNCTION OF THE PROVERB

A significant question in connection with proverbs, as with anything else, relates to their function. They undoubtedly have a function in society or they would not continue to live. A large number of primitive peoples, as well as civilized ones, have their proverbs, use them freely, and firmly hold to them. Solomon, often spoken of as the wisest of men, "sought out, and set in order many proverbs."[39] Nations outstanding for their literary monuments have not failed to cherish their proverbial heritage; nor have the illiterate tribes and races neglected them. All classes of society employ them. They are used by the learned and the unlearned. Among the Chinese, well-known for their proverbs, they are quoted by the most erudite teachers and by the most ignorant of coolies, having become the common heritage of all, and thus please all and form the ethical and moral standards which guide the people as a whole in their daily intercourse. "Proverbs are the wisdom of the streets."[40] Through them one can see the approach to ethical questions which have to be solved in daily life. Sir John Francis Davis in his translation of *Chinese Moral Maxims* points out that the Chinese have a saying which states "that as a man's conversation is the mirror of his thoughts, so the maxims of a people may be considered as a medium which reflects

[39] *Ecclesiastes* 12:9.
[40] John L. Rayner, *Proverbs and Maxims* (New York: Cassell and Co., Ltd., 1919), p. 171.

with tolerable accuracy the existing state of their manners and ways of thinking,"[41] and he believes that "there must ever be a close connection between the popular maxims, and the manners of a nation."[42]

To realize the importance of the proverb in society, it will be well again to turn to those who have made studies of proverbs among aborigines. The anthropologists have found that proverbs play an active part in the law, religion, education, and social life of primitive peoples, are bound up with the realities of the life of the native. Proverbs should be studied in context in order to get the full import, to see how, for example, they praise and encourage work, discourage the idler, check the erring, promote the good and help to mold public opinion. They furnish stereotyped, well-formulated phrases to be employed as a means of expressing emotions and feelings about happenings of daily life and current experiences and thus save the speaker from the need to invent original phraseology which will probably not be so cryptic and forceful. They fit well into conversation, serving as a neat argument, carrying with it the authority of tradition and custom. Aristotle said, "Proverbs are in the nature of evidence."[43]

The wisdom, philosophy, and experience of the community or tribe or race are passed on to the youth as a body of knowledge to guide them in their actions and help them in building their culture, while the older members make use of it in gaining the confidence and approval of one another. For example, orators, in participating in discussions which affect the interest of all, employ proverbs in order to help them win their audiences, for they realize the importance of tradition, of authority. Proverbs by their nature carry authority, for in order to exist they must have the sanction of society and express "the general sense of the people who adopt them."[44] Firth says in connection with this topic, "It is this weight of respect for traditional teaching which is the ultimate basis and sanction for the proverb, which provides its potency as a means of enforcement of social conduct."[45] Missionaries and other workers among the natives have discovered

[41] Published by John Murray, London, 1823, and reprinted by Gowans and Gray, Ltd., London, 1910, p. 9.

[42] *Ibid.*, p. 10.

[43] *Rhetoric*, I, xv, 14; Jebb, p. 63.

[44] Thomas Percy (translator), *A Collection of Chinese Proverbs and Apothegms* in *Hau Kiou Choaan* (London: R. and J. Dodsley, 1761), III, 183.

[45] *Op. cit.*, II, 258.

that the quickest way to gain their confidence is to learn their proverbs and use them. Firth defines the proverb in terms of its function and shows the real nature of the proverb and its living relation to social life. His definition reads: "A proverb is a concise and expressive, often figurative, saying in common use, which acts as a conveniently formulated means of expression, charged with emotional significance, to indicate and transmit the facts of experience, or to point out by injunction or prohibition an ideal of social conduct or behaviour."[46] That is, proverbs do play a significant role in the religious, social, moral, and economic life of the peoples they serve and give a picture of them. "They are trustworthy witnesses to the social, political, ethical, and religious ideals of the people among whom they originated and circulated."[47]

Lord Bacon said that "the genius, wit, and spirit of a nation are discovered in its proverbs," an exaggeration undoubtedly, for many proverbs are imported from foreign countries. On the other hand, the people in adopting a foreign proverb find it acceptable to their mode of life, or, if not, modify it in such a way that it fits into its new environment. "A genuine proverb may not embody a true ethical principle, yet it is an index to what the people regard as true, and presents their ideal of life and conduct."[48] Finally after it becomes a part of the life of the people, it begins to influence the thinking and the feelings of those who have adopted it. If it does not, it ceases to live. As Westermarck says, "Proverbs are not merely reflections of life, but play an active part in it."[49] The chief function is to influence the will and actions of people. One way to improve one's knowledge of a nation is to study its proverb.

PART II

INSTRUCTIONS FOR COLLECTING PROVERBS

"A friend in need is a friend indeed," "A kingdom divided against itself cannot stand," "No man can serve two masters," "A

---

[46] *Ibid.*, pp. 265–266.

[47] James A. Kelso, "Proverbs," *Encyclopaedia of Religion and Ethics*, edited by James Hastings, X, 414.

[48] *Ibid.*, p. 412.

[49] "The Study of Popular Sayings" in *The Frazer Lectures, 1922–32*, p. 205.

sleeping fox catches no poultry," "Chickens come home to roost," "The early bird catches the worm," "It's a long road that has no turning," "A watched pot never boils," "Beauty is but skin deep," and other proverbs like these are heard daily.

Speech is full of these pithy, epigrammatic sayings. No matter how up-to-date and forward-looking a person may think that he is, it is highly probable that when he comes to express himself in language, he makes use of a vast number of phrases and sentences that are actually proverbs, distilling the wisdom or supposed wisdom of antiquity or of more recent times. Most persons are entirely unaware how many proverbs or proverbial sayings they repeat in their everyday conversation, because they have never stopped to analyze their speech.

Consciously or unconsciously, one uses proverbs because such sayings serve to drive home a point or teach a lesson as nothing else will, for they are apt, concise, the "pith and heart" of observation, and compressed into a cryptic mold with a touch of fancy in the phrasing, a characteristic which helps in making them a permanent part of the language. Every section of America and Canada has a mine of proverbs, idioms, and phrases that represent its people and tell the story of their way of life.

Since proverbial lore does play such an important part in our language, the American Dialect Society, founded in 1889, is beginning a country-wide canvass in order to get a representative collection of these popular folk sayings from every possible corner. Will you help by sending in any proverb or proverbial saying that you yourself use or hear in your daily conversation?

A. WHAT TO COLLECT

Collect any saying in English, in the form of a proverb or idiomatic phrase, which is expressive of wisdom or descriptive as a metaphor or simile. Many proverbs are figurative in character, but not all. It is better to err on the side of collecting too many rather than too few. If in doubt, collect. Specimens are given below to be used as a guide. Sayings may be individual or traditional, handed down from generations past; but no one collector can be sure of their character. It is best to send in anything you hear or find, and the committees of the Dialect Society, by comparing your contributions with others in the district and elsewhere, will be able to decide how widely used the sayings are.

Examples:

(1) Folk proverbs appearing as complete sentences.

> "Barking dogs never bite."
> "Every rose has its thorn."
> "A task well begun is half done."

(2) Sententious sayings or proverbs of the learned in complete sentences.

> "Sweet are the uses of adversity."
> "None but the brave deserves the fair."
> "Distance lends enchantment."

(3) Proverbial rhymes.

> "Where cobwebs grow
> Beaux never go."
> "Man's work is from sun to sun
> But woman's work is never done."
> "Rain before seven, fair before eleven."

(4) Proverbial sayings, not complete sentences, involving a verb (usually in the infinitive form but with the first noun as the key word).

"To be in hot water."
"To count chickens before they are hatched." (Such an expression may also appear as a proverb in sentence form: "Don't count your chickens before they are hatched.")
"To raise the roof.'

(5) Proverbial sayings not involving a verb.

> "A bed of roses."
> "A fool's paradise."
> "A song and a dance."

(6) Proverbial comparisons and similes.

> "As greedy as a pig."
> "Blacker than soot."
> "To fight like a tiger."

(7) Wellerisms—comparisons like those made by Sam Weller in Dickens' *Pickwick Papers* (involving a quotation, often a well-known one, with a facetious sequel).

" 'Home sweet home!' as the vagrant said when he was sent to prison for the third time."
" 'All's well that ends well,' said the peacock when he looked at his tail."
" 'I punish her with good words,' as the man said when he threw the Bible at his wife."

(8) Modern facetious proverbs and rhymes.

> "Candy's dandy, but liquor's quicker."
> "Don't tell a woman, telephone or telegraph."
> "A ring on the finger is worth two on the 'phone."

Interesting collections of sayings may be found in Logan Pearsall Smith's *Words and Idioms* (1925), Thomas H. Russell's *The Sayings of Poor Richard: Wit, wisdom and Humor of Benjamin Franklin in the Prefaces, Proverbs, and Maxims of Poor Richard's Almanacks for 1733 to 1758* (1926), Archer Taylor's *The Proverb* (1931), Emma Louise Snapp's *Proverbial Lore in Nebraska* (1933), Harold W. Thompson's *Body, Boots and Britches* (1940).   For a fuller bibliography see "History of the Proverb," Part I.

B. WHERE TO COLLECT PROVERBIAL SAYINGS

Sources may be oral or written.   Proverbial lore may be found in travel books, journals, and magazines, where professional writers have made deliberate but authentic use of folk materials; in almanacs, newspapers, and so on, where local and popular tales and anecdotes are recorded.   Oral lore is to be found everywhere every day.   Rural or secluded districts are especially rich in proverbial lore, lore often peculiar to them.   Some proverbs have been translated and adapted from foreign languages into idiomatic English.   The various foreign strains blending to furnish our citizenry should be rich sources for this kind of saying.

C. HOW TO RECORD PROVERBIAL SAYINGS

(1) Use 3 x 5 cards or slips.   Write in ink, or typewrite.

(2) Write each saying on a separate card, exactly as you have heard it.   Do not polish it up.   If, however, you know any variations of the saying or expression, give those too.

(3) Add any helpful note as to where, when, and by whom this saying was used.   Be sure to record the fact whether it is peculiar to a particular foreign, social, religious, industrial, or other group.   If necessary, explain the meaning.

(4) In the upper left corner, write the key word of the sentence or phrase, usually the most important noun, sometimes a verb or adjective.

(5) In the upper right corner, write the state from which your contribution originally came.

(6) On the card give the proverb or saying and its meaning in parentheses, if the meaning is not perfectly obvious.   Give

also the details about the proverb or saying that are significant, such as the language from which it originally came, the occasion upon which it was heard, or the book or magazine from which it was copied.

(7) Carefully indicate all written sources. Give author (full name), book or manuscript (full title), year of publication or writing (as nearly as it can be ascertained), page in book or document (if numbered).

(8) On the back, write your name and address so that you will be credited with your contribution. A rubber stamp will save time in doing this.

SPECIMEN CARDS

Tongue Nebraska "At one's tongue's end." (Variant: On the tip of one's tongue.) Informant came from Nebraska in 1940.	*Cat Hole* Ohio "He flew to the cat hole." (Meaning: He retreated in a hurry.) Alexandria, Licking Co. Handed down from older generations who knew the function of the cat hole in pioneer cabins.
Slop water Minnesota "Don't be as independable as slop water in a trough." Borghild Dahl, *I Wanted to See*, Macmillan, 1944, p. 91.	*Gas* New York "To step on the gas." (Meaning: To hurry—to put one's foot on the gasoline accelerator.) Modern.

D. WHO MAY COLLECT PROVERBIAL SAYINGS

Anyone may collect and send in proverbs or proverbial sayings. The more people that can be enlisted in the project, the better. Each collector should send in to his State Chairman a card with biographical data, giving his name, present and permanent address, schooling, profession or position. This information may be helpful to the editors of the material when it is being prepared for publication. Use a card or slip 3 x 5 in size. Be sure, in addition, to sign all cards you send in or use a rubber stamp with your name and address.

Enlist the help of others—local historians, folklorists, school superintendents and principals, teachers, rural teachers in particular, alumni of various schools, newspaper editors, elderly people, chairmen of clubs and organizations, grange lecturers. Foreign language groups are particularly important. English teachers can be especially helpful and will in turn find the study of great value in their classes. Travel into districts where old country families have settled will be rewarding. In some states, folklorists connected with Writers' Projects, State Historical Societies, and other groups have begun such collections as the one contemplated. Get in touch with them. Have classes in forklore collect. Local records, histories, etc., often preserve the lore of previous generations. Put notices in folklore journals or other suitable magazines, such as those issued by historical societies. Letters in the name of a department (English, for instance) and the State Chairman, or the State Committee, might be sent to all students in a college or university. Candidates for an M.A. or a Ph.D. degree may be set to work on proverbs. Make sure your community is well represented. Do not worry if various collectors duplicate sayings; repeated occurrence shows the degree to which a saying is accepted, and the different places where it is found.

E. WHAT WILL BE DONE WITH THE PROVERBIAL SAYINGS COLLECTED

All sayings will be filed in the archives of the Society. From time to time pertinent collections will be printed in order to stimulate interest in further collecting. When an adequate amount of material has been compiled, it will be published in various regional studies and, at last, it is hoped, in a *Dictionary of American and Canadian Proverbs*.

To this end the Society needs the co-operation of hundreds of volunteers who in their particular localities will provide the material by sending the proverbial sayings in to the State Chairmen. The State Chairmen, when they have collected what seems to be a complete or interesting set of sayings for a given area or people or occupation, such as might be published separately, will then send the collection to the Chairman of the Committee on Proverbial Sayings of the American Dialect Society, Margaret M. Bryant, at her home address, One Montague Terrace, Brooklyn 2, New York, or at Brooklyn College, Brooklyn, New York.

THE AMERICAN DIALECT SOCIETY

Membership in the Society is conferred upon any person interested in the activities of the Society. Dues are $2.00 a year for persons or institutions. Members receive free all publications. The price of any issue when purchased separately will depend upon the production cost of the issue.

The *Publication of the American Dialect Society* is issued at intervals during the year.

PUBLICATION OF THE AMERICAN DIALECT SOCIETY

Number 5

A GLOSSARY
OF VIRGINIA WORDS

By

PHYLLIS J. NIXON

With a Preface By

HANS KURATH

The Secretary's Report

Published by the

AMERICAN DIALECT SOCIETY

May, 1946

Obtainable from the Secretary of the Society
Woman's College of the
University of North Carolina
Greensboro, North Carolina

OFFICERS

OF

THE AMERICAN DIALECT SOCIETY

Continued on Cover 3

PUBLICATION OF THE AMERICAN DIALECT SOCIETY

Number 5

A GLOSSARY
OF VIRGINIA WORDS

By

PHYLLIS J. NIXON

WITH A PREFACE BY

HANS KURATH

THE SECRETARY'S REPORT

Published by the
AMERICAN DIALECT SOCIETY
May, 1946

Obtainable from the Secretary of the Society
Woman's College of the
University of North Carolina
Greensboro, North Carolina

PREFACE

This glossary of Virginia words, by Phyllis Jones Nixon, though modest in scope, is a contribution to our knowledge of the Virginia vocabulary in more than one way.

First of all, 39 words that have not previously been booked for Virginia make their appearance:

coal scuttle	lay (of wind)
corn stack, "crib"	milk gap
doney	old-fields colt
dry-land frog, "toad"	paling fence
egg bread	pert
fishing worm	piece, piece meal
flannel cake	poke
foreigner	proud, "pleased"
freshen	pull flowers
gentleman cow	red-worm
ground worm	rock fence
guano sack	saw buck
hand irons	(sea) grass sack
hay cock	side meat
hay doodle	smear case
hommy	somerset
hunkers	stairsteps
jam across	trumpery
johnny house	woods colt
lamp oil	

Six of these, *corn stack*, *dry-land frog*, *grass sack*, *johnny house*, *milk gap*, and *old-fields colt*, have never been recorded in any dictionary or word list, either American or British, *lamp oil* only in the NED.

These numbers are not impressive in themselves. However, when we take into account the fact that Green's *Virginia Word Book* is the best regional glossary we possess in the field of American English, and that the *Linguistic Atlas*, from which these words were culled, merely samples the vocabulary to determine types of regional distribution, we are forcefully made aware of the wealth of regional and local vocabulary that awaits the hand of the lexicographer.

3

Mrs. Nixon's second contribution is in the nature of an innovation in American lexicography. She tells us briefly whether a word is current in all of Virginia or only in a part of it; whether it is used on all social levels, or restricted to the cultured or the simple folk; whether it is in common use or rare. Such statements can be made only when a systematic survey of an area has been carried out. But this type of information is of the greatest importance. Speech areas can be delimited in no other way, and the history of individual expressions in North America can be traced only in relation to settlement history, the growth of centers of trade and culture, the development of transportation facilities, etc. It is obviously essential to know whether a Virginia word is found only in the Tidewater area, or the Valley, or the Piedmont, or in any combination of such subareas, before one can undertake to relate its history to the history of the population. A good dictionary of American English should, therefore, provide this type of information. Such broad labels as "Southern" and "Western" have little significance.

About 40 per cent of the words in this glossary are not to be found in the recently completed *Dictionary of American English.* Many of these words are current not only in Virginia but in large parts of the South and the South Midland, some of them also in the North Midland and the North, e.g. the food terms *clabber cheese, green-beans, hasslet, pully-bone, snack;* the farm words *change, cut, boar hog, freshen, nicker, whinny, stud horse, rick,* and *bundle* ("sheaf"); names for things around the house such as *burlap sack, lamp oil, poke, spicket, whet-rock;* the weather terms *abate, bluster up, calm down, moderate, rise, squall;* and such expressions as *favor* ("resemble"), *kin folks, kin to, song ballad, woods colt.* Other items omitted from the DAE are more local in character or humble folk words, e.g. *base-born, buss, doney, doodle* ("hay cock").

All words in this glossary that have not found a place in the *Dictionary of American English* are labeled with an asterisk to emphasize the need of a *Dictionary of Spoken American English* to supplement the DAE, which is based almost entirely on printed sources. What we need is not a Dialect Dictionary in the narrow sense of the word but a full record of the vocabulary of spoken English in its regional and local manifestations and its social variations in which not only the meanings but also the geographic and social spread of each word are defined. The intimate tie-up between regional and local vocabulary and features of regional and local culture cannot be visualized in any other way; and, in turn, a history of the American vocabulary cannot be written until we shall know both the words and the things they denote.

The procedure that should be followed in the preparation of a *Dictionary of Spoken American English* would seem to be quite obvious.

We must have, first of all, comprehensive glossaries of the every-day vocabulary of carefully chosen active focal areas such as Eastern Massachusetts, the lower Connecticut Valley, the Hudson Valley, Delaware Bay, the Pittsburgh area, the Virginia Piedmont, the Low Country of South Carolina, etc., and similar glossaries of the more important relic areas such as the coast of Maine, the Green Mountains, the Eastern Shore of Maryland, Albemarle Sound, the Alleghenies and the Appalachians. The *Linguistic Atlas* will be an effective guide in choosing the vantage points, and the word lists already published by the Dialect Society and by *American Speech* as well as the vocabulary items in the *Atlas* will suggest topics on which the collecting should be centered in the various sections.

We need, furthermore, complete topical glossaries for such things and activities as food and cooking, general farming, dairy farming, cotton culture, fishing, seafaring, mining, etc. A single glossary for each topic from any part of the country will give us the basis for preparing the necessary questionnaires for the systematic collecting that must follow.

The preparation of regional and topical glossaries would involve little expense. It could be done to a large extent by scholars already located in different sections of the country. Intelligent informants can be easily secured, as the experience of the *Atlas* staff shows. There should, of course, be a guiding spirit for all such activity.

The regional and topical glossaries would provide the basis for planning systematic collecting in a larger number of points by means of questionnaires. When this stage has been reached, say in ten years, a central repository and planning agency would have to be set up in some university.

The writer of this preface is convinced that not much progress can be made along the road we have been traveling in the last 50 years in our attempts to lay the foundation for an American dialect dictionary. With few exceptions the published word lists are too scanty to be of much use. Whole sections of the country, e.g. Pennsylvania and the entire Southern Seaboard, are unexplored. The unevenness of the available material, in a geographical sense, is brought home by Mrs. Nixon's careful compilation in which many references to the Appalachians, the Ohio Valley, the Ozarks, and New England will be found but very few to the Southern Seaboard and the Gulf States where many of the words she presents are widely current. One therefore hopes that the Dialect Society may take a new perspective and steer the work of its members into more productive channels.

October   Hans Kurath
1945   *Brown University*

INTRODUCTION

This word list presents a sampling of the Virginia vocabulary with a description of the regional and the social spread of each term in Virginia and, as far as available dictionaries and word lists permit, in the rest of the United States and in the British Isles.

These terms are taken from the 138 Virginia field records of the *Linguistic Atlas*. For each term the geographic and the social spread in Virginia is described on the basis of the findings of the *Atlas*. Some of the expressions presented here occur in all parts of Virginia, others only on the Eastern Shore, the Tidewater, the Piedmont or the Valley, or in a combination of these sections. Some are used by speakers of all social classes, others only by the common folk or the cultured. Some expressions have general currency, others are rare. The list contains primarily regional and local words, but whenever a national or a literary synonym is current in Virginia by the side of the regional or local expression, it has been included to give a complete picture of Virginia usage. To omit such terms would be to give a false view of the actual situation.

It was planned originally to use the *Atlas* records to describe the occurrence of each term in all of the Eastern States, but since these records have been edited only in part, such statements cannot be made at present.

Each term was then looked up in the following sources, which are cited always in this order and with these abbreviations: B. W. Green's *Word-Book of Virginia Folk-Speech* (VWB), *Dialect Notes* (DN), *American Speech* (AS), the *Dictionary of American English* (DAE), Richard Thornton's *American Glossary* (T), the *New English Dictionary* (NED), the *Century Dictionary* (CD), and the *English Dialect Dictionary* (EDD).

Green's *Word-Book* is quoted first. This regional glossary is very good for the Piedmont, less so for the Valley, the Tidewater, and the Eastern Shore. It does not attempt to describe the geographic spread of the terms within Virginia.

Next come the references to the word lists from different parts of the country published in *Dialect Notes* and in *American Speech*. Items from the South are given first, then those from the Midland, finally those from the North. Because of the haphazard nature of these word lists the actual geographic spread of the terms in the United States cannot yet be determined.

7

References to the dictionaries are presented last, in the order given above. Definitions are quoted from these dictionaries when they are at variance with the meanings of the Virginia terms or when they contribute something specific. Whenever a term is assigned to a particular area, the proper notation has been made. Dates of the earliest and the latest quotations have been reproduced. Words which are not included in the *Dictionary of American English* have been starred.

The treatment of the terms presented here is as full as available published sources permit, but the picture is obviously incomplete.

PHYLLIS J. NIXON

A GLOSSARY OF VIRGINIA WORDS

*abate (see *calm down, lay, lower down, moderate, moderate down*):
Of the wind, subside; rare. NED (II.14) 1400–; CD (II.1).

aim (see *be fixing*): Intend; not common. VWB. Reported
from eAla (DN 3), wcWVa (AS 2.347), wNC Mts (DN 4), Tenn
Mts (DN 1), Cumberlands (AS 7.90), Ind (AS 16.22), wInd
(DN 3), sIll (DN 2), seMo (DN 2), swMo (DN 5), nwArk (DN
2), Me (AS 2.82; DN 5, *obsolete*). DAE Now chiefly *colloq.* or
dial., 1650–1908; NEDS (5.b) *Dial.* and *U.S.,* 1665–1909; CD
(II.2); EDD: Cum, Wm, Yks, Lan, Der, War, Wor, Hrf, Glo,
Dor, Som, Dev.

alter (see *change, cut*): Castrate; fairly common. VWB.
Reported from eAla (DN 3), La (DN 1), swMo (DN 5), wNY
(DN 3), cConn (DN 3). DAE *American;* NEDS (1.b) *U.S.*
and *Austral.,* 1889–1895; CD (3) *U.S.*

angleworm (see *earthworm, fishing worm, ground worm, red
worm*): Earthworm; on the Northern Neck. Reported from Mo
(DN 3), cNY (DN 3), NE (AS 8.12), wConn (DN 1), Vt (DN
3). DAE *American,* 1832–1918; CD.

andirons (see *fire dogs, dog irons, fire irons, hand irons*): Iron
utensils used to support the wood in a fireplace; common. VWB.
DAE 1640–1891; NED 1300–1878; CD; EDD: Yks, Lan; in dial.
pron. *endirons.*

ash cake (see *ash pone*): A cornmeal cake baked in the ashes;
common everywhere. VWB A loaf of cornbread baked in the
ashes. Reported from eAla (DN 3, *rare except in reminiscences*),
seMo (DN 2), nwArk (DN 3). DAE *American* 1809–1904;
T 1839–1861; NED (8.b); NEDS *U.S.,* 1824–1887; CD.

ash pone (see *ash cake*): A cornmeal cake baked in the ashes;
fairly common. DAE *American,* 1816–1840.

ashy (see *touchous, wrathy*): Angry; not common. VWB.
Reported from Va (DN 4), Ill (DN 5), sIll (DN 2), seMo (DN
2), Mo (DN 5), nwArk (DN 3). DAE *American, colloq.,* 1846–
1903.

attic (see *garret*): The top story of a house; used mostly by the
better educated. DAE 1841–1907; NED (3) The highest storey
of a house, or a room in it, 1817–1870; CD (2).

back a letter: Address a letter; common. VWB. Reported
from Va (DN 4), eAla (DN 3), wFla (DN 1), wcWVa (AS 2.347),

wNC mts (DN 4), SC (AS 18.66), Ky (DN 4), Ind (AS 16.21),
Ill (DN 1), sIll (DN 2, DN 3), neIa (DN 1), seMo (DN 2), nwArk
(DN 3), Ozarks (DN 5), Kan (DN 4), Neb (DN 4), Neb Pioneer
English (AS 8.51), wNY (DN 3), Me (AS 5.124). DAE (3)
1829–1902; T; NEDS (12.b) *U.S.*, 1859–1902, *So. and West;*
CD; EDD: Sc.

    back-house (see *garden house, johnny house*): A privy; common.
VWB. Reported from eAla (DN 3, also *backy*), wNY (DN 3),
cConn (DN 3), Me (DN 5, *obsolete*). DAE (b) *American*, quotations from Webster 1847, and Bartlett 1859; CD A building behind or back from the main or front building; hence, in country
places, especially in New England, a privy.

    ballet (see *song ballad*).

    bank-barn: A barn erected on sloping ground, with three sides
of the bottom story enclosed by earth; not common; in northern
part of the Blue Ridge. Reported from the English of the Pa
Germans (As 10.171), neO (DN 2). DAE *American*, 1894–1903;
NEDS *U.S.*, 1894–1909.

    barn lot, stable lot, lot: Barnyard; common everywhere except
in the Shenandoah Valley and on the Eastern Shore. Reported
from sIll (DN 2), nwArk (DN 3), wConn (DN 1). DAE; T A
piece of land; NED (6a) ... any piece of land set apart for a particular purpose, *now chiefly U.S.*, 1633–.

    barrow hog: A barrow; rare. DAE (2); NED (1.b), also
barrow-pig, 1547–1693; CD Now chiefly prov. Eng.; EDD: Lan,
Ken, Hmp; also *barrow-pig*.

    *base-born (see *oldfields colt, woods colt*): Illegitimate child;
on Chesapeake Bay; NED (3) 1645–1851; CD (a); EDD, *base-
child*, one base born.

    bateau: A flat-bottomed boat; in the Tidewater area and on the
Eastern Shore. VWB A flat, light-draught boat of planks. Reported from eVa (DN 2, *by negroes*), NJ (DN 1, *by oystermen*),
eMe (DN 3, *by loggers*), lumberjacks (AS 17.219, a boat used on
Eastern drives), early NE words (AS 15.226). DAE *American*,
1711–1902; T 1769–1870; NED A light river boat; esp. the long
tapering boats with flat bottoms used by the French Canadians,
1759–1884; CD (1) A light boat for river navigation, long in pro-
portion to its breadth, and wider in the middle than at the ends.

    batter bread (see *egg bread*): Cornbread made with eggs and milk;

east of the Blue Ridge. VWB. Reported from nwArk (DN 3, a soft corn bread containing lard or butter and served with a spoon, or a thick griddle cake of flour and meal), Cornell U. (DN 2, a preparation like hominy, eaten with butter, possibly like the *eggbread* of Tenn). DAE *American*, 1899–1904.

batter cake (see *flannel cake, griddle cake, hot-cake*): Pancake; common everywhere. VWB A thin cake of corn meal, milk, and eggs, and baked on a hot iron. DAE *American, chiefly Southern*, 1833–1897.

beholden: Under obligation; common. VWB. Reported from Ozarks (DN 5), nwArk (DN 3), Cape Cod (DN 2, DN 3). DAE *Now dial.*, 1835–1878; NED (1) 1340–1873; CD; EDD: Irel, Yks, Lan, Stf, Not, Lei, Nhp, War, Glo, Brks, eAn, Ken, Hmp, Dor, Som.

belling: Serenade after a wedding; in the northern part of the Blue Ridge and the central part of the Piedmont. Reported from O (DN 1), Neb (AS 8.22, 1870), NY (DN 1), NE (AS 8.24, *rare*). DAE *American*, 1862.

*bite (see *piece, snack*): A lunch eaten between meals; scattered in the Tidewater area. Reported from wcWVa (AS 2.348, a cold lunch), sIll (DN 2, sometimes also a regular meal), Western Reserve (DN 4), nwArk (DN 3, sometimes also a regular meal), NH (DN 4). NED (2) ... *concr.* food to eat; chiefly in the phrase *bite and sup*, 1562–1861; CD (5) Food; victuals: as, three days without either *bite* or sup; EDD: Sc, Nhb, Dur, Cum, Wm, Yks, Lan, Stf, Lin, Hmp, Wil, Som, Dev Slang; (1) A mouthful, a small portion of food; (2) *bite and sup*, food and drink, a slight repast.

blinds, window blinds (see *curtains, shades*): Roller shades for windows; common west of the Blue Ridge. *Blinds* reported from swPa (AS 7.19), DAE 1845–1902, NED (2) 1786–; *window blinds* NED (5.a) 1730–1865, CD.

*(be) blustering up (see *brewing up, ketchy*): Of the weather, look stormy; used among older people, rare. VWB, *blustering*, stormy. NED (II.2), *bluster*, of the wind: To blow boisterously or with stormy violence, 1530–.

*boar hog (see *male, male hog*): Boar; in the northern Blue Ridge, rare. Reported from Va (DN 4), eAla (DN 3, *used always*).

bonny-clabber (see *clabber*): Curdled milk; scattered. Reported from eAla (DN 3), Cape Cod (DN 2, *barney-clabber*). DAE, also *bony clabber, bonny clapper*, 1731–1904; NED 1631–1883; CD (1); EDD, *Obs.*, Irel, Chs.

bottom, bottoms (see *bottom land, low grounds, flats*): Low land; common everywhere. VWB Low land near a river; or between two hills; a valley. Reported from Va (AS 15.157, low land formed by alluvial deposits along a stream), nwArk (DN 3, generally used of low land). DAE (1) A stretch of low-lying land, usu. along a river or other stream, now *dial.*, 1634–1907; NED (4.b) Low-lying land, a valley, a dell; an alluvial hollow, 1325–1803; CD (3); EDD, Var. dial. uses in Sc, Irel, and Eng, also colonies; (1) the lowest part of a valley; a gully, ravine; low-lying land subject to inundation. Freq. in *pl.*

bottom land (see *bottom, low grounds, flats*): Low ground; west of the Blue Ridge and on the Rappahannock. Reported from Va (AS 15.158, rich flat land on the banks of streams; a flood plain; a bottom), swMo (DN 5). DAE *American*, 1738–1890; NEDS *U.S.*, A stretch of level land beside a river; an alluvial plain forming a river bottom, 1785–1903; CD, *bottom* (3).

branch (see *creek, run*): A small stream; common everywhere. VWB a small stream of water, brook. Reported from Va (AS 15.158–9: (1) a principal tributary of a river, creek, or other stream, (2) an arm of a cove or swamp, (3) a stream smaller than a creek; a brook or run), eAla (DN 3), Md (AS 10.256–9, most familiar in the plateau), Ohio River valley (AS 9.320, a small stream), eKy (DN 3), wInd (DN 3), sIll (DN 2, a small tributary of a small stream), Cumberlands (AS 15.47), Great Smokies (AS 15.47), seMo (DN 2), swMo (DN 5), nwArk (DN 3), Ozarks (AS 15.47). DAE A tributary of a creek or river, one of the streams which unite to form a river; *American*, a small stream, 1663–1913; T a brook; NED (2.b) *U.S.*, a small stream or brook, 1825; CD (3) In the southern and some of the western United States, the general name for any stream that is not a large river or a bayou.

*break up, break (see *let out, turn out*): *Of school*, be over; mostly in the eastern Piedmont. NED (56.e) 1535–1882; CD.

breakdown (see *frolic, hoedown, shindig*): A dance; not common. VWB, A riotous dance. Reported from eAla (DN 3), southern negroes (AS 3.209), wInd (DN 3), nwArk (DN 3), cConn (DN 3). DAE *American*, (a) To dance or perform a dance in a violent, stamping manner, 1838–1873; NED (2) *U.S.*, but frequently humorously in England, 1864–1881; CD (2), A noisy, lively dance, sometimes accompanied by singing, as in the southern United States; *U.S.*

*breast: Chest; fairly common. Reported from sIll (DN 2). NED (3) *Obs.*, 1340–1766; CD (2).

breeze up (see *getting up*): *Of the wind*, rise; along the shore, and on the Eastern Shore. VWB. Reported from Cape Cod (DN 2, *to breeze up fresh*). DAE 1752–1879; NED (2) *Naut.*

*(be) brewing up (see *blustering up, ketchy*): *Of the weather*, look stormy; not common. NED (4.c) 1530–1765; CD (II.2).

buck: Ram; west of the Blue Ridge, and on the lower Rappahannock. Reported from Va (DN 4), wcWVa (AS 2.349), Western Reserve (DN 4, *ram* considered scientific), swMo (DN 5, See *male* "bull"). DAE *American*, 1812–1881; NED (1) The male of several animals; CD.

bucket: A pail; regularly, among all classes. VWB Wooden or metal vessels, usually carried by a handle over the top. Reported from the Ohio River valley (AS 9.320, *universal*), Western Reserve (DN 4, usually a wooden bucket without a bail), the South (DN 4), eAla (DN 3), sIll (DN 2), seMo (DN 2), nwArk (DN 2), Kan (DN 4, any vessel with a bail used for carrying liquids), Neb (DN 4), wNY (DN 3, a wooden pail), Cape Cod (DN 2, a wooden pail), Hampstead, NH (DN 3, a wooden pail), West Brattleboro, Vt (DN 3, a wooden vessel without a handle or bail and having flaring sides; usually deeper than it is wide). DAE (1) A vessel for holding liquids; a pail. "The term is applied in the South and West, to all kinds of pails and cans holding over a gallon" (Bartlett, 1859), 1622–1904; NED . . . The local application of the word varies greatly; in the south-east of England and in the U. S. a bucket is a round wooden pail with an arched handle; in the south of Scotland it is a four-sided vessel for salt, coal, ashes, etc., 1300–1852; CD (1) . . . a pail or open vessel of wood, leather, metal, or other material, for carrying water or other liquid; EDD Var. dial. uses in Sc, Eng, and Amer; (1) a wooden pail, quotation from Bartlett as given in DAE above.

*bundle (see *sheaf*): A sheaf of wheat; common everywhere. Reported from Western Reserve (DN 4), nwArk (DN 3), eNeb (AS 12.106, *of hay*), wNY (DN 3). CD (1) . . . a *bundle* of hay; EDD Var. dial. uses in Sc, Eng, and Amer.

*burlap bag (see *crocus bag, grass sack, guano sack, sack bag,* *tow sack*): A large bag made of coarse canvas; not common except along the Potomac. NED, *burlap* 1695–1880.

*buss (see *smouch*): To kiss; fairly common. Reported from eAla (DN 3, *not common*), English of the Pa Germans (AS 10.172), Tenn Mts (DN 1, *bussy*, sweetheart, *also* AS 14.89), App Mts (DN 5, also *bussy*), Ozarks (DN 5, *not common*, perhaps by former Tenn people), Ozarks (AS 5.424). NED *Arch.* and *dial.*, 1571–1866; CD (II); EDD: Sc, Nhb, Cum, Yks, Lan, Chs, Stf, Der, Lin, Lei, Nhp War, Shr, eAn, Ken, Sus, Hmp, Dor, Cor.

butterbeans (see *lima beans*): Lima beans; common everywhere. DAE *American*, 1841–1911; NEDS 1884–1906; CD *U.S.*

*calm down (see *abate, lay, lower, moderate, moderate down*): *Of the wind;* not common. NED (1); CD (II).

carry (someone home): Escort (someone home); common east of the Blue Ridge. Reported from Va (DN 1, DN 4, lead, ride, drive), swVa (AS 8.23), eAla (DN 3), Miss Intelligencer (DN 4, to lead a quadruped), La (DN 1), wcWVa (AS 2.350), Md (DN 1), NC (DN 5), NC Mts (DN 4, AS 8.23), Ky (DN 1), Cumberlands (AS 7.90), seArk (AS 13.5), nwArk (DN 2, DN 3), Me (DN 4, to lead). DAE *Southern and dial.*, 1622–1896; NED (5) *arch.* and *dial.*, 1513–1886; CD (3); EDD: Ir, wCrk, Cum, wYks.

*catty-bias (see *catty-cornered, catty-wampered, cattawampus*): In a diagonal position; not common. Reported from wKy (DN 1).

catty-cornered (see *catty-bias, catty-wampered, cattawampus*): In a diagonal position; common. VWB. Reported from eAla (DN 3), nwArk (DN 3), Neb (DN 3), NY (DN 1), wNY (DN 3). DAE *American*, 1837–1875; T; NED *dial.*, 1878–1881; EDD: wYks, Der, Not, Bdf, neLan, Lei, War, Shr, sChs; U.S.A.

*catty-wampered (cattawampus) (see *catty-bias, catty-cornered*): In a diagonal position, or awry; not common. Reported from SC (AS 18.66, out of order), eAla (DN 3), NC Mts (DN 4), Ky (DN 4), Ind (AS 16.21), sInd (AS 14.266, DN 3), wInd (DN 3), Ill (DN 4), sIll (DN 2), seMo (DN 2), nwArk (DN 3), Kan (DN 4, awry), Neb (DN 3), NE (DN 4).

chamber (see *front room, living room, parlor, room, sitting room*): A sitting room on the first floor, usually with a bed; in the Tidewater area, among older people. DAE 1863–1902, *Southern*; NED (I.1) . . . in some English dialects, the "parlour" or better room as distinguished from the kitchen; EDD (3) A bedroom on the ground floor: Chs, Shr.

*change (see *alter*, *cut*): Castrate; fairly common. Reported from Va (DN 4).

chittlins: Hogs' intestines; in general use east of the Blue Ridge. VWB, Hog's intestines prepared for food, linked into knots and boiled, then put into vinegar. Reported from eAla (DN 3, *also chitlin-bread*), nwArk (DN 3), Ozarks (AS 5.17). DAE *chitlings, chetlins*, etc., (1) 1880–1909; NED *chitling* (1) Another form of *chitterling*; widely used in Eng. *dial*. and in *U.S.*, 1886–1888; CD *chitterling* (1) . . . part of the frill-like small intestine, as of swine, fried for food; also a kind of sausage; EDD *chitterlings*, Sc and gen. dial. use in Eng.

Christmas gift!: Merry Christmas !, a greeting used on Christmas morning; the person who says it first receives a gift; common everywhere. Reported from Va (DN 4), eAla (DN 3), seMo (DN 2), nwArk (DN 3, used by the negroes and lower whites, a kind of begging formula). DAE *American*, 1844–1908.

clabber (see *bonny-clabber*): Curdled milk; common everywhere. VWB, also *clobber*. Reported from sIll (DN 2), nwArk (DN 3). DAE 1828 (Webster)—1894; T, otherwise *bonny-clabber*, *Sc;* NED (2) 1624–1884; CD; EDD (2) Mun.

*clabber cheese (see *cottage cheese, curd, home-made cheese, smear-case*): Cheese made of the drained curd of sour milk; not common; in the Blue Ridge, the northern Piedmont, and the Southern Neck. Reported from nwArk (DN 2).

*clean (across) (see *clear across, jam across, plum across*): Entirely (across); fairly common east of the Blue Ridge. VWB. Reported from Ky (DN 5), Cumberlands (AS 7.90). NED (5) *Obs.*; EDD (13) Sc, Irel, Eng.

clear (across) (see *clean across, jam across, plum across*): Entirely (across); common in the western Piedmont and the Blue Ridge. Reported from eAla (DN 3), Western Reserve and Ind (*clear done*), seMo (DN 2), nwArk (DN 3). DAE *clear through*, 1842–1901; NED (5).

clever: Good-natured; common. VWB. Reported from Va (DN 4, generous), NC (DN 4), Ky (DN 4), eKy (DN 3), sInd (DN 3, AS 14.263), Miss (DN 4), Ozarks (DN 5, AS 4.204, AS 5.425), nwArk (DN 2), Neb (DN 4), Mass (DN 2, of horses), cConn (DN 3), NH (DN 2, of horses; DN 3, of animals, and of persons who are good-natured and perhaps a little deficient mentally), Me (AS 3.140); DN 4, of oxen), Dunglison's Glossary

(DN 5.)   DAE (1) Of horses, etc. well made; (2) good-natured
. . . *colloq.*, 1758–1904; (3) honest, conscientious . . . *colloq.*, 1804–
1818; T 1768–1850; NED (III.c) *U.S. colloq.*, 1773–1846; CD
(4) *colloq. U.S.;* EDD : Gall, Hr, eAn, Hrf, Suf, Cor.

coal hod (see *scuttle*): Along the Potomac; not common. Reported from NY (DN 1,—In the stove and hardware trade *coal
hod* is universal, and this form is more common in cities; in the
usage of country families in central N.Y. *coal scuttle* seems to
predominate.), cConn (DN 3).   DAE 1848–1895; CD.

coal oil (see *lamp oil*): Kerosene oil; common between the
Potomac and the Rappahannock, and in the Shenandoah Valley,
scattered elsewhere.   Reported from New Orleans, La (DN 4),
language of the oil wells (DN 2), Pa (DN 4), O (DN 1), Ill (DN
1), nwArk (DN 5), Neb (DN 4), Neb pioneer English (AS 7.167),
English Canada (DN 1).   DAE *American*, petroleum or oil
refined from it, especially kerosene, 1858–1908; NED *U.S.*, Shale-
oil, petroleum, 1858–1926; CD.

comfort: A thick bed quilt; regularly everywhere. VWB.
Reported from eAla (DN 3).   DAE 1843–1913; NED (8) *U.S.*;
CD *comfortable* (II) A thickly wadded and quilted bedcover.
Also *comfort* and *comforter, U.S.*

corn bread (see *corn pone, pone bread*): Cornmeal bread; common everywhere. VWB. DAE *American*, 1796–1898; NED
U.S., 1823–1913; CD *U.S.*

corn cakes (see *hoe cake, johnny cake*): Cornmeal griddle cakes;
fairly common.   DAE *American*, 1791–1863; NED *U.S.*, 1850–
1854; CD *U.S.*

corn crib (see *corn house, corn stack*): West of the Blue
Ridge.   VWB.   Reported from nwArk (DN 3), cConn (DN 3).
DAE *American*, 1687–1908; T 1809–1849; NED *U.S.* 1849–
1883; CD.

corn dodger (see *dodger, pone*): A hard, hand-shaped cake of
cornbread; west of the Blue Ridge and in the northern parts of the
Piedmont and Tidewater. VWB A dumplin' made of corn
meal and boiled in a pot with ham and cabbage.   Reported from
eAla (DN 3), Ky (DN 1), wInd (DN 3), seMo (DN 2), nwArk
(DN 3, plain cornbread or cornbread baked in a skillet), Neb
pioneer English (AS 6.250, AS 7.168).   DAE *American*, Bread
made of Indian corn meal baked hard in small cakes or pones,
1834–1909; NED *U.S.*, 1856–1885; CD *So. U.S.*

corn house (see *corn crib, corn stack*): Corn crib; everywhere east of the Blue Ridge except south of the lower James. Reported from wNY (DN 3). DAE *American*, 1699–1891; NED (2) *U.S.*; CD *U.S.*

* **corn stack** (see *corn crib, corn house*): Corn crib; on the Eastern Shore.

corn pone (see *corn bread, pone bread*): Corn bread; common everywhere. DAE *American* and *Southern*, bread made of Indian corn meal, water or milk, and salt, usu. baked in small loaves or masses, 1859–1904; NED *So. U.S.*, 1860–1890; CD *So. U.S.*

* **corruption:** Pus; common. VWB. Reported from Va (DN 4), eAla (DN 3), sIll (DN 2), seMo (DN 2). NED *Obs.* exc. *dial.*, 1526–1888; CD (2); EDD: NI, nYks, Chs, nLin.

cottage cheese (see *clabber cheese, curd, home-made cheese, smear case*): Cheese made of the drained curd of sour milk; regarded as a modern term. DAE *American* 1848 (Bartlett)—1917; CD *U.S.*, also called *Dutch cheese, pot cheese, smear case*.

counterpane (see *coverlid*): A bedspread; common. VWB. Reported from wcWVa (AS 2.352), NC Mts (DN 4), Ky (DN 4). DAE 1687–1900; NED A coverlet, a quilt 1464–1885; CD . . . a quilt; now, *spec.*, a coverlet woven of cotton with raised figures, also called Marseilles quilt.

coverlid (see *counterpane*): A bedspread; rare. VWB A cover for a bed, bed quilt, coverled. DAE 1640–1913; NED 1300–1862; CD; EDD: eYks, Chs, nLin, Nhp, War, Hnt, Ken.

cow pen (see *cow pound, cuppen, milk gap*): Pen for cows; common. DAE 1661–1904; NED 1635–1876.

cow pound (see *cow pen, cuppen, milk gap*): Pen for cows; on the Eastern Shore and on the point of land east of Norfolk. VWB *pound* A farm pen. DAE *pound* An enclosure built and maintained at public expense for impounding stray or trespassing stock, 1633–1902; NED *pound* (I.1.c) An enclosure for sheltering or in any way dealing with sheep or cattle in the aggregate, 1780–1890; CD *See* DAE; EDD *pound* (1) A small enclosure; a sheepfold; a pig-sty: Sh I, Yks, Stf, War, Shr, Hrf, Glo, Sur, Sus, Hmp, Som, Dev, and Amer.

creek (see *branch, run*): A fresh water stream, common everywhere; a narrow salt water inlet, on the Tidewater and Eastern Shore. VWB a small stream where there is an ebb and flow of the tide. Reported from Va (AS 15.168: (1) in the lower Tidewater an arm of the sea ... also a stream opening into a large river and subject to the tide, (2) a fresh-water stream normally smaller than a river and larger than a brook in the same general locality; usually distinguished from river and branch), SC (DN 4), Pa (DN 4), Md (AS 10.256–9, most frequent in the coastal plain), Western Reserve (DN 4), Mo (DN 1), nwArk (DN 3), Kan (DN 4), Neb (DN 4), Cal (DN 5), wNY (DN 3), NY (DN 4), Aroostook, Me (DN 3); Dunglison's Glossary (DN 5,—a small river, southern and middle states; "In New England it has the correct English signification; a part of a sea, lake, or river running into the land."). DAE (1) an inlet of the ocean or of a river, common in New England records of the 17th century and still in local use; (2) *American*, a stream forming a tributary to a larger river: a small stream, brook, or rivulet, 1638–1843; T A small river, 1674–1869; NED (I.1) A narrow recess or inlet in the coast-line of the sea, or the tidal estuary of a river; (2.b) in *U.S. and Brit. Colonies*, a a branch of a main river, a tributary river; a rivulet, brook, small stream, or run, 1674–1848; CD (1) A small inlet ... ; (2) A small stream; a brook; a rivulet; common in this sense in the United States and Australia, but now rare in England.

crocus bag, crocus sack, croker sack (see *burlap bag, grass-sack, guano sack, sack, sack bag, tow sack*): A large bag made of coarse canvas; common in the southern Piedmont, scattered in the northern Piedmont. Reported from eAla (DN 3, coker-sack), wFla (DN 1). DAE *crocus*, *American*, a kind of coarse, heavy cloth, *Obs.*, 1689–1790; NED (5) *crocus ginger-bagg* 1699.

cuppen, cow-cuppen (see *cow pen, cow pound, milk gap*): A pen for cows; the Piedmont and the Northern Neck. VWB (2) An enclosure in which animals are kept. DAE *American, Southern*, 1823–1899; NED (I.1.c) An enclosure for sheltering or in any way dealing with sheep or cattle in the aggregate, 1780–1890; EDD: Sh, Yks, Stf, War, Shr, Hrf, Glo, Sur, Sus, Hmp, Som, Dev, and Australia, (1) A small enclosure; a sheepfold; a pig-sty.

cur-dog (see *fiste*): A mongrel dog; common. VWB A cur, worthless dog, of unknown breed and blood but mean stock. Reported from sInd (DN 3), sIll (DN 2), nwArk (DN 3). DAE 1791–1885; NED (1.c) 1225–1859; CD; EDD (2) A collie or shepherd's dog, Cum.

curds, curd cheese (see *clabber cheese, cottage cheese, home-made* *cheese, smear-case*): Cheese made of the drained curd of sour milk, especially that fed to turkeys or chickens; mostly in the Tidewater area. DAE; CD (1).

curtains (see *blinds, shades*): Roller shades for windows; common in the Tidewater and the eastern Piedmont. Reported from nwArk (DN 3), seIa (DN 2), wNY (DN 3), Me (DN 5, AS 2.79). DAE (1) 1640–1902; NED (1) 1300–1827.

*** cut** (see *alter, change*): Castrate; common. VWB. Reported from wcWVa (AS 2.351), Western Reserve (DN 4), eNeb (AS 12.104), Cal (DN 5, *common at U. of Cal.*). NED (26.a) 1465–1865; CD (9); EDD (4) wYks, Chs, nLin, swLin, sWor, Shr, Ess, wSom.

dike up (see *fix up, primp up, prink*): Get dressed up; fairly common. VWB. Reported from Va (DN 4, *dike*, n and vb), Charlottesville, Va (DN 2), Wedgefield, SC (DN 6), eAla (DN 3), wTex (DN 4), Tex (DN 1), wcWVa (AS 2.352), nwArk (DN 3), NJ (DN 1, *dicked, on a dike*, showing one's finery in public). DAE *American* 1851–1923; NEDS s. and vb., *U.S. slang* or *colloq.*, 1871–1923.

dip: A pudding sauce; not common. Reported from NJ (DN 1), eKy (DN 3, cream for coffee), nwArk (DN 3), Ozarks (DN 5, sweetened cream, eaten with pie, apple dumpling, cobbler, and the like), ranch diction of the Texas panhandle (AS 8.27). DAE (3) A sauce or dressing, *local*, 1846–1894; NED (9) *local Eng.* and *U.S.*, 1825–1884; CD (5.b) *local, U.S.*; EDD (10): nCy, cYks, wYks, Chs, nwDer, Lei, Nhp, War, Hnt, eAn, Nrf, Amer; also *brandy-dip*.

dirt-daubers (see *masons, mud-daubers*): Wasps; common. Reported from Va (DN 4), eAla (DN 3), Ozarks (AS 8.48). DAE *American* and *Southern*, a sand-wasp or mud-dauber, 1844–1902; NED (2) A species of sand-wasp.

disremember: Not remember; common. VWB. Reported from south (DN 1, *common, though considered vulgar*), eAla (DN 3, *common*), Miss (DN 4), wTex (DN 4, *widely used*), wInd (DN 3), sIll (DN 2), nwArk (DN 3, *rare*), Ozarks (AS 5.425), Sherwood's Provincialisms (DN 5), Dunglison's Glossary (DN 5). DAE chiefly *dial.*, 1815–1917; T *dial.* in England and common in the north of Ireland; NED Chiefly *dial.*, 1836–1880; CD *Vulgar*; EDD: Sc, Irel, Lan, Lin, Oxf. Brks, Sus, Hmp, Corn, Amer.

dodger (see *corn dodger, pone*): A hard, hand-shaped cake of cornbread; west of the Blue Ridge and in the northern Piedmont and Tidewater. Reported from eAla (DN 3), Ky (DN 1), seMo (DN 2), nwArk (DN 3). DAE *American*, 1831–1894; T A soft cake of wheat or maize, somewhat resembling a pancake, 1834–1864; NED (2) *U.S.*, a hard-baked corn-cake, 1852–1882; CD (3) *U.S.*

dog irons (see *andirons, fire dogs, fire irons, hand irons*): Iron utensils used to support the wood in a fireplace; common from the Blue Ridge westward, and south of the lower James—less common in the Piedmont. Reported from swMo (DN 5), Ozarks (AS 8.48), Newfoundland (DN 5). DAE 1790–1884; NED 1883; EDD See *fire dogs.*

* **doney:** Girl friend; not common. Reported from NC Mts (DN 4, AS 15.46, also *doney-gal*), Ky Mts (DN 5, usually *doney-gal*). NED *Doña* (2) *Slang*, 1873–1894.

* **dry-land frog** (see *hop-toad, toad-frog*): A toad; common.

earthworm (see *angleworm, fishing worm, ground worm, redworm*): On the lower James. Reported from NE (AS 8.12, *general and literary term*). DAE 1737–1883; NED (1); CD (1).

egg bread (see *batter bread*): A soft bread made of corn meal and eggs; mostly south of the lower James and in the northern Piedmont. Reported from sMiss (DN 2), Tenn (DN 2). DAE *American*, 1854–1904; T 1862; NEDS (7) *U.S.*, 1862.

evening: Afternoon, from noon until sunset; common. Reported from eAla (DN 3), Barbourville, Ky (DN 3), wInd (DN 3), sIll (DN 2), seMo (DN 2), swMo (DN 5), Ozarks (AS 8.48), nwArk (DN 2), Newfoundland (DN 5), Dunglison's Glossary, labeled "southern states" (DN 5). DAE (2) *S. & W., dial.*, 1790–1904; NEDS (2.c) *dial.* and *U.S. local*, 1836–1888; CD (3) England and so. U.S.; EDD (1) Wor, Shr, Sur.

fair up: Of weather, to clear; used among older people, not common. VWB. Reported from Shenandoah Valley (AS 12.287) eAla (DN 3), Ozarks (AS 8.49), Vt (DN 5, *fair off*). DAE *dial.*, 1859–; NED (1.b) *rare exc. dial.*, 1842–1891; CD (II.2) *fair . . .* followed commonly by *up* or *off* (Scotch); EDD (16) Cai, Nhb, eDur, nYks, neYks, wYks, Amer (Bartlett).

falling weather: Bad weather, rain; not common. Reported from Lynchburg, Va (DN 4), NC (DN 4), wVa (DN 4), wcWVa (AS 2.353), sInd (DN 3), sIll (DN 2), seMo (DN 1), seArk (AS 13.5), nwArk (DN 3), Ozarks (AS 8.49), Kan (DN 4). DAE *American* 1732–1919; EDD (7) War, sWor, Hrf, Glo.

* **favor (someone):** Resemble (someone); common. VWB. Reported from eAla (DN 3, *universal*), wcWVa (AS 2.354), Springdale, Pa (DN 1), Tenn Mts (DN 1), seMo (DN 2), swMo (DN 5), nwArk (DN 3, *the favor to you*), nNH (DN 4), Me (AS 5.127), Me rural (DN 4). T; NED (8) *now colloq.* 1609–1866; CD *now chiefly colloq.*; EDD Sc, Eng, Amer.

fire dogs, dogs (see *andirons, dog irons, fire irons, hand irons*): Iron utensils used to support the wood in a fireplace; in the southern part of the Blue Ridge and all of the Piedmont. VWB. Reported from seMo (DN 2), nwArk (DN 3), Ozarks (AS 8.48). DAE *fire dogs*, 1792–1905, *dogs* (2.a) 1641–1884; T *fire dogs* 1792–1840; NED *fire dogs* 1840, *dogs* (8) 1596–1862; CD; EDD *dogs* (10) . . . also in comp., *dog-irons:* nCy, Dur, Nhp, War, Brks, eAn, Sus, Hmp, Dor, wSom.

fire irons (see *andirons, dog irons, fire dogs, hand irons*): Iron utensils used to support the wood in a fireplace; not common. DAE Implements, usually made of iron, for use about a domestic fire; also, andirons, 1648–1885.

fishing worm, fish worm (see *angleworm, earthworm, ground worm, red worm*): Earthworm; common everywhere except on Chesapeake Bay. Reported from eAla (DN 3), nwArk (DN 3), NE (AS 8.12). DAE *American* 1870–1913; CD.

fiste (see *cur-dog*): A mongrel dog; scattered everywhere. VWB A small worthless dog. Reported from eAla (DN 3, *faust, faust-dog, fausty, fice, fice-dog*), NC Mts (DN 4, *feist, feisty*), Ky (DN 1), Tenn Mts (DN 1, also *fisty*, low or mean), sIll (DN 2, an under-sized, vicious dog), Shurtleff College, Ill (AS 3.217, *fisty*, peevish, teasing, of persons), seMo (AS 17.248, *fiesty person*, an uppish person; DN 2, *fist*, cur), nwArk (DN 3), Okla (AS 18.111, A *feisty person*, a willful person), Kan (DN 4, *feisty*, worthless; AS 17.248, cowardly), eNeb (AS 12.103, *fyst*, a bad-tempered horse), Wisc (AS 18.111, *fees*, repugnant). DAE *American*, 1805–1886; T *So.*; NED (2) *U.S. dial.*, 1872; CD (Quotation from Trans. Amer. Phil. Ass. XVIII): "*Fice* is the name used everywhere in the South, and in some parts of the West, for a small worthless cur."

(be) fixing to (see *aim to*): Plan or intend to; common. Reported from Va (DN 4), eAla (DN 3), New Orleans, La (DN 4), NC (DN 4), Ill (DN 4), nwArk (DN 2), Kan (DN 4), Sherwood's Provincialisms (DN 5), Dunglison's Glossary (DN 5). DAE *colloq.*, 1716–1914; NEDS (16.a) *U.S.* 1716–1904.

fix up (see *dike up, primp up, prink*): Get dressed up; fairly common. VWB. Reported from Ozarks (AS 11.315, *fixy*, well-groomed). DAE *American* 1834–1871; NEDS (16.b) To put oneself in proper trim; to spruce up, *U.S.*; CD (b) *colloq., U.S.*

flannel cake (see *batter cake, griddle cake, hot-cake*): A pancake; mostly west of the Blue Ridge, also on Chesapeake Bay. DAE 1847–1916; T A soft thin cake usually eaten with molasses; NED (6.c) 1792; CD A kind of thin griddle-cake made with either wheat-flour or corn-meal and raised with yeast, *U.S.*; EDD (3) A coarse oatcake, wYks.

flats (see *bottom, bottom land, low-grounds*): Low level land; common in the Piedmont and on the Northern Neck. VWB A shoal or sand bank, a part of the shore uncovered at low tide. Reported from Va (AS 15.178: (1) a piece of level ground, (2) a level tract lying at a little depth below the surface of the water or alternately covered and left bare by the tide), wNY (DN 3), cConn (DN 3). DAE Low land, valuable as pasture or farm land, 1651–1829; NED (5) A piece of level ground . . . the low ground through which a river flows, 1296–1877; CD (2) . . . in the United States, a low alluvial plain near the tide-water or along a river, as the Jersey . . . flats; also the part of a shore that is uncovered at low tide; EDD (5) A hollow in a field; a small valley: neLan, Glo, Sus; Glo smaller than a *bottom*.

foreigner: A stranger, or a person from another state; fairly common. Reported from So App Mts (AS 15.46 *furrin*, anything strange), seMo (DN 2), Ozarks (AS 4.203, AS 15.46 *furrin*, anything strange), nwArk (DN 3). DAE . . . a non-native, an outsider, 1626–1886; NED (2) Now *dial.*, 1460–1875; CD (2) One who does not belong to a certain class, association, society, etc., an outsider; EDD Gen. *dial.* use in Sc, Irel, Eng, Amer.

(be) fresh, (come) fresh (see *freshen, hommy*): Calve; common. Reported from Va (DN 4), swMo (DN 5). DAE (2) 1884–1896; NEDS (10.c) *U.S.*, 1884–1896.

* freshen (see *fresh, hommy*): Calve; common. Reported from wcWVa (AS 2.354), swMo (DN 5), eMe (DN 3). NED (1.d) *U.S.*, 1931; EDD: wYks, nwDer.

* frogstool: Toadstool; not common. VWB. Reported from eAla (DN 3), Tenn Mts (DN 1), nwArk (DN 3). NED (8.b) 1661–1865; CD; EDD: Glo, sWil.

frolic (see *breakdown, hoedown, shindig*): A party; fairly common. VWB. Reported from eAla (DN 3, a country dance), seMo (DN 2, a country dance), Humphrey's Glossary (DN 5, country festival sports); DAE (1) 1711–1898; T 1767–1854; NED (2) 1645–1895; CD (2); EDD eAn, Any kind of entertainment or outing; not necessarily with the idea of amusement.

front room (see *chamber, living room, parlor, room, sitting room*)*:* A living room; in the James Valley and southward.—Reported from swMo (DN 5), eNeb (AS 12.102), Me (AS 5.127). DAE 1679–.

galluses (gallowses): Suspenders; common. VWB. Reported from eAla (DN 3), wcWVa (AS 2.355), Ky (DN 1), sIll (DN 2), nwArk (DN 3, s and vb), swMo (DN 5), wNY (DN 3, *less common than formerly*), NY (DN 1, to *gallows up* one's breeches), Cape Cod (DN 2), West Brattleboro, Vt (DN 3), nNH (DN 4), Me (DN 4, DN 5, AS 5.120), Aroostook, Me (DN 3), Newfoundland (DN 5), New Brunswick (DN 1, to *slip one's gallows,* lose a button). DAE *gallows, colloq.,* usu. *pl.,* 1806–1891; *gallus dial.,* usu. *pl.,* 1835–1888; T 1806–1867; NED (6) Now *dial., Sc* and *U.S.,* in form *gallowses,* whence occas. *gallows* for a single brace; CD (I) *pl., colloq.;* EDD (6): Sc, Bnff, Frf, eFif, Lnk, Edb, Gall, Ir, NI, sDon, sIr, Nhb, Dur, Cum, Yks, Lan, Chs, Der, nLin, Nrf, Suf, IW, Wil, nDev, (Amer., slip one's gallows "lose a button," DN 1).

* **garden house** (see *back-house, johnny house*): A privy; common everywhere except the southern part of the Piedmont. VWB. NED (1.b) *dial.* and *U.S.;* EDD (2) wSom "the usual name amongst farmers' wives and women of the class above labourers."

garret (see *attic*): The top story of a house; common. Reported from Cape Cod (DN 2), Me (AS 2.79). DAE 1637–1890; NED (2) A room on the uppermost floor of a house; an apartment formed either partially or wholly within the roof, an attic, 1483–1874; CD (2); EDD (2) A half-open upper room; wYks "Not precisely the same as *attic,* which is an upper room."

* **gentleman cow** (see *male, ox, steer*): A bull; on the Middle Neck in the presence of women. Reported from wInd (DN 3, used by squeamish women). NED *gentleman* (7.b).

* **getting up** (see *breeze up*): *Of the wind,* rising; not common. NED (72.d) 1556–1890.

> **goobers, goober peas** (see *ground peas*): Peanuts; fairly com-

mon. Reported from Va (DN 5), eAla (DN 3), Ky (DN 5),
NC (DN 5), Tenn (DN 1), seMo (DN 2), swMo (DN 5), nwArk
(DN 3). DAE *goober* or *gouber*, *American*, *S.* and *SW*, 1848–1904;
goober pea, *American*, 1871–1901; NED *U.S.*, 1885–1888.

> **granny, granny-woman:** Midwife; common everywhere. VWB.
Reported from NC Mts (DN 4, *granny-doctor*), App Mts (DN
5), swMo (DN 5), Ozarks (DN 5). DAE *American* (1) 1794–
1824; NED *U.S.*, *local*, 1794.

* **grass sack, sea grass sack** (see *burlap bag*, *crocus bag*, *guano
sack*, *sack*, *sack bag*, *tow sack*): A large bag made of coarse canvas;
on the Rappahannock and the Potomac. CD *grass cloth* (2) A
thick fabric made in the Canary islands of some vegetable fiber.

* **green-beans** (see *snaps*, *string beans*): String beans; west of
the Blue Ridge.

griddle cake (see *batter cake*, *flannel cake*, *hot-cake*): A pancake;
in the Piedmont and Tidewater among cultured people, rare.
DAE 1783–; NED (4) 1783–1852; CD *U.S.*; EDD (3.2) Ir,
wYks, nCy, Amer.

> * **grindrock:** Grindstone; rare. Reported from NC Mts (DN
4, *grindin' rock*), Tenn Mts (DN 1).

grist (of corn) (see *turn of corn*): The amount of corn taken to
(or from) the mill at one time; in the Shenandoah Valley. VWB
That which is ground; corn to be ground; grain carried to the
mill to be ground separately for the owner. The quantity ground
at one time, the grain carried to the mill for grinding at one time.
Applied to small quantities. DAE 1640–1905; T A quantity of
anything, 1833–1910; NED (2) Corn which is to be ground; also
(with *pl.*) a batch of such corn, 1430–1896, (3) Corn that has been
ground 1566–1887; CD See VWB; EDD In *gen.* dial. and prov.
use in Sc and Eng, (1) The quantity of corn sent to a mill to be
ground; meal or flour after grinding; the fee paid at a mill, *gen.*
in kind, for grinding.

> **ground peas** (see *goobers*): Peanuts; common. VWB. Re-
ported from eAla (DN 3, not as common as *goober*), seMo (DN 2),
nwArk (DN 3). DAE *American*, 1769–1892; NEDS 1769–1854;
CD.

> **ground worm** (see *angleworm*, *earthworm*, *fishing worm*, *red-
worm*): An earthworm; on the Eastern Shore and on the shore of
the Middle Neck. DAE *American*, cut worm, 1708–; NEDS
U.S., cut worm.

guano sack (see *burlap bag, crocus bag, grass sack, sack, sack bag, tow sack*): A large bag made of coarse canvas; in the northern Piedmont. CD *guana*.

gully-washer (see *squall*): A thunderstorm; not common. Reported from sInd (AS 14.263), nwMo (DN 5), Ozarks (AS 8.49). DAE 1903.

handirons (see *andirons, dog irons, fire dogs, fire irons*): Iron utensils used to support the wood in a fireplace; on the Eastern Shore, and south to the James in the Piedmont and Tidewater. DAE 1649–1836; NED *Obs.*, 1475–1731; CD.

*** hasslet** (see *pluck*): The edible inner parts of a pig or calf; in general use east of the Blue Ridge. VWB. Reported from eAla (DN 3, *haslet*, the windpipe of an animal, or the liver and lights of a slaughtered pig), Zebulon, NC (AS 17.77), Cape Cod (DN 2, *haslet*, the liver, lights, and tongue of a killed pig), nNH (DN 4), Me (DN 4). NED A piece of meat to be roasted, esp. the entrails of a hog, 13. .–1872; CD; EDD: Sc, Chs, Lin, Nhp, War, Wor, Shr, Hrf, Glo, Brks, Suf, Ken, Hup, IW, Wil; (1) the liver and lights of a pig, (2) a dish of pigs' entrails.

hay cock (see *hay doodle, shock*): A pile of hay in the field at haying time; west of the Blue Ridge, on the Middle Neck and on the Eastern Shore. Reported from eNeb (AS 12.107). DAE 1684–1904; NED 1470–1851; EDD (13) Wil.

*** hay doodle** (see *hay cock, shock*): A pile of hay in the field at haying time; in the Blue Ridge, rare. Reported from eNeb (AS 12.106, a small stack of leftover bundles of hay).

hoe cake (see *corn cake, johnny cake*): A griddle cake made of corn meal; mostly in the Tidewater and on the Rappahannock. VWB Bread of cornmeal, water and salt, baked on the bottom of an old weeding-hoe. Reported from eAla (DN 3, baked in a flat pone in an open vessel), seMo (DN 2, baked on a board or in an open vessel before the fire), nwArk (DN 3). DAE *American, chiefly Southern;* also a similar cake of wheat, 1774–1916; T A flat cake formerly baked on a hoe over coals, 1787–1857; NED *U.S.*, 1793–1885; CD Coarse bread, generally in the form of a thin cake, made of Indian meal, water, and salt: originally that cooked on the broad, thin blade of a cottonfield hoe; *So U.S.*

hoedown (see *breakdown, frolic, shindig*): A lively dance; fairly common. Reported from wcWVa (AS 2.357), sInd (DN 3, a rough dance), wInd (DN 3, an evening of old-fashioned dancing;

more familiar than breakdown), sIll (DN 2), nwArk (DN 3, a rough or "lowclass" dance), Neb pioneer English (AS 8.48). DAE *American, originally and chiefly Southern,* (1) a lively dance 1849–1898, (2) a party of such dances 1870–1887; T A negro dance 1855–1885; NED *U.S.* A noisy, riotous dance, 1860–1885; CD Same as *breakdown, So U.S.*

> **hog's head cheese** (see *pudding, souse*): A sausage of pig's entrails; fairly common. DAE *American,* 1859 (Bartlett)–1870.

* **home-made cheese** (see *clabber cheese, cottage cheese, curd, smear case*): Cheese made of the drained curd of sour milk; in the Shenandoah Valley, uncommon.

* (**have a**) **hommy,** (**find a**) **hommy** (see *fresh, freshen*): Calve; in the northern Blue Ridge, rare. Reported in the English of the Pa Germans (AS 10.169).

hoppergrass: Grasshopper; in the eastern Piedmont and the Tidewater. VWB. Reported from eAla (DN 3), So App Mts (AS 15.53), seMo (DN 2), Ozarks (AS 15.53), wTex (DN 3), Neb (DN 3, *facetious*), Cape Cod (DN 2, a troublesome woman or child), Dunglison's Glossary (DN 5, "often used in the South ...a *vulgarism*"), Americanisms of a Hundred Years Ago (AS 7.96). DAE *American, colloq.,* 1829–1899.

> **hop-toad** (see *dry-land frog, toad frog*): A toad; common. Reported from sInd (DN 3, *common*), sIll (DN 2), nwArk (DN 3), Neb (DN 3, *common*). DAE *American, colloq.,* 1827–1906; T 1827–1861; NEDS *Local U.S.,* 1827–1913.

hot-cake (see *batter cake, flannel-cake, griddle cake*): A pancake; on the Eastern shore, rare. Reported as a westernism (AS 1.150). DAE (1) 1683–1835.

* **hunkers** (**hunkles**): Haunches; fairly common. Reported from So App Mts (AS 15.46, *hunker down,* to squat), SC (AS 18.67), Tenn (DN 4), Erie Canal (AS 6.98, *hunkered*), sInd (DN 3, knees), Ind (AS 16.23), swMo (DN 5, *hunker down*), Ozarks (AS 8.50 and AS 15.46 *hunker down*), nwArk (DN 3, *usually of animals*), Kan (DN 4), wTex (DN 4). NED 1785–1898; CD *Scotch;* EDD: Sc, Irel, nCy, Nhb, Dur, Cum, Yks, Suf; Amer.

* **Irish potatoes:** White potatoes; fairly common. VWB. Reported from Va (DN 4), NC (DN 4), Tenn (DN 4), Ill (DN 4), New Orleans, La (DN 4), Iowa (DN 4).

jacket (see *weskit*): A vest; fairly common among older people in the southern part of the Blue Ridge. VWB A short coat or body garment; any garment for the body coming not lower than the hips. DAE (2) *Obs.*, 1705–1738; NED (1.d) *locally* in *U.S.*; CD (3) *local, U.S.*; EDD (2) Nhb, Dur.

jam (across) (see *clean across, clear across, plum across*): Entirely (across); on the Middle Neck. Reported from eAla (DN 3), nwArk (DN 3). DAE *American*, 1882–; NED (2) 1835–1921; EDD *jam full.*

johnny cake (see *corn cake, hoe cake*): A corn meal griddle cake; on the Northern Neck. VWB A cake made of corn meal and water or milk and salt, baked on a board set on edge before the fire. Reported from eAla (DN 3), Neb pioneer English (AS 7.168), cNY (DN 3), cConn (DN 3). DAE *American* (1) A flat cake of corn meal etc. cooked in various ways, on a board before the open fire, on a griddle, in a pan or oven, 1739–1903; T; NED (a) *U.S.*, a cake made of maize-meal, in the So. states toasted before a fire, elsewhere usu. baked in a pan; (b) *Austr.*, a cake made of wheat-meal, baked on the ashes or fried in a pan, 1775–1892; CD (1) In *So. U.S.* a cake of Indian meal mixed with water or milk, seasoned with salt, and baked or toasted by being spread on a board set on edge before a fire; (2) in other parts of the U.S., any unsweetened flat cake of Indian meal, sometimes mixed with mashed pumpkin (esp. in New England) and usu. baked in a pan.

* johnny house (see *back-house, garden house*): Privy; fairly common in the James Valley and the southern part of the Blue Ridge.

ketchy (see *blustering up, brewing up*): Of the weather, stormy; used among older people, rare. Reported from Ozarks (AS 11.315), NJ (DN 1, *catchy*, irritable), NY (DN 1). DAE *catching*, Variable, uncertain, unexpected, 1868–1876; NED (4) Occurring in snatches, fitful, spasmodic, 1872–; *catchy wind* 1883.

kick (see *mitten, sack*): Jilt (someone); common. VWB. Reported from eAla (DN 3). DAE *American, colloq.*, 1848; NED (4.c) *U.S. Slang*, 1860–1895; CD *Vulgar, So. U.S.*

* (no) kin (to someone): (Not) related (to someone); common among all classes. VWB. Reported from eAla (DN 3), sInd (DN 3), sIll (DN 2), seMo (DN 2), swMo (DN 5), nwArk (DN 3), Cape Cod (DN 2, not *like* someone). NED 1597–1870; CD (3); EDD: Sc, nCy, Cum, Yks, Lan, Sur, Som, Dev.

* kinfolks: Relatives; common among all classes. VWB. Reported from eAla (DN 3), Cumberlands (AS 7.93), sIll (DN

2), seMo (DN 2), swMo (DN 5), nwArk (DN 3).   NED *kins-folk*, now *rare*, 1450–1855.

* **lamp oil** (see *coal oil*): Kerosene oil; in the southern parts of the Blue Ridge and the Piedmont.   NED Oil used for burning in a lamp, 1581–1895.

* **(be) laying** (see *abate, calm down, lower down, moderate*): Of the wind, subside; fairly common.   Reported from Ky (DN 5), sInd (DN 3), sIll (DN 2), nwArk (DN 3).   EDD *lay*, sb. (26) Of waves, a temporary lull, Cai.

let out (see *break up, turn out*):   *Of school*, be over; everywhere, but not common south of the James.   VWB.   Reported from Ind (AS 16.22 *to let out school*).   DAE *American* (4.b) 1867–1898; NED (34.a) *Obs.*, 1154–1889; CD (II.c) *Rural, U.S.;* EDD (III.1.10.g) Abd.

light-bread: Wheat bread; common.   VWB.   Reported from Va (DN 4), eAla (DN 3), wFla (DN 1), wcWVa (AS 2.359), sIll (DN 2), seMo (DN 2), nwArk (DN 2), seKan (DN 4). DAE *American, Southern*, 1821–1920.

lighterd, lightwood: Kindling; everywhere east of the Blue Ridge.   VWB Very resinous pine wood.   Reported from wcWVa (AS 2.359), eAla (DN 3, *liderd*), nwLa (DN 4), Chicago people of NE antecedents (DN 3).   DAE *American, Southern*, 1705–1905; T 1705–1856; NED *North Amer.* and *West Indian* (a) any wood used in lighting a fire; in the Southern states, resinous pine-wood, 1693–1888; CD . . . in the *So. U.S.*, very resinous pine wood.

lightning-bug: Firefly; common among all classes.   Reported from wInd (DN 3).   DAE *American* 1778–1899; T 1787–1860; NED 1806–1850; CD.

lima beans (see *butterbeans*): Considered a modern term. DAE 1822–1901; NED 1858.

living room (see *chamber, front room, parlor, room, sitting room*): Used among younger, better educated people.   DAE 1857–1910; NEDS (2) *U.S.*, 1867–1911; CD.

* **load** (see *turn*): The total amount (of wood, etc.) that can be carried by a person at one time; in the Shenandoah Valley, rare.   VWB A large quantity of anything.   NED (2) 1225–1882; CD (1); EDD (2) A measure of weight varying according to the district and commodity.

log fence (see *rail fence, worm fence*): A rail fence; rare.   DAE *American* 1651–1902.

* **lot** (see *patch*): A field (of tobacco, etc.); not common.   NED
(6.a) . . . any piece of land set apart for a particular purpose, *now
chiefly U.S.*, 1633–.

* **lower down** (see *abate, be laying, moderate, moderate down*):
Of the wind, subside; rare.   NED (4.a) *lower*; CD (II) *lower*.

low-grounds (see *bottom, bottom land, flats*): Low land; com-
mon south of the Rappahannock in the Piedmont and Tidewater.
VWB Meadow or bottom land.   Reported from Va (AS 17.281).
DAE 1659–1898; NED (IV.20) 1897.

* **lucky-bone** (see *pull bone, pully bone, wishbone*): Wishbone;
east of the Blue Ridge, scattered.   Reported from Cape Cod
(DN 2).   EDD A bone in the sheep's head worn for luck.

lumber (see *trumpery*): Junk; common everywhere.   VWB.
DAE 1642–1900; NED Disused articles of furniture and the like,
which take up room inconveniently, or are removed to be out of
the way, 1552–1884; CD (1), also *lumber-room*; EDD sb. and vb.:
Sc, Wm, Yks, Lan, Chs, Not, Lin, Rut, Nhp, Shr, Oxf, Bdf, eAn,
seCy, Sur.

* **male** (see *gentleman cow, ox, steer*): Bull; used everywhere,
mostly in the presence of women.   Reported from Va (DN 4),
swMo (DN 5, any male animal kept for breeding.   *Bull, boar,
stallion* and *jack* are not used in mixed company, although *buck*,
a male sheep or goat, and *crower*, rooster, are not considered ob-
jectionable); also *male-cow, male-brute*, etc. from NC Mts (DN 4),
Ky (DN 4), Ill (DN 4), Kan (DN 4).

* **male, male hog** (see *boar hog*): Boar; used in the presence of
women, not common.   Reported from NC Mts (DN 4), Ky (DN
4), sInd (DN 3), seMo (DN 2), swMo (DN 5), nwArk (DN 3),
Kan (DN 4), eNeb (AS 12.104, *male-pig*).

* **male horse** (see *stud, stud horse*): Stallion; used mostly in the
presence of women, fairly common.   Reported from wcWVa (AS
2.360), seMo (DN 2, *male brute*).

* **masons** (see *dirt-daubers, mud-daubers*): A kind of wasp; not
common.   VWB.   NED (3.b) In the names of animals, esp.
certain insects which build a nest of sand, mud, or the like; CD
mason bee.

middlin, middlin meat (see *side meat*): Salt pork; common
everywhere.   VWB.   Reported from eAla (DN 3), wcWVa (AS
2.360), seMo (DN 2), swMo (DN 5), Ozarks (AS 5.19, nwArk
(DN 3).   DAE (2) *American, S & SW,* 1777–1904; NED (4)
U.S., 1859 (Bartlett); CD (II.2) *West. and So. U.S.*

* **middling** (see *tolerable*): Fair, in answer to "how are you?"; common everywhere. VWB. NED (B.2) 1810–1894; CD (2) Not in good health, yet not very ill; also, in Scotland, in fairly good health, *Rural*; EDD (2) *Colloq.* in Sc, Irel, and Eng.

* **milk gap** (see *cow pen, cow pound, cuppen*): Pen for cows; in the southern part of the Blue Ridge.

(give someone) the mitten (see *kick, sack*): Jilt (someone); common. VWB *get the mitten*. Reported from wcWVa (AS 2.360) Ark (DN 5), nwArk (DN 3), Neb (DN 5), NY (DN 5), wNY (DN 3), Conn (DN 5), cConn (DN 3), Me (AS 5.124). DAE (2.a) To get the mitten, *colloq.*; (b) to give the mitten, *colloq.*, 1847–1902; T 1838–1855; NED (3) *Slang*, or *colloq.*, 1838–1884; CD *Colloq*; EDD Can.

* **moderate, moderate down** (see *abate, calm down, be laying, lower down*): *Of the wind*, subside; rare. Reported from wcWVa (AS 2.360), Western Reserve (DN 4), Cape Cod (DN 2), Me (AS 5.127). NED (1.b) 1678–1897; CD (II.1); EDD *moderate*, adj. (5) of the weather, calm, Sh.

mosquito hawk (see *snake doctor*): Dragon fly; on Chesapeake Bay. VWB. Reported from eAla (DN 3), seMo (DN 2), nwArk (DN 3). DAE *American, Southern*, 1737–1842; T; NED (2.b) *U.S.*; CD (1.A) *U.S.*

mud daubers (see *dirt daubers, masons*): Wasps; not common. VWB. Reported from nwArk (DN 3). DAE *American*, 1856–1899; T; NED (5.b) 1856–; CD A digger wasp.

* **new year's gift!**: Happy new year!; not common. Reported from eAla (DN 3), seMo (DN 2), nwArk (DN 3).

* **nicker** (see *whicker, whinny*): Noise made by a horse at feeding time; everywhere except south of the lower James. VWB. Reported from Va (DN 4), eAla (DN 3), Erie Canal (AS 6.99), sInd (DN 3), wInd (DN 3), sIll (DN 2), seMo (DN 2), swMo (DN 5), nwArk (DN 3). NED Chiefly *Sc.* and *north. dial.*, (1) 1774–1880; CD (1); EDD *Gen. dial.* use in Sc, Irel, and Eng.

oldfields colt (see *base-born, woods colt*): Illegitimate child; in the southern Piedmont. VWB *oldfield*, cleared land some distance from the house. DAE (2.a) *oldfield, American.*

* **ox** (see *gentleman cow, male, steer*): Bull; on the lower Rappahannock, in the presence of women.

paling fence (see *picket fence*): A fence made of pales, pointed slats; common everywhere. Reported from eAla (DN 3), seMo

(DN 2), nwArk (DN 2). DAE (1) 1806–1925; NED *paling*
(4) 1805; EDD (1) Sc, Yks.

paper sack (see *poke*): A paper bag; not common. Reported
from Va (DN 4), eAla (DN 3), sIll (DN 2), seMo (DN 2), nwArk
(DN 2), Washington (DN 2), as "Westernism" (AS 1.152).
DAE (II.8.b).

parlor (see *chamber, front room, living room, room, sitting room*):
(a) A family living room, (b) a "best room"; common everywhere.
DAE 1640–1923; NED (2) . . . Formerly often simply the "room"
or "chamber," sometimes a bedchamber, 1374–1886; CD (3) . . .
In Great Britain the common sitting-room or keeping-room of a
family as distinguished from a drawing-room intended for the
reception of company. In the U.S., where the term drawing-
room is little used, parlor is the general term for the room used for
the reception of guests; EDD (2) The inner room of a cottage or
farmhouse of the ground floor, used either as a sitting or a bed-
room: eYks, sYks, Lin.

patch (see *lot*): A field (of tobacco, etc.); common. VWB (2).
Reported from sIll (DN 2), nwArk (DN 3). DAE *American* (1),
1653–1904; NED (2.b) 1577–1894; CD (6); EDD (4) Sc, Chs,
nWil.

peckerwood: Woodpecker; in the Piedmont. Reported from
Va (DN 4), Shenandoah Valley (AS 12.287), eAla (DN 3, *universal*), wTex (DN 4), South (DN 4), Ky (DN 5), So App Mts (AS
15.53), seMo (DN 2), Ozarks (DN 5, AS 15.53), nwArk (DN 3),
central west (DN 5). DAE *American*, 1859 (Bartlett)—1909.

* **pert** (see *spry*): Lively; common everywhere. Reported from
wcWVa (AS 2.361), SC (AS 18.67), Tenn (AS 18.67), sInd (DN
3, AS 16.24, AS 14.264), seMo (DN 1, DN 2), nwArk (DN 3),
NY (AS 5.152). NED Since 17th cent. *dial.*, 1500–1889; CD
(2); EDD Lakel, Lin, Hrf, Oxf, Bdf, Hmp.

picket fence (see *paling fence*): A fence made of pales, pointed
slats; rare except among the cultured. Reported from App Mts
(DN 5, *picketin fence*), Aroostook, Me (DN 3). DAE *American*,
1800–1917; NED (IV.7), 1857; CD.

* **piece, piece meal** (see *bite, snack*): A lunch eaten between
meals; in the Blue Ridge south to the James. Reported from
wInd (DN 3, *to piece*, eat between meals). NED (15.b) short
for "piece of bread" (with or without butter, etc.), *spec.* such a
bread eaten by itself, not with a regular meal, *Sc* and *Eng. dial,*

1787–1903; CD (4.f) *prov.* or *colloq.*; EDD (8) A slice of bread or bread and butter, etc., esp. that given to children and carried in the pocket, to be eaten as lunch; also *piece-time*, lunch-time, Sc.

pluck (see *hasslet*): The heart, liver, and lights of a sheep, ox, or other animal; east of the Blue Ridge, not common. VWB. Reported from Conn (DN 1). DAE (1) 1772–1873; NED (III.6) 1611–1904; CD (4) . . . also used figuratively or humorously for the like parts of a human being; EDD (11) *fig.*, of human heart and lungs.

plum (**across**) (see *clean across, clear across, jam across*): Entirely (across); in the southern part of the Blue Ridge. VWB. Reported from NC (DN 5), Barbourville, Ky (DN 3), Tenn Mts (DN 1), eAla (DN 3), sInd (DN 3), sIll (DN 2), Mo (DN 1, also familiar in Mich), nwArk (DN 3), eNeb (DN 3). DAE *Colloq.*, 1845–1925; T 1601–1893; NED (B.2.c) Chiefly *U.S. Slang*, 1587–1897; CD (3) *Colloq. U.S.*; EDD (8) *Obs.*

plunder: Household or personal effects, baggage; common everywhere except the Northern Neck and the Eastern Shore. VWB. Reported from Ohio River Valley (AS 9.320 household effects,—used figuratively sometimes for goods in general), eAla (DN 3), Tenn Mts (AS 14.91 *house plunder*), sIll (DN 2), seMo (DN 2), nwArk (DN 3), Wichita, Kan (DN 4), Me (DN 4), Sherwood's List of Provincialisms (DN 5). DAE *American* 1805–1856; T; NED (3) *U.S., Local*, 1817–1873; CD (1) *Local U.S.*

** **poke, paper poke** (see *paper sack*): A paper bag; west of the Blue Ridge. Reported from swPa (AS 7.20), wcWVa (AS 2.362), eKy (DN 3), Tenn Mts (DN 1), Tenn (AS 11.373), So App Mts (AS 15.45), seMo (DN 2), swMo (DN 5), nwArk (DN 3), Ozarks (AS 4.204, AS 5.427, AS 15.45), wTex (DN 4), Underworld Jargon (DN 5, pocketbook). NED Now chiefly *dial*, 1276–1902; CD (1) A pocket, pouch, bag, sack; EDD In gen. dial. use in Sc, Irel, and Eng, (1) a bag, sack; a wallet; a pocket.

pone (see *corn dodger, dodger*): A hard, hand-shaped cake of corn bread; common everywhere. VWB. Reported from Ga (DN 3), Fla (DN 3), wTex (DN 4), seMo (DN 2), swMo (DN 5), nwArk (DN 3), Neb pioneer English (AS 7.168, a thick pancake baked in a covered skillet). DAE *American, Southern*, (2) A patty or cake of corn or wheat bread, 1796–1903; NED Orig.

the bread of the North American Indians, made of maize flour in thin cakes, and cooked in hot ashes; now in southern U.S., any bread made of maize, esp. that of a coarse or poor kind; also very light bread, enriched with milk, eggs, and the like, and made in flat cakes, 1612–1861; (b) a cake or loaf of such bread, 1796–1887; CD *sw U.S.*

pone bread (see *corn bread, corn pone*): Corn bread; common everywhere. DAE *American,* cornbread in the form of pones, 1785–1833.

poor (see *puny, scrawny*): In poor health; common everywhere. VWB. Reported from wcWVa (AS 2.362, *porely*), Ind (AS 16.22), sInd (AS 14.264, *porely*), Martha's Vineyard (DN 5), Me (AS 2.80). DAE *American, Obs.,* 1758; T Nearly *obs.* in England, 1778–1878; NED *obs.,* 1758; CD (3.c); EDD gen. of live-stock: Sc, Cum, Yks, Chs, Der, War, Oxf, Sus, Som.

* pretty day: Pleasant day; common everywhere among all classes. Reported from Va (DN 1), Ill (DN 1, DN 4), New Orleans, La (DN 4), seArk (AS 13.6), nwArk (DN 2), Ia (DN 4), Kan (DN 4). EDD (4) Sus, Amer (DN 1).

primp up (see *dike up, fix up, prink*): Get dressed up; common everywhere. DAE *American,* 1881–1906; NED *dial.,* 1801–1880; CD (I); EDD Sc, nCy, Cum, Glo.

* prink (see *dike up, fix up, primp up*): Get dressed; not common. VWB Dress ostentatiously or fantastically. Reported from cConn (DN 3). NED (2.b) *colloq.,* 1709–1898; CD (I.1) To prank; dress for show; adorn one's self; II, *trans.*; EDD: Sc, nCy, Yks, Shr, Glo, eAn, Ken, Som Dev, Corn, Amer.

* proud (to see someone): Pleased (to see someone); common everywhere. Reported from eAla (DN 3), La (AS 11.368), wcWVa (AS 2.362), Ky (DN 4), NC Mts (DN 4), Tenn Mts (DN 1), Tenn (AS 11.373), seMo (DN 2), swMo (DN 5), nwArk (DN 2), cConn (DN 3), Sherwood's Provincialisms (DN 5). NED Early use (and still *dial.*), 1250–1593; EDD Clc, Cum, Chs, IW, Som, wCor; Amer.

pudding (see *hog's head cheese, souse*): A sausage of pig's entrails, cereal, etc.; fairly common. DAE 1859–; NED (I.1) Now chiefly *Sc.* and *dial.,* 1305–1819; CD (1); EDD (2) Sc, Sh I, Per, Fif, Dmf, Der, sDev.

* pull flowers: Pick flowers; common everywhere. Reported from eAla (DN 3, *universal*), sInd (DN 3), sIll (DN 2), Norse

dial. of Wisc (DN 2), nwArk (DN 3). NED (I.1.c) Now chiefly
Sc., 1340–1854; CD (2); EDD Sc, Ayr, Cum, Yks, nLin.

pull bone, pulling bone (see *lucky-bone, pully bone, wishbone*):
Wishbone; east of the Blue Ridge. DAE *American, local;* NEDS
(2) *U.S.*, 1906; EDD *pull bone,* wYks, *pulling bone* Shr.

* **pully bone** (see *lucky-bone, pull bone, wishbone*): Wishbone;
west of the Blue Ridge and in the southern Piedmont. Reported
from Va (DN 4), eAla (DN 3), wInd (DN 3), swMo (DN 5),
nwArk (DN 3), Ozarks (AS 8.51).

* **puny** (see *poor, scrawny*): In poor health; common everywhere. VWB. Reported from Va (DN 4), eAla (DN 3), Cumberlands (AS 7.191, AS 7.94 *puny-lookin'*), sInd (DN 3), seMo
(DN 2), swMo (DN 5), nwArk (DN 3), La (AS 11.368). T;
NED (4.c) 1866–1904; CD (2).

rail fence (see *log fence, worm fence*): Common everywhere except on the Eastern Shore. VWB *Rail.* Reported from nwArk
(DN 3, *railin fence*). DAE *American;* NEDS *U.S.*, 1649–1902.

reckon: Suppose; common everywhere among all classes.
VWB. Reported from eAla (DN 3), Miss (DN 4), Ky (DN 3),
wInd (DN 3), sIll (DN 2), seMo (DN 2), swMo (DN 5), nwArk
(DN 2, DN 3), Ozarks (AS 5.19, AS 5.428), cConn (DN 3). DAE
(1) To suppose, 1707–1917; (2) I reckon, used parenthetically
or as an affirmative reply, Eng. *dial.* and *southern U.S.*; T 1811–
1908; NED (6) 1513–1875; CD (6) ... Though regularly de-
veloped and used in good literature, has come to be regarded as
provincial or vulgar because of its frequency in colloq. speech in
some parts of the U.S., esp. the South; EDD: Sc, Eng, Amer.

* **red-worm** (see *angleworm, earthworm, fishing worm, ground
worm*): Earthworm; only west of the New River. Reported from
swMo (DN 5), nwArk (DN 3, *common*). NED 1450–1856.

* **rick.** A stack of hay, usually long and rectangular; common everywhere except the Tidewater south of the Rappahannock and the Eastern Shore. VWB. Reported from sIll (DN
2), seMo (DN 2, DN 5, also of wood), nwArk (DN 2, of wood;
DN 3, of hay, grain, or wood), eNeb (AS 12.106), nwLa (DN 4,
of wood). NED 900–1895; EDD sb. and vb., In Gen. dial. use
in Sc, Irel, and Eng for a stack of hay, Cum "a long pile."

* **rising:** A small boil; fairly common. VWB. Reported
from Va (DN 4), sIll (DN 2), seMo (DN 2), swMo (DN 5),
Ozarks (AS 5.20), nNH (DN 4), Me (DN 4). NED (11.b) Now
dial., 1563–1847; CD Now *colloq.*, or *dial.*; EDD wCy, Som.

(throw a) rock: (Throw a) stone; common everywhere. VWB A stone of any size larger than a pebble. Reported from Va (DN 4), eAla (DN 3), NC (DN 5, *to rock*), Barbourville, Ky (DN 3), Tenn Mts (DN 2), seMo (DN 1, *to rock*), swMo (DN 5, *to rock*), nwArk (DN 3, *to rock*), nwArk (DN 1), Ottawa, Kan (DN 2, *to rock*), cConn (DN 3), eMe (DN 3), Miss Intelligencer (DN 4), Sherwood's Provincialisms (DN 5), Dunglison's Glossary (DN 5). DAE (2) *local*, 1817–1882; NED (I.1.b) *U.S.* and *Austr.*, a stone of any size, 1700–1895.

rock fence (see *stone fence*): A fence of loose stone; everywhere, but not common north of the Rappahannock. Reported from eAla (DN 3), nwArk (DN 3), NY (DN 1). DAE (11) 1896 (DN 1).

(the) room (see *chamber, front room, living room, parlor, sitting room*): The living room; among older people, rare. NED See *parlor*; EDD (3) The best sitting-room: neCs, Cae, eSc, Slk, Dmf, sYks, eYks, sNot.

run (see *branch, creek*): A stream; in the Shenandoah Valley, the northern Piedmont, and the Tidewater north of the James. VWB. Reported from Va (AS 15.386–7: (1) a brook, (2) a creek or small river, (3) a bottom or meadow, (4) a canal, (5) a tributary of a stream, (6) the flow of a stream), Md (As 10.256–9, *most frequent in the mountains*), Ohio River Valley (AS 9.320), Cumberlands (AS 15.47), Great Smokies (AS 15.47), Ozarks (AS 8.51, AS 15.47), Dunglison's Glossary (DN 5). DAE (1) 1605–1908; NED (II.9) Chiefly *U.S.* and *north. dial.*, 1581–1877; CD (10); EDD (26) Lnk, nCy, nYks, nLin, Nrf.

* **sack (someone)** (see *kick, mitten*): Jilt (someone); fairly common. VWB. Reported from sIll (DN 2), seMo (DN 2), nwArk (DN 3), Ozarks (AS 5.20). NED (I.4) *Slang*, 1825–1902; CD (4) *Slang*.

sack (see *burlap bag, crocus bag, grass sack, guano sack, sack-bag, tow sack,*): A large bag made of coarse canvas; not common. Reported from Va (DN 4), swPa (AS 7.20), eAla (DN 3), sIll (DN 2), seMo (DN 2), nwArk (DN 2). DAE 1645–1912; NED (I.1) 1000–1864; CD (1); EDD Var. *dial.* uses in Sc, Irel, and Eng.

* **sack bag** (see *burlap bag, crocus bag, guano sack, sack, tow sack*): A large bag made of coarse canvas; rare. VWB A bag holding three bushels of grain.

sallet: Greens cooked for food; common everywhere except west of the Blue Ridge. VWB. Reported from Va (DN 4), wcWVa (AS 2.363), App Mts (DN 5, salad), So App Mts (AS 15.45, salad), seIll (DN 2), seMo (DN 2), Ozarks (AS 4.204, AS 15.45, salad), NY (DN 2), NE (DN 5, provincialism). DAE (1.b) *American, Southern*; NED *obs.* form of *salad*; CD *salad*, formerly also *sallet*, (2) herbs for use as salad: colloq. restricted in the United States to lettuce; EDD *sallet*: Edb, Yks, Lan, Chs, War, Wor, Shr, Hrf, Glo, Bch, Sus; *sallit*: Yks, eLan, seWor.

saw buck, wood buck, buck (see *saw horse*): A rack upon which wood is laid for sawing by hand; in the Shenandoah Valley, not common. DAE *American*, 1839–; NED (7) *U.S.*, 1860, Bartlett; CD (6.a), also called *sawhorse, U.S.*

saw horse, wood horse, horse (see *saw buck*): A rack upon which wood is laid for sawing by hand; common everywhere. VWB. Reported from Canada (DN 1). DAE 1848–1920; NED *saw horse* (d) 1778–1883, *horse* (L.7.b) 1718–1769; CD; EDD *saw horse* wYks, Wil, Amer, *horse* wSom.

scrawny (see *poor, puny*): In poor health; fairly common. VWB. DAE *American*, mean, meager, thin, 1833–1897; NED *U.S.*, variant of *scranny*, 1833–1883; CD A *dial.* form of *scranny* now prevalent.

* **scrooch down, scrutch down:** Crouch down; common everywhere. VWB. Reported from Va (DN 4), eAla (DN 3), NC (DN 1), wInd (DN 3), swMo (DN 5), Kan (DN 4), Neb (DN 3), West Brattleboro, Vt (DN 3), Me (DN 4). NED *dial.* and *U.S.*, 1882–1911; EDD: Yks, Not, Amer.

scuttle, coal scuttle (see *coal hod*): Coal hod; common everywhere. Reported from wNY (DN 3), cNY (DN 1, *coalscuttle*). DAE 1833–1889; NED (2.b) 1849–1909; CD *coalscuttle*; EDD (2) A shallow wooden or wicker basket for produce or corn, occasionally coal: Cum, Yks, Lan, Der, Not, Lin, Lei, War, Oxf, Bdf, eCy, Suf, sCy.

shades (see *blinds, curtains*): Roller shades for windows; regularly in the Piedmont, less commonly elsewhere. DAE *American*, 1645–1889; NED (III.11.a) *U.S.*; CD (10); EDD (6) eDur, nYks, wYks, Amer.

* **sheaf** (see *bundle*): Fairly common west of the Blue Ridge and on the Middle Neck. NED (1) 725–1862; CD; EDD.

shindig (see *breakdown, frolic, hoedown*): A party; common everywhere. VWB A ball or dance; especially with much uproar and rowdyism. Reported from eAla (DN 3, an entertainment),

wTex, (DN 4, an entertainment), wcWVa (AS 2.364), Ky (DN
1), swMo (DN 5, *shinadig*), nwArk (DN 3, an entertainment),
Neb (DN 3, a dance or party; a row), Neb pioneer English (AS
8.48), Mich (DN 1), wNY (DN 3, an entertainment) cConn
(DN 3, any public or social entertainment). DAE *American,
Slang*, (2) 1873–1911; NED *U.S.* 1859 (Bartlett)—1899; CD
Western U.S., *shindy*, a row or rumpus, *Slang*.

shock (see *hay cock*, *hay doodle*): A pile of hay in the field
at haying time; common everywhere. VWB. Reported from
Western Reserve (DN 4), sInd (DN 3), sIll (DN 2), nwArk
(DN 3). DAE shock of corn, *American*, 1863–1920; NED; CD;
EDD gen. *dial.* and *colloq.* use in Sc and Eng.

(get) shut of (someone): (Get) rid of (someone); common
everywhere. Reported from Shenandoah Valley (AS 12.287),
wcWVA (AS 2.355), NC (DN 4), Tenn (DN 4, also from Tenn
Mts), seO (DN 4), wInd (DN 3), sIll (DN 2), Ill (DN 4), seMo
(DN 2), swMo (DN 5), Kan (DN 4), Neb (DN 4), Sherwood's
Provincialisms (DN 5).—T; NED *dial.* and *colloq.*, 1500–1892;
CD *prov.* Eng. and U.S.; EDD gen. *colloq.* use.

side meat (see *middlin*): Salt pork: in the Blue Ridge and south
of the lower James. Reported from eAla (DN 3), seMo (DN 2),
nwArk (DN 3). DAE *American* 1873–1912; NEDS *U.S.;*
CD (1.12.b) *Colloq.*, *western U.S.*

simlin: A kind of squash having a scalloped edge; common everywhere. VWB *cymblin*, a small eatable gourd. Reported from
seMo (DN 2, a small kind of squash), nwArk (DN 3, a bitter
gourd, mock melon . . . sometimes mistaken for a melon). DAE
cymbling, American, 1804–1911; NED *U.S.*, 1794–1896; CD (2)
A kind of small squash *S. and W. U.S.; also simnel* (1) a rich
sweet cake offered as a gift at Christmas and Easter and Mothering
(Simnel) Sunday; (2) a variety of squash . . . resembling the cake:
now called *simlin, So. U.S.;* EDD A rich cake.

sitting room, setting room (see *chamber, front room, living room,
parlor, room*): A living room; common everywhere among all
classes. Reported from Hampstead, NH (DN 3). DAE 1771–
1925; NED 1806–1894; CD.

skillet (see *spider*): Now a cast iron frying pan, formerly a three
legged, long handled pan for use in the fireplace; common in the
western Piedmont and westward, scattered elsewhere. VWB Of
brass, cast not beaten, a semi-globe in form, having three short,

straight legs of about three inches in length cast on its bottom. The handle is tapering but flat and quite straight . . . only suitable to be used with a wood fire on the hearth. Reported from Tenn Mts (DN 1, a fry-pan with legs), eAla (DN 3, with three legs, and a cover, for baking), sIll (DN 2, *skillit*, any kitchen utensil), seMo (DN 2, a shallow iron vessel with a cover, used for baking). DAE (1) A cooking utensil having a long handle: (a) a small saucepan having three or four legs, *Obs.;* (b) a frying pan, 1630–1917; NED (1) A cooking utensil of brass, copper, or other metal, usually having three or four feet and a long handle, used for boiling liquids, stewing meat, etc.; 1403–1866; CD (1); EDD gen. *dial.* use in Sc, Irel, Eng, and Amer.

slop bucket: Garbage pail; common everywhere. Reported from Va (DN 4, *slop*), eAla (DN 3). DAE *slop-basin, slop-bowl;* NED (6) 1856; CD A pail or bucket for receiving slops or soiled water.

smear case (see *clabber cheese, cottage cheese, curd, home-made cheese*): Cheese made of the drained curd of sour milk; west of the Blue Ridge. Reported from the English of the Pa Germans (AS 10.169), Ohio River valley (AS 9.319), nwArk (DN 3). DAE *American*, 1829 (Royall, *Pennsylvania:* "A dish, common amongst the Germans . . . is curds and cream. It is very palatable, and called by the Germans smearcase")—1894; NED *U.S.* 1848 (Bartlett)—1893; CD See *cottage cheese*.

smouch (see *buss*): Kiss; fairly common everywhere. VWB. Reported from Tenn Mts (DN 1). NED 1575–1825; CD *Obs.* or *prov.* Eng.; EDD: nCy, Yks, Lan, Chs, Der, Lin, Lei, Nhp, War, Wor, Hrf, eAn, Sur, Dor, Amer.

snack (see *bite, piece*): A lunch eaten between meals; common everywhere. VWB. Reported from eAla (DN 2), wcWVa (AS 2.364), Ky (DN 5, a light, cold repast, originally a Gypsy cant term, meaning a share or division of plunder), eKy (DN 3), Tenn Mts (DN 1, also *snack-houses*), wInd (DN 3), nwArk (DN 3). NED (4.b) 1757–1874, also *snack-houses;* CD (3); EDD Sc, Irel, Eng, and Amer.

snake doctor (see *mosquito hawk*): A dragon-fly; common everywhere except on Chesapeake Bay and west of the New River. VWB. Reported from eAla (DN 3). DAE *American* (1) 1862–1899; NED (11.b); CD *Local, U.S.*

snaps, snapbeans (see *green-beans, string beans*): String beans;

common everywhere. VWB. Reported from Va (DN 5), eAla (DN 3), wcWVa (AS 2.364), nwArk (DN 3). DAE *snap bean, American,* 1775–1910.

snits: Apples cut in quarters and dried; in the northern part of the Blue Ridge, rare. Reported from the Shenandoah Valley (AS 12.287, slices, of oranges, etc.), wcWVa (AS 2.364, apples quartered for drying or for apple butter), Kan (DN 4, pieces of fruit quartered and dried). DAE *American, Local,* from Pa German *schnitz,* sections of apple, slices of dried fruit, 1848–1903.

*somerset: A somersault; common everywhere. Reported from eAla (DN 3), wNY (DN 3), Hampstead, NH (DN 3). NED 1596–1874; CD.

*song ballad, song ballet: Used with various meanings: a folk-song or ballad, or the actual manuscript copy of it; not common. Reported from Va (DN 4, a song or ballad), Miss (AS 4.87, a manuscript copy of a song; in the So Appal meant a written copy made by children), wcWVa (AS 2.348: (1) the words of a song (2) a ballad or old song), swNC (DN 1, *song-valet,* the words of a song), Cumberlands (AS 7.94, the long-hand copy of the words of a ballad), So App Mts (AS 15.50, ballad), Ozarks (AS 15.50, ballad), southern negroes (AS 3.213, an elaboration of an older folk song . . . mostly written by negroes), NJ (AS 12.231, by negroes). NED *ballad* 1492–1855; EDD (1) A song, a ballad; sometimes applied to the sheet upon which several songs are printed: Cum, Yks, Lan, Chs, Der, Nhp, War, Shr, Hrf, Brks, Ess, Ken, Sus, Wil, Som, Dev.

souse (see *hog's head cheese, pudding*): Pig's feet, ears, etc., either pickled or jellied. VWB (pickled). Reported from nwArk (DN 3, a jellied compound, a great delicacy). DAE 1805–1895; T; NED Now *dial.* and *U.S.,* the various parts of a pig, prepared for food by means of pickling, 1391–1872; CD (2) The head, ears, and feet of swine pickled; EDD (6) The ears, feet, tail, etc., of a pig pickled: nCy, Nhb, Cum, Yks, Chs, Der, Not, Lin, War, Glo, Brk, Suf, Hmp, IW; also *souse-cheese.*

spicket: Faucet; in general use everywhere. VWB The inner plug of a wooden tap. NED *Obs.,* 1530–1725; CD . . . any plug fitting into a faucet used by drawing off liquor; EDD in *comb.,* Sc, Nhb, Dur, Lan, Chs, Shr.

spider (see *skillet*): Now a cast iron frying pan, formerly a three legged, long handled pan for use in the fireplace; in the Tidewater area and on the Eastern Shore.   VWB.   Reported from Miss (DN 3), nwLa (DN 4), Ill (DN 3), Mo (DN 3), Neb pioneer English (AS 7.169), NY (DN 3), cConn (DN 3), Cape Cod (DN 2, a frying pan with high sides), Vt (DN 3), Me (DN 5), Aroostook, Me (DN 3).   DAE (2) *American*, An iron frying pan or skillet, sometimes provided with long legs, 1790–1905; NED A kind of frying pan having legs and a long handle; also loosely, a frying-pan, *Orig. U.S.*, 1830–1869; CD (4) A cooking utensil having legs or feet to keep it from contact with the coals: named from a fancied resemblance to the insect ... the ordinary frying-pan is, however, sometimes erroneously termed a *spider*.

*spry (see *pert*): Lively; common everywhere.   VWB.   Reported from nwArk (DN 3), cConn (DN 3), Miss Intelligencer (DN 4, as a Yankeeism), Humphrey's Glossary (DN 5).   T 1815–1846; NED Current in English dialects, but more familiar as an Americanism, 1746–1892; CD *Prov. Eng.* and *U.S.;* EDD In gen. *dial.* and *colloq.* use in Sc, Eng, and Amer.

*squall (see *gully-washer*): A hard storm, mostly wind; not common.   VWB A sudden shower of rain or snow, not necessarily accompanied by wind.   NED (1) A sudden and violent gust, a blast or short sharp storm, of wind (Orig. *Naut.*), 1719–1886; CD A sudden and violent gust of wind ... usually accompanied by rain, snow, or sleet.

*stairsteps: Stairway; common everywhere among all classes.   Reported from eAla (DN 3, *universal*), NY (DN 1), Chicago people of NE antecedents (DN 3).

*steer (see *gentleman cow*, *male*, *ox*): A bull; on the Eastern Shore, on the lower Rappahannock, and in the southern Piedmont, in the presence of women.

stone fence (see *rock fence*): A fence of loose stone; on the Middle Neck, in the Piedmont north of the Rappahannock, and the lower Shenandoah Valley.   DAE (1) 1682–1905.

*stout: Strong; common everywhere.   VWB Broad and strong. Reported from scPa (DN 4), sIll (DN 2), Ozarks (DN 5), nwArk (DN 3), cNY (DN 3), wConn (DN 1), seNH (DN 4).   NED (A. II.6) Strong in body, of powerful build, *?Obs.*, 1386–1842; (b) in robust health, strong ... *Obs. exc. Sc.*, 1697–1884; CD (4) Hardy, vigorous, lusty; (5) Firm, sound ... strong; EDD Var. *dial.* uses in Sc, Irel, Eng, and Amer; (1) strong; healthy; well-grown; convalescent.

> **string beans** (see *green-beans, snaps*): North of the Rappahannock, not common. DAE *American*, 1759–1891; NED (32) *U.S.*, 1842; CD.

stud (see *male horse, stud horse*): Stallion; common everywhere. VWB. Reported from eAla (DN 3), nwArk (DN 3), New Brunswick (DN 1), Dunglison's Glossary (DN 4). DAE *American* (1) 1803–1891; NED (4.b) *U.S.* 1803–1891; CD (3) *Colloq.*

*****stud horse** (see *male horse, stud*): Stallion; fairly common everywhere, a breeders' term. VWB. Reported from eAla (DN 3), Aroostook, Me (DN 3). NED 1000–1891; CD.

sundown: Sunset; common everywhere. VWB. Reported from eAla (DN 3), sInd (DN 3), sIll (DN 2), seMo (DN 2), nwArk (DN 3), NJ (DN 1), wNY (DN 2), Me coast (AS 3.139), early New England words (AS 15.230). DAE (1) 1712–1906; T 1796–1878; NED (1) Chiefly *U.S.* and Eng. and Colonial *dial.*, 1620–1896; CD (1); EDD: Abd, Rxb, Gall, Ir, Yks, nLin, War, Wor, Glo, Nrf, Som, Dev; Amer, Austr.

sunup: Sunrise; common everywhere, mostly among older people. VWB. Reported from Cumberlands (AS 7.94), eAla (DN 3), sInd (DN 3), sIll (DN 2), seMo (DN 2), nwArk (DN 3), NJ (DN 1), Me coast (AS 3.139). DAE 1712–1901; T; NED *Local*, chiefly *U.S.*, 1847–1899; CD *local, U.S.;* EDD also *sunbreak.*

take up: *Of school*, begin; not common. Reported from Va (DN 4), wcWVa (AS 2.365), Western Reserve (DN 4), nwArk (DN 3). DAE (10.e) 1876–1903; NED (90.s) *trans.*, to begin afresh, 1604–1902; CD.

*****toad frog** (see *dry-land frog, hop toad*): Toad; not common. Reported from Va (DN 4), eAla (DN 3, *universal*), La (DN 4), NC (DN 4), Cumberlands (AS 7.94, a tailless, jumping amphibian, resembling the frog and often mistaken for a toad), sIll (DN 2), seMo (DN 2), Ozarks (DN 5, either a toad or a frog), nwArk (DN 3), Kan (DN 4).

*****tolerable** (see *middling*): Fair, in answer to "how are you?"; common everywhere. VWB. Reported from eAla (DN 3), Ky (DN 1), sInd (AS 14.264), seMo (DN 2, *universal*), swMo (DN 5). NED (5.b) 1847; CD (4) *colloq.;* EDD; wCy, Dev, and Amer.

> **tote:** Carry (a load) in one's arms or on one's back or shoulders; common everywhere. VWB. Reported from the South (AS 8.23, not from WVa), eAla (DN 3), Miss (DN 4), La (DN 5), w-Tex (DN 4), eKy (DN 3), NC (DN 5), seMo (DN 2), swMo

(DN 5), Ozarks (AS 5.429), eMe (DN 3). DAE *American,* chiefly *southern,* 1677–1920; T 1676–1892; NED *U.S. colloq.,* 1676–1892; CD *So. U.S., colloq.* or *prov.,* also humorous use in the North and West.

*touchous (see *ashy, wrathy*): Easily angered; common everywhere. VWB. Reported from eAla (DN 3), Ky (DN 1), seMo (DN 2), swMo (DN 5), Ozarks (AS 4.204). EDD: Irel, Nhb, Lakel, Cum, Yks, Lan, Chs, Der, Amer.

tow sack (see *burlap bag, crocus bag, grass sack, guano sack, sack, sack bag*): A large bag made of coarse canvas; in the Norfolk area. DAE *tow* 1646–1842; NED *tow* 1530–1896, *tow cloth* 1822; CD *tow;* EDD *tow:* Sc, Irel, Nhb, Wm, Yks, eAn.

*trumpery (see *lumber*): Junk; on the Middle Neck, rare. Reported from West Brattleboro, Vt (DN 3). NED (2) 1531–1807; CD (3); EDD (2) Sc, Irel, Yks, Hrt, Wil, Dor, Som, Cor.

turn (see *armful, load*): The amount (of wood, etc.) that can be carried by a person at one time; everywhere, but not common in the southern part of the Blue Ridge. VWB. Reported from NC (DN 5), SC (DN 6), eAla (DN 3), La (DN 1), wcWVa. (AS 2.366), nNH (DN 4, of water), Me (DN 4, of water), Aroostook, Me (DN 3, two pailfuls, of water). DAE (2) 1800–, *dial.;* NED (VII.37) A measure of various commodities, the quantity dealt with at one "turn" or stroke of work, 1805–1905; CD (19); EDD (7) As much as is done or fetched with one return—two ridges in plowing, two pitchers of water: Sus, Hmp, IW, Cor, Amer.

turn of corn (see *grist*): The amount of corn taken to (or from) the mill at one time; common everywhere except in the Shenandoah Valley and the Tidewater area. VWB. Reported from eKy (DN 3, about two bushels), Ky (DN 4), Tenn Mts (AS 14.92), NC Mts (DN 4), seMo (DN 2), swMo (DN 5). DAE 1800–1896.

*turn out (see *let out, break up*): Of school, be over; everywhere, but not common north of the James. Reported from Ga (DN 3), Fla (DN 3), Ind (AS 17.130, *turn over*), nwArk (DN 3, *universal*). NED (75.g) *trans.*

*(to have) weather: (To have) bad weather; not common. VWB. Reported from Va (DN 1), sIll (DN 2), seMo (DN 2), nwArk (DN 3), Tex (DN 1), wTex (DN 4), Sarah Orne Jewett (DN 2). CD.

*(to) weather: To storm; not common. Reported from swMo (DN 5), Tex (DN 1). EDD: nYks.

weskit (see *jacket*): A vest; common among older people. Reported from Va (AS 6.100). DAE *waistcoat* (2) 1640–1912; NED *Colloq.* or *vulgar*, 1519–1869; EDD An undercoat worn by either sex: Kent, Yks, Dev.

*whetrock (see *whetstone*): Whetstone; mostly in the southern part of the Blue Ridge, and the southern Piedmont. Reported from Va (DN 4), eAla (DN 3), Ky (DN 4), NC Mts (DN 4), Ill (DN 4), nwArk (DN 3).

whetstone (see *whetrock*): In the northern Piedmont and in the Tidewater. DAE 1643–1923; NED (1) 725–1896; CD (1); EDD: Nhb, Cum, Yks, Chs, Lei, Som, Dev.

*whicker (see *nicker, whinny*): Noise made by a horse at feeding time; on the Tidewater and Eastern Shore. VWB. Reported from NC (DN 5), eAla (DN 3), sInd (DN 3), sIll (DN 2), swMo (DN 5), nwArk (DN 3). NED (2) 1808–1912; EDD: Sc, Wm, Yks, Glo, Brks, Hmp, IW, nCy, Wil, Dur, Som, Amer.

*whinny (see *nicker, whicker*): Noise made by a horse at feeding time; scattered on the Eastern Shore and in the Shenandoah Valley. NED (1) 1530–1894; CD; EDD To cry, as a child.

wishbone (see *lucky-bone, pull bone, pully bone*): Fairly common among younger people. VWB. Reported from eNeb (AS 12. 104). DAE *American*, 1853–1905; CD.

*woods colt (see *base-born, oldfields colt*): An illegitimate child; west of the Blue Ridge. Reported from wcWVa (AS 2.366), Winchester, Ky (DN 1), Tenn Mts (AS 14.92), Nc (AS 18.68), NC Mts (DN 4), SC (AS 18.58), Ind (AS 16.25), seMo (DN 2, a horse or person of unknown paternity), swMo (DN 5), nwArk (DN 3), Me (AS 5.124).

worm fence (see *log fence, rail fence*): A zigzag rail fence; fairly common in the northern Piedmont and on the Eastern Shore. VWB. Reported from Va (DN 4), swMo (DN 5), Aroostook, Me (DN 3). DAE *American*, 1652–1913; T 1817–1867; NED (IV.f) *U.S.*, 1796–1842; CD.

wrathy (see *ashy, touchous*): Angry; common everywhere. VWB. Reported from eAla (DN 3), nwArk (DN 3), cConn (DN 2). DAE *American, Low colloq.*, 1828–1900; T 1834–1888; NED *Orig.* (and chiefly) *U.S.*, 1828–1887; CD *colloq.;* EDD: Sc, Irel, Brks, IW, Amer.

THE SECRETARY'S REPORT

A. THE CHICAGO MEETING

The annual meeting was held in Chicago at the Stevens Hotel, December 27, 1945, 2:00–3:30 P. M. The meeting was well attended, more persons being present than could be seated. Although there was discussion of each paper, a number of persons told the Secretary or later wrote him that they felt that the meeting had not had enough time allotted to it to allow for unhurried presentation of papers and full discussion of them.

The following papers were read:

"Some Observations on Eastern Canadian Dialect," Henry Alexander, Queen's University, Ontario.

"Some Questions and Opinions on Place-Name Study," Frederic G. Cassidy, University of Wisconsin.

"In the Wake of the *DAE*," M. M. Mathews, University of Chicago.

Reports were given by the Secretary and the President. The Auditing Committee sent in its report, which stated that the Secretary's bookkeeping was correct.

The officers recommended for 1946 by the Nominating Committee were elected. The principal officers are: President, Kemp Malone, Johns Hopkins University; Vice-President, Atcheson L. Hench, University of Virginia; Secretary-Treasurer, George P. Wilson, Woman's College of the University of North Carolina. Members of the Executive Council are: Kemp Malone, Johns Hopkins University; Atcheson L. Hench, University of Virginia; George P. Wilson, Woman's College of the University of North Carolina; Harry Morgan Ayres, Columbia University; Hans Kurath, Brown University; Stith Thompson, Indiana University; Albert C. Baugh, University of Pennsylvania.

The next meeting will be held in Washington, D. C., in conjunction with the Modern Language Association.

B. SOME MATTERS REPORTED ON AT THE MEETING

1. *Deceased members.* The President of the Society asked that the group rise and remain silent a few moments in memory of four

members who had died during the year: Professor B. J. Vos, Dr. Thomas A. Knott, Dr. John L. Lowes, and Dr. C. C. Rice.

2. *Work of committees.* The Secretary commended the marked industry and achievements of two chairmen and the members of their committees: Dr. Margaret M. Bryant, chairman of the Committee on Proverbial Sayings; and Dr. I. Willis Russell, chairman of the Committee on New Words. He expressed the hope that other committees would show similar results now that the war is over.

3. *Activities of individual members.* The following is a paragraph from the Secretary's report as read: "During the year I learned that so many members had written articles and books and had engaged in other valuable activities that I thought it would be of interest to all members if I made a report on these doings. Accordingly, in October I sent a form letter to each member requesting that if he had 'committed' any good acts, he cognize me of them. I stand before you a poor psychologist and a frustrated man: only three persons responded to my request. In his *Supplement I to the American Language* Mr. Mencken concludes a discussion on our Society and its members in these judgmatical words: 'Thus the society stands in the first years of its second half-century, rejuvenated and indeed reincarnated. It is still small, but its members include all American philologians who are really interested in American English, and it has more ambitious plans than ever before.' I hope that in *Supplement II* Mr. Mencken will add that our members are too modest to testify to their good deeds."

4. *"Indecent" material.* The Secretary raised the question as to whether so-called "indecent" dialect and proverbs should be collected and published by the Society. All who voiced their opinions thought that such material should be collected and published.

5. *Membership.* During the year several members were good enough to send in the names of persons who later joined the Society. Those who have been most helpful in this respect are: Dr. James F. Bender, Dr. Margaret M. Bryant, Dr. Josiah Combs, Dr. Thomas A. Kirby, Miss Mamie J. Meredith, Dr. Robert Price, and Dr. Francis Utley.

Here are some figures on our membership for 1945:

Life	18
Members paid through or beyond 1945	156
Members paid through 1944	25
Unpaid but probably good	58
Libraries	122
Exchange and complimentary	8
Total	387

6. *Financial report.* This report is as of December 15, 1945.

Receipts

Money brought over from last year	$746.33
Dues from persons	411.00
Dues from libraries	304.00
Gifts: A. W. Read and C. L. Barnhart	5.00
Sale of *Needed Research in American English*	.25
Sale of *PADS* No. 1	2.75
Sale of *PADS* No. 2	21.62
From Ency. Brit. Co. for new words	100.00
Interest on money in bank, June 30	4.44
Total	$1595.39

Disbursements

For 1000 envelopes (6½ x 9½)	$3.83
" express	1.18
" miscellaneous	8.20
" paper	4.44
" postals and stamps	57.09
" *PADS* No. 2	325.35
" *PADS* No. 3	169.45
" secretarial work	4.50
" stencils	1.19
Total	$575.23
Balance on hand	$1020.16

7. *Change of address.* The Secretary would be most grateful to all members who change their address if they would notify him immediately of their full new address. Such an act of charity would save time, energy, postage, and copies of *PADS*.

THE AMERICAN DIALECT SOCIETY

Membership in the Society is conferred upon any person interested in the activities of the Society. Dues are $2.00 a year for persons or institutions. Members receive free all publications. The price of any issue when purchased separately will depend upon the production cost of the issue.

The *Publication of the American Dialect Society* is issued at intervals during the year.

PUBLICATION OF THE AMERICAN DIALECT SOCIETY

Number 6

A WORD-LIST FROM VIRGINIA AND NORTH CAROLINA

By

C. M. WOODARD

WORDS FROM *A Glossary of Virginia Words*
CURRENT IN MAINE
BY B. J. WHITING

Published by the
AMERICAN DIALECT SOCIETY
November, 1946

Obtainable from the Secretary of the Society
Woman's College of the
University of North Carolina
Greensboro, North Carolina

OFFICERS

OF

THE AMERICAN DIALECT SOCIETY

PRESIDENT
KEMP MALONE — *Johns Hopkins University*

VICE-PRESIDENT
ATCHESON L. HENCH — *University of Virginia*

SECRETARY-TREASURER
GEORGE P. WILSON — *Woman's College of the University of N. C.*

EDITING COMMITTEE
KEMP MALONE — *Johns Hopkins University*
I. WILLIS RUSSELL — *University of Alabama*
THE SECRETARY, *ex-officio*

EXECUTIVE COUNCIL
KEMP MALONE — *Johns Hopkins University*
ATCHESON L. HENCH — *University of Virginia*
GEORGE P. WILSON — *Woman's College of the University of N. C.*
HARRY MORGAN AYRES — *Columbia University*
HANS KURATH — *Brown University*
STITH THOMPSON — *Indiana University*
ALBERT C. BAUGH — *University of Pennsylvania*

CHAIRMEN OF THE RESEARCH COMMITTEES
REGIONAL SPEECH AND LOCALISMS — *George P. Wilson, Woman's College of the University of N. C.*
PLACE-NAMES — *Harold W. Bentley, Columbia University*
LINGUISTIC GEOGRAPHY — *Hans Kurath, Brown University*
USAGE — *Robert C. Pooley, University of Wisconsin*
NON-ENGLISH DIALECTS — *J. M. Carrière, University of Virginia*
NEW WORDS — *I. Willis Russell, University of Alabama*
SEMANTICS — *S. I. Hayakawa, Illinois Institute of Technology*
PROVERBIAL SAYINGS — *Margaret M. Bryant, Brooklyn College*

REGIONAL SECRETARIES
NEW ENGLAND — *Hans Kurath, Brown University*
MIDDLE ATLANTIC STATES — *C. K. Thomas, Cornell University*
SOUTH ATLANTIC STATES — *Atcheson L. Hench, University of Virginia*

Continued on Cover 3

PUBLICATION OF THE AMERICAN DIALECT SOCIETY

Number 6

A WORD-LIST FROM VIRGINIA AND NORTH CAROLINA

By

C. M. WOODARD

Words from *A Glossary of Virginia Words*
Current in Maine
By B. J. Whiting

Published by the
AMERICAN DIALECT SOCIETY
November, 1946

Obtainable from the Secretary of the Society
Woman's College of the
University of North Carolina
Greensboro, North Carolina

INTRODUCTION

It has been and still is the wish of the Secretary to publish material representing each of the eight research groups, and he had expected to publish as *PADS* No. 6 one of two long works in other fields than dialect and proverbs (thus far all issues have been devoted mainly to these two fields). But neither of these manuscripts is yet ready. The Secretary makes this statement in no way derogatory to or apologetic for Dr. Woodard's contribution but merely as an explanation to members so that they may appreciate why another number contains dialect.

Most of Dr. Woodard's words and sayings come from Pamlico County, North Carolina, and from Salem, Virginia, the one on the coast of North Carolina and the other in the mountains of Virginia. Items marked "Pamlico" unless otherwise dated were heard by Dr. Woodard 1900–1910. The fact that an item is given a specific date and a specific locale does not imply that that item is not heard at other times and in other places (counties and states).

Editorial comments, as heretofore, are placed in double parentheses. These comments are not intended as criticisms but as some slight enlargement of information. The Editor has not made so many comments here as he might have made. Much that he has said in *PADS* No. 2 by way of general observation is also applicable here.

GEORGE P. WILSON

3

A WORD-LIST FROM VIRGINIA AND NORTH CAROLINA

C. M. WOODARD

Quartermaster School, Camp Lee, Virginia

A. GLOSSARY

a [a]: *pronc.* The broad *a* appears in the following words in some families: *master, pasture, trample, wrapped.* Pamlico, 1890's.

a many a: *phr.* Many a. "I've seen him *a many a* time." Pamlico. Common.

act off: *vb.* To cut up, to act silly before company. Said of children. "You decided to try *to act off.*" Pamlico.

all the: *phr.* The only. "That's *all the* pencil I have." Pamlico. Occasional among children.

all the farther: *phr.* As far as. "That's *all the farther* I went." Salem, 1930.

alley: *n.* The space between two rows of corn, cotton, etc.; the sloping, concave area made by plowing out the middle or balk. The space is called an *alley* after the crop is laid by. During the growing season of the crop, the space is a ridge, called a *middle*, if made by a cotton plow. If made by a turning plow, the ridge is called a *balk*. Pamlico. Common.

antney over: *phr.* Words spoken by a player as he throws a ball over the house to be caught by a player on the opposite side of the house. The full expression: "Antney, antney, and over she goes." Pamlico. Common among teen-age children. ((In some parts of Va. and N. C. *antney* (or *anty*) is the name of the game also.))

as: *conj.* Than. "This pen is better *as* as that one." Region around Salisbury, N. C., 1920.

asafetida bag: *n.* A small bag (one inch by two inches) containing a piece of asafetida and hung around the neck inside the clothing to give immunity to diphtheria. Worn by children. Pamlico, 1900–05.

ashamed: *adj.* Bashful. Said of timid children. Pamlico. Occasional.

ashy: *adj.* Ill-tempered, ill-humored. Pamlico. Common.

as long as: *phr.* Inasmuch as; regardless of how long (many times). "*As long as* he said so, it's all right." "*As long as* I've lived here, I didn't know that."

4

as many as: *phr.* Notwithstanding how. "*As many* times *as* I've been here, I've never seen this house before." Pamlico. Common.

baby: *n.* The youngest member of the family regardless of age. Usually a term of affection. Pamlico. Common.

backhouse: *n.* A privy. Pamlico. Common.

back-talk: *n.* Impudent talk; mumbling, murmuring complaint. Pamlico. Common.

bad: *adv.* Very much. "He wants to see her mighty *bad.*" Pamlico. Common.

bad off: *adj.* Very ill. Pamlico. Common.

bag: *n.* The scrotum. Probably because of the association, *bag* was almost never used for *sack* until rather recently. Pamlico.

balk: *n.* A strip (about six inches wide) of unplowed ground between two rows. The sides are cut vertically by a turning plow. The earth thrown away by a cotton plow from the row of plants is called an *alley* or a *middle.* Pamlico. Common among farmers.

bamly Gillyard tree ['bæmlɪ 'gɪljəd, -əd]: *n.* The *balm of Gilead tree.* Pamlico, 1900–46. Mainly among Negroes.

bamly Gillyard salve: *n.* A salve made from the exudation of the balm of Gilead tree. Pamlico, 1900–46. Mainly among Negroes.

bar [bɑr, bɑ:]: *n.* A *barrow,* a castrated hog. Pamlico, 1900's. The usual word.

bat: *n.* A woman of ill repute. Pamlico. Occasional.

bateau ['bæˌto]: *n.* A small boat. Beaufort Co., N. C., 1934.

bed up ground: *phr.* To form rows of four furrows with a turning plow. Pamlico. Common.

bearer: *n.* A horizontal support for a bridge across a field ditch two to ten feet wide. Pamlico. Common.

being; being that: *conj.* Since. "*Being that* you are here, I'll stay." Pamlico. Common.

belong: *vb.* To be supposed. "We (don't) *belong* to do that." Pamlico. Common among children.

Bessie bug: *n.* A handsome black bug whose habitat is rotten wood. It is about one inch long. To children it seems to say "Bessie" when touched with a blade of grass. Pamlico. Common among children.

big: *vb*. To make pregnant. Pamlico. Occasional among Negroes.

big-bug: *n*. A rich, influential person; a small-town tycoon. Used somewhat disparagingly. Pamlico. Common.

biggety: *adj*. Conceited, bossy. Pamlico. Common.

bill: *n*. Visor for a cap. Salem, 1942.

bird snow: *n*. Late spring snow. Salem, 1942. Occasional.

blackberry summer: *n*. The season when blackberry vines are in bloom. Rainy weather is said to prevail. Near Williamsburg, Va.

black grape: *n*. An unimproved variety of *Muscadinia rotundifolia*, of which the scuppernong is an improved variety. The black grape is sometimes cultivated. Pamlico.

bless out: *vb*. To rebuke unmercifully. Pamlico. Common.

blind: *vb*. To ask questions that students are unprepared to answer. "The professor *blinded* me today." University of N. C., 1912. Common.

blind, to go: *phr*. To become blind. Pamlico. Common.

blind-bridle: *n*. A bridle with flaps to prevent the horse from seeing towards the side from the corner of his eye. This bridle is used only with buggy harness. Pamlico. Common.

blinky: *adj*. Beginning to turn sour; said of milk. Salem, 1942. Reported.

blobber-lipped: *adj*. Thick-lipped; voluptuous-looking. The term usually applied to a Negro man having such lips. Pamlico. Occasional.

blowing fly: *n*. A large green fly that lights on freshly killed meat. (*Calliphora erythrocephala*.) Pamlico. Common.

blue hen's chickens: *phr*. Local aristocracy. Salem, 1890's.

bob jack ((jack rock)): *n*. A right-angled metal crisscross used in the game of bob jacks. Four jacks are used. They are tossed a few inches in the air, and caught, if possible, on the back of the hand. They are swept up with one hand (one or more at a time) from the floor or ground while a bounced rubber ball is in the air. Pamlico. Common.

bone: *vb*. To study hard. University of N. C. Student language.

bone, to have a —— to pick: *phr*. Verbal settling of a real or supposed injury done one by another. Cf. *to pick a crow*. Pamlico.

bone felon: *n.* Whitlow. (*Paronychia.*) Pamlico. Somewhat rare.

booger ['bʊgɚ, -ə]: *n.* A baby; a term of affection. "You little *booger.*" Pamlico. Common.

boogers: *n.* Mythical bad man; a term sometimes used by mothers to children to induce obedience. Pamlico.

boot: *n.* and *vb.* A favor; to seek a favor. "He had a *boot* on the professor." "He *booted* the professor." University of N. C., 1912.

born days: *n.* Lifetime. Always with *never.* "In all my *born days* I never saw the like!" Pamlico. Common.

break all to flinders: *phr.* To break to pieces, smithereens. Pamlico. Fairly common.

breath harp: *n.* A harmonica, a mouth harp. Salem.

brier hook: *n.* A thin curve-bladed ax used for cutting bushes, etc. Pamlico.

broken stick: *n.* An unreliable person or thing. "If you're counting on me, you're counting on a *broken stick.*" Pamlico, 1900–. Common.

bronical: *adj.* *Bronchial.* "I had *bronical* trouble." Pamlico. Common.

broom grass: *n.* Long grass of savannas, used for making brooms. Pamlico. Common.

buck: *vb.* To tame a tough or mommock a small boy by seizing his arms and legs and banging his fundament against the fundament of another boy or against a tree or wall. It takes two "initiators" to do the bucking. Pamlico. Common among boys.

buffalo soldier: *n.* A Southerner who, near the end of the Civil War, fought for, or sympathized with, the North in order to curry favor with the probable winner. Pamlico, 1900–. Occasional.

bug-eye: *n.* A small boat with a triangular sail. Pamlico. Common.

bull-tongue: *n.* A plow used to break up ground containing reed roots. Pamlico. Rare or obsolete.

burying: *n.* The burial. The funeral might be held months after the burial. Pamlico. Rare.

bush ax: *n.* A thin, curve-bladed ax used for cutting bushes, etc. Pamlico. Common.

butcher knife: *n.* A large kitchen knife used for cutting meat, scaling fish, etc.

butt-headed: *adj.* Hornless; applied to cattle. Pamlico. Common.

calathump ['kælə'θʌmp]: *n.* See *serenade.* Salem. Reported, 1940.

calico horse: *n.* A reddish horse with irregular stripes. Pamlico. Common.

call at a home without going in: *vbs. for*—**call by, drop by, stop by.** Salem, 1930–43. Common.

cal-log ['kæ 'lɑg]: *n. Carry-log,* a log carrier. A cart with wheels eight or more feet high used for hauling timber logs. The axle was arched to allow the cart to straddle the five-foot butt of a log. The tongue was split from the end to nearly halfway, and the split portions were spread and fastened to the axle. The log was lifted by a lever fastened to a windlass above the axle. In the top end of the lever was a shiv (sheave) through which a rope ran. The cart was drawn by oxen. Pamlico, about 1900. Obsolete.

cam [kæm]: *adj. Calm.* Pamlico. Common.

carried away: *adj.* Very much impressed by someone or something. Pamlico. Common.

carry: *vb.* To furnish with provisions during the growing of a crop. Done by country merchants. Salem. Reported, 1940.

carry a tune: *phr.* To be able to sing a tune in tempo. Pamlico. Common.

carryings-on: *n.* Mischievousness; playfully audacious behavior. "I heard about your *carryings-on* yesterday." ((In some parts of Va. and N. C. the expressions refers to immorality, drinking, gambling, and such other conduct as the speaker does not approve of.))

cart wheel: *n.* A sort of handspring among boys. "To turn the *cart wheel.*" Pamlico, 1900–05. Among boys.

cattle beast: *n.* General term for a bovine animal. Pamlico, 1900–05. Common. ((The eastern part of the state has fewer double terms each element of which has the same meaning than does the western part.))

cattle penning: *n.* Semiannual event when cattle were driven from grazing grounds in woods and salt marsh hammocks to be marked by owners, sold, etc. Pamlico before 1905. Common.

cat-west, to knock: *phr.* To knock out of the way; to settle "the hash of"; to threaten "to fix up the flint of a teaser." "The car hit him and *knocked* him *cat-west.*" "I'll *knock* you *cat-west* if you don't stop pestering me." Pamlico. Occasional among teen-age boys.

chance: *n.* A large number. "A whole *chance* of children." Salem. Reported, 1940.

Christmas Eve morning: *n.* The morning of December 24. Pamlico. Common.

Christmas gift: *phr.* Greeting heard on a few occasions on the morning of December 25. I interpreted it to mean "Merry Christmas." Pamlico. ((The Editor has heard it in s. Va., c. N. C., and c. Ga. When two persons meet on Christmas morning, the one who first says "Christmas gift!" is supposed to be given a present by the other. Jocular.))

chunk: *vb.* To throw, toss, fling. Pamlico. Common.

circumstance, not to be a: *phr.* Not to be compared with in importance or strength. "That earthquake was *not a circumstance* to this one." Pamlico. Common.

clatterwhacking: *n.* Clatter, palaver. Salem. Reported several times, 1940.

clatty: *adj. Clattered.* Salem, 1943. Reported. Common.

clean up: *interj.* Begone! Used in driving away an unwanted dog. Pamlico. Occasional.

clivvy: *n. Clevis.* Pamlico. Common.

clod-knocker: *n.* A heavy shoe. ((In some parts of the South also applied to a countryman in a derogatory sense.))

cold hurt: *adj.* Nipped or frozen by the cold. Said of potatoes that have been slightly affected before being dug or after they have been banked during the winter. Never applied to Irish potatoes. Pamlico, 1900–. Common.

come through: *vb.* To be converted religiously, generally after much shouting and other emotional display. Pamlico. Negroes.

come up: *vb.* 1. To germinate and come through the ground. 2. To command a horse to move faster. Pamlico. Common.

compost: *n.* Fish scrap and small fish used for fertilizing gardens. Pamlico.

congestive chill: *n.* A severe chill? Pamlico, 1900. Occasional.

contrary: *vb.* To disobey; said of children. Salem region. Reported, 1940.

coon oyster: *n.* A long, narrow sharp-shelled oyster found in marshes. Usually in clusters, sometimes a dozen to a cluster. Pamlico and Carteret counties, 1900–46. Common.

corn rows: *n.* Braids formerly used by Negro women in their hair-dos. Pamlico.

co, wench [ko]: *interj.* A call used for a cow when she is only a short distance away. Pamlico. Common.

cork: *vb.* *Calk.* Pamlico. Common.

crack the door: *phr.* To open the door slightly. Pamlico. Common.

crack-a-loo: *n.* A game played with pennies, nickels, or dimes. The coin is pitched against the ceiling and falls to the floor. The person whose coin comes to rest on or nearest a chosen crack wins. Pamlico.

crawfish chimney: *n.* The mud or clay cylinder-shaped structure made by a lobster-like crustacean that lives in low, damp places. The chimney is about six inches high and three inches in diameter. Pamlico. Common.

creeses ['krɪsɪz]: *n.* Cress or cress greens. Hopewell, Va. Common. ((S. Va. and c. N. C. Common.))

creesy salad ['krɪsɪ]: *n.* Same as *cresses.*

creeter ['krɪtɚ, -ə]: *n.* A horse; sometimes a cow. Pamlico.

cringle: *n.* The glass insulator to which a telephone or telegraph wire is attached. Pamlico. Common.

crocus bag: *n.* A tow sack. Eastern S. C. Among Negroes and older persons. ((Also in s. Va. and c. N. C.))

crock: *n.* A terra cotta drain pipe. Pamlico. Common.

crop: *vb.* To cut off the tip of the ear of a hog or a bovine animal. Pamlico. Common.

cross-jaw: *vb.* To chatter, palaver, clatterwhack. Used mainly in reference to women. Pamlico.

cross-vine: *n.* A scaly-bark porous vine that twists around trees. Boys cut it into pieces and smoke it. (*Bignonia capreolata.*) Pamlico. Perhaps obsolete now.

curtain: *n.* A window shade. Pamlico. Obsolete.

cut: *n.* A piece of arable land enclosed by ditches, generally from one-half acre to three acres. Pamlico. Common.

cut (any, no) ice: *phr.* To make any difference; to exert influence. "That *cuts no ice* with me." Pamlico. Common.

cut down: *vb.* To go up one place in a spelling class; that is, to take the place of the student who has just misspelled a word. Pamlico.

cut out: *vb.* To get the best of—supersede. "He *cut* me *out* with my girl." Pamlico. Common.

cut the buck: *phr.* To move rapidly, as in driving a car. Salem. Reported, 1940.

cut the short dog: *phr.* To caper and frisk around when tipsy. Pamlico. Occasional among *bons vivants.*

cut up lard: *phr.* To cut hog fat into small pieces to be fried. Pamlico. Common.

cuttyhole: *n.* A small room or corner for holding plunder. Pamlico. Occasional.

cypress knee: *n.* The branchless and top root-growth of the cypress tree from one to three feet high. The top is round and looks like the nub of a finger or an amputated leg. Pamlico. Common.

daisy: *n.* A fine specimen of potato, etc.; a ludicrous-looking person. Pamlico. Common.

dead: *vb.* To chop the bark around the circumference of a tree to cause it to die. A tree so treated is *deaded.* Pamlico. Common.

dead men: *n.* The parallel layers of the insides of a crab. Pamlico, 1900–. Common.

dead-rise: *n.* A boat whose bottom slopes to a slight, inverted peak—deeper in the center than on the sides. Pamlico. Common.

delicun squinton ['dɛləkn̩ 'skwɪntn̩]: Whisky. "*Delicun squinton* makes you speak the truth and gives you everlasting remembrance." Pamlico. Occasional among drinkers.

dew poison: *n.* Sores on the feet, usually between the toes; caused by parasitic mites. Among barefooted boys. Pamlico. Common.

diarrhea of words: *phr.* A superabundance of pointless words. Salem, 1940.

dib; dibby: *n.* A small chicken. W. S. C., 1945. Occasional.

diddy bag: *n.* A reticule of articles used by a midwife. Salem. Reported, 1946.

dinky: *n.* The small boat of a ship; perhaps from *dinghy*. Pamlico. Common among boatmen.

disfurnish: *vb.* To inconvenience. Used by persons who borrow something from a neighbor who may also need the article. Pamlico, 1905—.

doing of: *phr.* *Doing.* "What you *doing of?*" Pamlico, 1900—.

do-less: *adj.* Lazy. Salem. Reported, 1942.

done and: *phr.* Already. "He's *done and* done it." Pamlico. Common among uneducated.

doodle-ant: *n.* A small fuzzy-looking insect that burrows in soft dry earth. It is supposed to come to the surface when entreated with the words: "Doodle-ant, doodle-ant, house is afire," repeated several times. ((In s. Va. and c. N. C.: *doodle-bug. Myrmeleonia.*))

doubled and thribbled: *phr.* *Doubled and tripled.* Pamlico. Rare.

double-jointed: *adj.* Big, strong, muscular. Pamlico. Occasional.

down-the-country: *n.* A severe tongue lashing, usually when the victim is absent. "She gave him *down-the-country.*" Pamlico. Occasional.

draw: *n.* The gap in a bridge, together with the water beneath, that appears when the drawbridge is opened. Pamlico. Common, 1900—.

dress (one) down: *phr.* To scold one, to give one a tongue-lashing. Pamlico. Occasional.

drunken horrors: *n.* Delirium tremens. Pamlico. Occasional.

dumpling: *n.* A flattened cake of corn meal boiled with meat and vegetables. Pamlico. Common.

dunger ['dʌŋgɚ -ə]: *n.* A cultivated area that was formerly the site of a dwelling, sometimes abounding in kitchen middens. Probably the same word as *dunghill*. Pamlico, about 1900. Older persons.

east: *n.* *Yeast.* Pamlico. Common.

euchre out of: *vb.* To flimflam or trick. Pamlico, 1920. Occasional.

fancy woman: *n.* A woman of ill repute. Guilford Co., N. C., 1943. ((Also in s. Va.))

fat-back: *n.* Fatty, bony fish used for oil and fertilizer. Pamlico. Common.

fau't: *n.* and *vb.* *Fault.* "I don't *fau't* him for doing that." Pamlico. Occasional. Uneducated.

feel on the bum: *phr.* To feel worthless, unfit for work. Pamlico. Occasional.

fence lock: *n.* An angle made by the interlocking rails of a fence. Pamlico, 1900—. Common.

fetch: *vb.* To bring a sail into the wind in making a tack. If the sail is successfully handled, the boat is said to have *fetched.* Pamlico. Common in sailing days, about 1900.

fifty-O (-oh): *n.* A school game in which the leader counts aloud to fifty while the other children hide. The leader closes his eyes and stands with his back to those hiding. When he reaches fifty, which he shouts at the top of his voice, he opens his eyes and tries to tag each player before the player can touch base. Pamlico, around 1905. Common.

find: *vb.* To give birth to. A euphemism. Pamlico. Common.

finger—little, ling, long, lick-pot, and thumb-ball: *n.* The little finger, ring finger, long finger, index finger, and thumb. Pamlico. Common among children.

fire board: *n.* A cover made of wood to conceal the fireplace when not in use.

fish for a compliment: *phr.* To maneuver the conversation in such a manner as to receive a compliment. Pamlico. Common.

fitified: *adj.* Afflicted with fits, that is, epilepsy. Pamlico. Common.

flam: *n.* The five-degree slant in the sides of a small skiff. Pamlico, 1908. Rare.

flat-break land: *phr.* To plow all around a piece of ground with a turning plow, throwing all furrows toward the margin, ditch, hedge, etc. Pamlico. Occasional.

flesh crawl, to make the: *phr.* To make one shudder or quiver at the report or imagination of anything unpleasant to the nerves. Pamlico. Common.

flitter: *n.* A fritter, usually made of fried oysters and flour. Pamlico. Common.

fly off the handle: *phr.* To become angry and excited about a trifle. Pamlico. Common.

flying jenny: *n.* The merry-go-round. A sixteen-foot pole five inches in diameter with a hole through the center. In this hole was a wooden or metal peg, which rested on a stump or some other wooden foundation. The jinny was rotated by some children while others rode it. Pamlico. Common among children.

folkses: *n.* *Folks*, people. Baby talk used by mothers to their children. Pamlico. Common.

fore: *vb.* Past tense of *fare*. "The crops *fore* bad during the drouth." ((Cf. O. E. *fōr*, past tense singular of *faran*.)) Pamlico, about 1900. Occasional among older people.

fore part of the day: *phr.* The early part of the forenoon. Pamlico. Common.

fox grape: *n.* A wild grape that grows in a cluster like the scuppernong; much smaller than the scuppernong. (*Muscadinia rotundifolia*.) Pamlico. Common.

fractious: *adj.* Unruly, stubborn. Applied to nervous, temperamental horses. A horse with more than one white foot is liable to be fractious; hence the saying—

> "One, buy him;
> Two, try him;
> Three, let him alone."

Pamlico. Common.

frail: *vb.* To whip (a child). Pamlico. Common.

fram: *vb.* To strike a person with a book or some other object. Pamlico. School children.

fresh-water mosquito: *n.* A long-legged, slender mosquito that has a sharp bite. (*Anopheles maculipennis*.) Pamlico. Common.

frog in the throat: *phr.* A slight change or break in the voice due to a need for clearing the throat before speaking. Pamlico. Common.

frog the eyes: *phr.* To blink the eyes as a frog does in rain. Said of a surprised, naive person. Salem. Reported, 1942.

funny: *adj.* Pretty, as applied to a baby. Salter Path, near Moorehead City, N. C. Older people.

gall bush: *n.* A small evergreen bush (about three feet high) that grows abundantly in low flat lands. Bears berries. ((*Myrica gale?*)) Pamlico. Common.

gamble: *n.* *Gambrel*. A fifteen-inch stick sharpened at the ends and inserted between the bone and the tendon of the hind legs of a hog to suspend the hog from a device called a *gallows*. Pamlico. Common. ((In s. Va. and c. N. C. called *gambling stick*.))

geenavy [dʒəˈnevɪ]: *n.* A large number. Jocular. Pamlico. Common.

gentleman cow: *n.* A bull. An old-time euphemism. Pamlico. Occasional.

get-together: *n.* A small assembly of congenial persons. Pamlico. Common.

get-up: *n.* Initiative. "He has no *get-up*." Pamlico. Occasional.

give in (**taxes**): *phr.* To list property for taxation. Pamlico. Common.

give out: *vb.* To call out words to be spelled in a contest. Pamlico. Common.

glut: *n.* A wooden wedge used to split wood (usually rails), made of oak or ash ((or dogwood)). Now replaced by the iron wedge. Pamlico. Common.

go to do: *phr.* To intend. Used negatively. "I did*n't go to do* that." Pamlico, 1910—.

go-to-hell collar: *n.* A wing collar. Pamlico. Common about 1900.

gone gosling: *n.* A person hopelessly in difficulties. Pamlico. Occasional.

good fashion: *adv.* Thoroughly. Used with threats. "I'll spank you *good fashion*." Pamlico.

goose bumps: *n.* Bumps on the human skin due to cold or fright. Pamlico. Common.

goslings: *n.* The frequent break in an adolescent boy's voice. Salem, 1938. Common.

gospel fowl: *n.* A chicken. ((So named probably because fried chicken is customarily fed to the preacher and taken to "protracted meetings.")) Salem. Reported, 1940.

grabble: *vb.* To finish digging with the hands potatoes that have been turned up by a turning plow. Pamlico. Common. ((In s. Va., w. and c. N. C.: to take a few potatoes from the hill and fill in with dirt the hole so made.))

grass, go to: *phr.* A friendly rebuke. Used by children when annoyed with questions of other children. Pamlico. Occasional.

grat: *n.* and *vb.* Missing a scheduled class, said of the teacher in charge; a gratuity. To miss such a class. "We got a *grat* today." He *gratted* us." University of N. C., 1912. Common.

great hand for: *phr.* One fond of or susceptible to. "He's a *great hand for* speculating in cotton." Pamlico. Common.

green: *vb.* To become green. "The tobacco is *greening.*" Pamlico. Common among farmers.

grinding smoke: *phr.* An evasive answer given a child who inquisitively asks what one is doing. Salem. Reported, 1940. ((A similar response in Vance Co., N. C.: *sowing wheat.*))

ground itch: *n.* See *dew poison.* Pamlico. Common.

ground skinner: *n.* A batted baseball that skips along the ground from batter to infielder. Pamlico. Common.

grubbing hoe: *n.* A heavy, narrow hoe for digging up reeds, bushes, and small stumps. Pamlico. Common.

gumption: *n.* Courage, enterprise, initiative. Pamlico. Common. ((The more common meaning elsewhere in the state is, perhaps, common sense.))

gut: *n.* A shallow, narrow, winding arm of a creek in a salt-water region. Pamlico. Common.

gyp: *n.* A female dog. Salem. Reported, 1942.

hack: *vb.* To discomfit, to daunt, to faze. ((*Hawk*, Southern dialect, has the same meaning.)) Pamlico. Common.

half-leg high: *adj.* Half the distance from the sole of the foot to the knee. Used by farmers in speaking of the height of plants. Pamlico. Common.

half strainer: *n.* A social climber. Salem, 1890's.

hammock: *n.* An acre or two of trees and other vegetation in a large area of salt marsh. Pamlico. Common.

hand-hold: *n.* The grip of the hand on an object. Pamlico. Common.

hand-speak: *n.* A black-gum pole six to eight feet long, three inches thick at the center, and tapering to about an inch and a half at each end. Used by two men for toting logs or bunching logs (one man) at logrollings. Pamlico, 1900–05. Common among farmers.

hard ague: *n.* A severe chill. Pamlico. Common.

Hardshell: *n.* A Primitive Baptist. Pamlico. Now rare.

harvest: The following forms are used to mean to harvest:

gather **corn,** *pick* **cotton,** *dig* **potatoes,** *pick* **peas,** *take* **in fodder.** Pamlico.

haul off: *vb.* To act unexpectedly or impulsively. "He *hauled off* and gave us a quiz." Pamlico. Common.

have: *vb.* To accept as a gift; to tolerate. "I wouldn't *have* the thing." Pamlico. Common.

have off: *vb.* To take off (one's coat, hat, etc.). "*Have off* your things and stay a while." Pamlico. Common.

head cap: *n.* The platform in the bow of a skiff or other small boat. Pamlico. Common.

heading: *n.* 1. A pillow. 2. A piece of tow sack used for closing the top of a barrel of potatoes, fastened by a hoop and nailed to the barrel. Pamlico. Common.

head-mark: *n.* A merit-mark for being at the head of a class in spelling at the end of the day. Pamlico.

heap: *adv.* Much; very much. "He's a *heap* larger than I am." "I'd a *heap* ruther not go." Pamlico.

heat: *n.* Children's summer rash. Pamlico. Common.

heel string: *n.* Achilles' tendon. Pamlico. Common among old people.

heel-stave: *n.* The inner pasteboard support at the back of a shoe heel. Pamlico. Occasional.

hemorrhagic fever: *n.* Probably typhoid or malarial fever. Pamlico, 1910.

hether ['hɛθɚ, -ə]: *vb.* Command to a horse to turn to the left. Pamlico. Common.

hickey: *n.* A seesaw. Pamlico. Common among rural children.

hickey: *n.* A small festered spot on the skin of a person. Salem. Reported, 1942.

high muckety muck: *n.* A pompous-looking person. ((May be singular or plural.)) Slang. Pamlico.

hilling hoe: *n.* A hoe used for working newly broken stumpy ground. Wider and shorter than a grubbing hoe. Pamlico. Common.

hockey: *n.* and *vb.* Excrement; to defecate. Mainly a child's word. Pamlico. Common.

hominy snow: *n.* Tiny pieces of winter ice or hail. Pamlico. Common.

hook: *n.* Account, accord. "He did that on his own *hook*."

horse, on a high: *phr.* Proud and haughty. Pamlico. Occasional.

horses, not to set: *phr.* Not to agree; to be incompatible. Pamlico. Occasional.

how-do-piece: *n.* The visor of a cap. Pamlico. Common.

hunch: *vb.* To nudge (with the elbow). Pamlico. Common.

hurang [ˈhjuˈræŋ]: *n.* A household rumpus among children. "It's a continual *hurang* around here." Pamlico, 1900–.

hushpuppies: *n.* "Plain corn meal to which salt and hot water are added and so cooked in hot, deep fat in which fish have been fried."—Ann Chamberlain. Williamsburg, Va.

huss [hʌs]: *n.* Euphemism for *hell*. "I'll knock the *huss* outen you." Pamlico. Occasional among boys.

ice pebble: *n.* Hail. Salem. Reported, 1940.

ill: *n.* Cross, in a bad humor. Said of children. Pamlico. Common.

infinitive with **to** *after* **had:** "He *had* a horse *to die* last night." Pamlico. Common.

innding: *n.* *Inning,* in baseball. Heard among ball players. Pamlico.

jack: *n.* A small-sized, small-type translation of the classics (Cicero, Vergil, etc.). In a number of schools and colleges in N. C.

jack-leg: *adj.* Inferior, inefficient. "He's a *jack-leg* carpenter." Pamlico. Common.

Japan peas: *n.* Soy beans. Pamlico. Obsolete.

jigger: *n.* A small mite infesting chickens. Pamlico. Common.

jim sweetener: *n.* A fine specimen. A jocular expression. Salem.

jimmy-jawed: *adj.* Prognathous. Salem. Reported as occasional, 1942.

Job's teeth: *n.* Small, hard beans on a string for a teething child. Salem. Reported, 1940.

Johnny Gaugghy [ˈgɔgɪ]: *n.* A long-legged bird sometimes seen wading in shallow water of creeks and ponds. Probably a member of the heron family. (*Arcidae.*) Pamlico.

johnny house: *n.* A privy. Salem, 1942–.

jump: *n.* A start, an advantage. "We got the *jump* on him.' Pamlico. Common.

jump: *vb.* To start an animal from its lair. Pamlico. Common.

just so: *conj.* If only. "It doesn't matter, *just so* we get there on time." Pamlico. Common.

knock down ground: *phr.* To plow down (flatten out) last year's rows. The plowing is down with two furrows. Pamlico. Common.

knock down to: *phr.* To introduce one person to another. Pamlico.

lace curtains: *n.* Window curtains. Used to distinguish curtains from shades, which are also called curtains. Pamlico. Obsolescent.

laid up: *adj.* Abed for a long while with some form of sickness. Pamlico. Common.

lamp shade: *n.* A lamp chimney. Pamlico. Common.

lard stand: *n.* A large (twelve to sixteen quarts) tin can used to hold lard derived from hog killings. Pamlico. Common.

lay: *vb.* To settle (dust). "The rain will *lay* the dust." Pamlico. Common.

lay by: *vb.* To plow a crop for the last time. Pamlico. Common among farmers.

lay off: *vb.* To intend. "I *laid off* to tell you." Pamlico. Common.

leader: *n.* A tendon in the neck. Pamlico. Common.

leaf: *n.* Permission; reward. "Give me *leaf* to 'skin the cat'?" Pamlico. School children.

least little: *phr.* Least. Used with a few nouns, such as *thing, noise*. Pamlico. Common.

leastways: *adv.* At least. Pamlico. Occasional.

lickety-split: *adv.* Rapidly (to go). "He went down the road *lickety-split*." Pamlico. Occasional.

like to have: *phr.* Almost. "We *like to have* got run over." Pamlico. Common.

limber jack: *n.* Jumping jack. Pamlico, 1900. Rare.

lodging: *n.* A sleeping place on the floor. Pamlico. Common.

look at you: *interj.* An exclamation used in scolding a person for carelessness. Pamlico. Common.

'lowance [laᴜns]: *vb.* *Allowance.* Pamlico. Occasional.

low-bush lightning: *n.* Whisky hidden by "blind tiger" in bushes. Pamlico. Common for a while after 1908, the year of the beginning of prohibition in N. C.

low cotton: *adj.* Puny. "I'm feeling sort o' *low cotton* today." Craven Co., N. C., 1941–42.

mad fence: *n.* A boundary fence between adjoining farms. Albemarle Co., Va. Used about 1890.

mad money: *n.* Money taken along by a girl on a date to be used in case she falls out with her companion and wants to come home early. Also money used by a girl or woman for small purchases. Petersburg, Va., about 1920.

make out like: *phr.* To pretend. Pamlico. Common.

making down: *phr.* Snowing hard. (Cf. *putting down.*) Salem. Reported, 1940.

mash, to make a: *phr.* To get a crush on. Salem. A Salem girl selling mustaches at a frolic in 1890:

> "Buy a mustache,
> Cut a dash,
> And *make a mash.*"

May pop: *n.* The May apple. (*Podophyllum peltatum.*) Pamlico. Occasional among farmers about 1900.

melt: *n.* *Milt* (of a hog). Pamlico. Common among farmers. ((Common in many sections of the South. A butcher in Guilford Co., N. C., once told the Editor that beating a stuttering child with a melt would cure him of stuttering.))

middle: *n.* The ridge of earth made between two rows of corn, cotton, etc., by throwing a furrow from each of the adjoining rows. Pamlico. Common.

mill days: *n.* Days of moodiness, gloominess, and grouchiness Pamlico.

mind: *n.* Attention. "He paid me no *mind.*" Pamlico. Mainly among Negroes.

mind: *n.* Inclination, desire. "I could do that if I had a *mind* to." Pamlico. Common.

miration: *n.* Exaggerated and pretentious wonderment, a carrying-on. "They made a great *miration* about my killing that squirrel." Pamlico. Occasional.

miss: *vb.* To misspell a word in a contest. Pamlico. 1900–08.

Miss Nancy: *n.* An effeminate boy or man. Salem. Reported, 1940.

misty moisty, to be: *phr.* To be threatening rain. Salem. Reported, 1940.

mommock ['mɑmək]: *vb.* To tease, annoy, torment, "impose on." A large boy *mommocks* a small boy. A cat *mommocks* a mouse before killing it. Pamlico. Common.

mosey along: *vb.* To saunter along; to start along on a journey. Pamlico. Occasional.

mosquito hawk: *n.* The dragon fly. (*Diplax elisa.*) Pamlico. Common.

mountain oyster: *n.* Sheep's testicle. Salem. Reported, 1940.

mouth: *n.* Impudent talk, back talk. Pamlico. Occasional.

mubble-squibble ['mʌbḷ 'skwɪbḷ]: *n.* To tease (mommock) a smaller person (male) by running one's knuckles heavily through the victim's hair in order to make the hair "pull" and hurt. Pamlico. Common among school boys.

mud turkle ['tɜ·kḷ]: *n.* A small turtle found in muddy bottoms, in either fresh or salt water. Pamlico. Mainly among Negroes.

multiply words: *phr.* To whine and argue with parents when told to do something. Salem. Reported, 1942.

mumble peg: *n.* A contest among boys as to who can throw his knife to make it stick in a wall. Pamlico. Occasional.

muscle out: *vb.* To raise a weight in the hand with the arm extended till it is horizontal. Pamlico, 1900–05. Occasional.

mutton-ham sail: *n.* A triangular sail used on a bug-eye boat. Pamlico. Common.

natural-born: *adj.* Born. "He's a *natural-born* fiddler." Pamlico. Common.

nellify: *vb.* To rise on the hind legs and then come back on all fours repeatedly, meanwhile refusing to move forward. Said of a horse. Pamlico. Occasional.

new ground: *n.* Ground recently put under cultivation. Called "new ground" for about five years after removal of timber and beginning of grubbing and plowing. Corn and watermelons are always the first crops grown. Pamlico. Common till about 1900. ((In s. Va. the first crop is usually tobacco. Common and current.))

nibby: *adj.* Inquisitive. Used disparagingly. Salem. Reported, 1942.

nicket: *n.* A small amount of articles like sugar, coffee, flour, meal, etc. Randolph Co., N. C., 1941.

norate: *vb.* To bruit around. Pamlico. Rare.

number: *vb.* To count off in a spelling class at the end of the day: "first, second, third," etc. Pamlico, 1900–08.

of: *prep.* Used after the verbs *feel, smell,* and *taste.* Pamlico. Common.

off against: *adj.* and *prep.* Opposite, in front of, near. Pamlico. Common.

oh, hush: *interj.* Equivalent to: "Is that so?" "No kidding!" "You don't say so!" "Well, I'll declare!" Pamlico. Occasional.

old bad man: *n.* Satan. "The *old bad man*'ll get you if you don't behave." Pamlico, 1900–. Used in talking to children. Common.

Old Christmas: *n.* January 6. Celebrated as late as 1915 by some families I knew. Pamlico.

old stick in the mud: *phr.* A stupid person. ((In s. Va. and c. N. C.: an old-fashioned person.)) Salem. Reported, 1940.

one: *pron.* One or the other. "You'll have to work or go to school *one.*" Pamlico. Common.

open a grave: *phr.* To dig a grave. Salem, 1944.

orey-eyed: *adj.* Blear-eyed. Salem, 1946.

out: *adv.* Already. Used only in stating ages. "I'm twenty-one *out* and in my twenty-two." Pamlico.

outdone: *adj.* Disappointed, exasperated. Pamlico. Common.

paper shaver: *n.* A person who discounts commercial papers for profit. Used derogatorily. Salem. Reported, 1942.

parze: *vb. Parse.* The only pronunciation used by teachers in the section around 1900. ((Common elsewhere in N. C., and also Va.)) Pamlico. Common.

passel: *n.* A group of nondescript boys and girls. Used derogatorily. Pamlico. Common.

patteroll: *n. Patrol.* A term used in the South in slavery days.

> "My old mistress promised me
> When she died she'd set me free;
> She lived so long, she died so po'
> She didn't have sugar in the coffee-O.
> (Refrain)
> Run, Nigger, run, don't the *patteroll*'ll catch you;
> Run, Nigger, run, for it's almost day."

Pamlico, 1900.

pea: *n.* A sliding weight (counterpoise) used on scales and steelyard(s). Pamlico, 1900–. Common.

pear pad: *n.* A variety of cactus which grows in sandy soil on the N. C. coast. Pamlico. Common.

pear pad apple: *n.* A sort of seed or fruit produced by the pear pad. Carteret Co., N. C. Heard a few times, 1941.

peckish: *adj.* Somewhat hungry. Pamlico, 1925.

peeling: *n.* Peel. *Peel* is never used as a noun. Pamlico. Common.

peepies: *n.* Chickens. Salem. Reported, 1940.

penniwinkle: *n.* *Periwinkle.* Pamlico. Common.

permeeter [pə'mitɚ, -ə]: *n.* *Palmetto.* Pamlico. Common till 1880; rare now.

pethy: *adj.* *Pithy* (wood). Pamlico. Common.

phthisic: *n.* Croup. Pamlico, 1900–05.

pig's eye, in a: *phr.* Indeed not; "not on your life." Richmond, Va., 1944. Occasional. ((Cf.: *"pig's eye,* n., euphemistic name for the very prevalent symbol for the female pudendum, an upright diamond with a longitudinal slit in the middle. 'In a pig's eye' was used by some in preference to the preceding saying, but to those conscious of the yoni sign the improvement seemed hardly noticeable."—W.L. McAtee, *Supplement to Rural Dialect of Grant County, Indiana, in the 'Nineties.*))

pig's whisper, in a: *phr.* Quickly. Salem. Reported, 1940.

pillentary tree ['pɪlən'tɛrɪ]: *n.* A small tree having rough bark, which is astringent. Grows near mouth of Neuse River. Pamlico. Occasional.

pine straw: *n.* Pine needles. Pamlico.

pin-toed: *adj.* Pigeon-toed. Pamlico. Common.

pitch a crop: *phr.* To plant a crop. Pamlico. Old farmers. Obsolete. ((Still heard in s. Va. and c. N.C.))

pitch pine: *n.* The longleaf pine. Pamlico.

pizer: *n.* *Piazza;* a one-story porch attached to a one-story house. Pamlico, around 1900's.

play fiddledewinks: *phr.* To waste time on trifles. Roanoke, Va., *Times,* 1942.

play-pretty: *n.* A plaything. Pamlico. Common.

pluggy: *adj.* Frail and puny. "I'm feeling sort o' *pluggy.*" Pamlico.

poison vine: *n.* A variety of yellow jessamine. Thought to be poison. (*Gelsemium sempervivens?*)) Pamlico. Common.

pole around: *vb.* To go around from place to place. Said of gangs of small boys prowling around and bent on mischief. Pamlico, 1900–.

pon hosh ['pɑn 'hɑʃ, -'hɔʃ]: *n.* Grease from hog-killing mixed with corn meal, fried, and sliced. "Scrapple." "Solidified liquid leavings from liver pudding, etc., cooked (fried) with corn meal." Rural region of Salem, 1940, 1946.

pony penning: *n.* The semiannual driving of "bank" ((wild)) ponies into a compound, where they are captured, to be branded or sold. On the banks of eastern N. C. Current.

pop: *vb.* To break. "He *popped* the stick in two." Pamlico. Common.

pop-lash: *n.* A rawhide whip used on oxen. Pamlico. Among timbermen around 1890.

'possum grape: *n.* A bluish-purple berry about the size of a buckshot. It grows on vines in jungle-like areas and ripens after frost. Opossums are said to like it. (*Vitis cordifolia.*) Pamlico. Occasional.

pound: *vb.* To victual an (incoming) parson. Salem, 1940. Occasional.

pretty come-off: *n.* An unfortunate outcome, referred to scoldingly and sarcastically. Pamlico. Common.

pretty plenty, a: *phr.* A good deal. Randolph Co., N. C., 1941.

progue [prog]: *vb.* To probe, as in a wound. Pamlico. Common.

progue around [prog]: *vb.* To go around somewhat at random, as if in some way bent on mischief and creating a little suspicion. Said of gangs of small boys. Pamlico. Occasional.

projeck ['prɑdʒɛk]: *vb.* To meddle with. "Quit *projecking* with that typewriter." Pamlico.

pull (strip) fodder: *phr.* To pull corn leaves from the stalk, tie them in bundles, and hang them on the stalk to dry. Pamlico. Common.

pullikins: *n.* Forceps. Pamlico. Occasional.

pullybone: *n.* The wishbone. Eastern N. C.

purpose, a: *phr.* On purpose. ((The early English preposition *a* (or *an*) survives in a number of Southern phrases.)) Pamlico. Common.

pussy ['pʌsɪ]: *adj.* *Pursy;* fattish, bay-windowed. Said of middle-aged men who have gained weight. Pamlico. Common.

put one's foot down: *phr.* To be firm. Pamlico.

put one's head under the fence: *phr.* To be subservient or easily suggestible. An expression used by parents when scolding their children for being led by the nose by playmates. "You'd *put your head under the fence* if he told you to." Pamlico, 1900. Rather common.

putting down: *phr.* Raining hard. (Cf. *making hard.*) Salem. Reported, 1940.

quates [kwets]: *n.* *Quoits;* a game similar to "horseshoes." Pamlico. Rare.

rake over the coals: *phr.* To deal unmercifully with the reputation of a person absent. ((In s. Va. and c. N. C. the victim may be present.)) Pamlico. Common.

reap up: *vb.* To bring up an old topic for rediscussion, usually a rankling topic. Pamlico. Common.

reckon when: *phr.* "When do you reckon?" Among children asking older persons details about a report or a story. Pamlico, 1900–44.

ride ragamuffin: *phr.* To ride horseback in a Christmas frolic while dressed in antiquated clothing. Salem. Indulged in in 1890's. Reported, 1940.

riverjack: *n.* A rock from a river bed. Salem, 1940.

roach: *vb.* To comb the hair back from the front smooth and straight. Pamlico, about 1905. Common.

robin worm: *n.* A long, slender, reddish worm used for fishing. Pamlico. Common.

rouser: *n.* A healthy, hefty baby, or a fine large fish. Pamlico. Occasional.

roust out: *vb.* To wake a person early and get him out of bed. Pamlico. Among men. Occasional.

run-down: *n.* A sweet potato planted in the furrow in the center of a plowed row. Run-downs were usually covered with earth by a hoe, but more recently by a plow. They produce vines, not slips, for transplanting. Pamlico. Common.

run around with: *phr.* To associate with, consort with. Used in a tone of disapproval. Pamlico. Common.

run into (in) the ground: *phr.* To overdo; to carry nonsense too far; to make conversation ridiculous. Pamlico. Common.

run-mad dog: *n.* A mad dog. Pamlico. Mainly among children.

salt-water mosquito: *n.* A small mosquito that thrives in salt-water marshes or brackish water marshes. Does not produce malaria. (*Culex cantator, Culex sollicitans.*) Pamlico. Common.

sand fiddler: *n.* A small, crab-like crustacean that uses in the sands of the ocean, sounds, and creeks. Pamlico. Common.

sand spur: *n.* The spiny bur of beach grass. Carteret Co., N. C., Common, 1940.

say for: *vb.* To request, tell, command. Used mainly in the past tense. "She *said for* us to be there by eight o'clock." Pamlico. Common.

scrapegallows: *n.* A man given to various kinds of skulduggery. Applied to a person like a forger of checks. Pamlico. Occasional.

scare up: *vb.* To spare, to get hold of (money, mainly). "Ah'll go with you if Ign ((I can)) *skeer up* a dollar." Pamlico. Old people. Occasional.

scat: *interj.* Said to a small child who has just sneezed. Pamlico. Common.

schnitts and kanaps: *n.* Fried apples cooked with dough, dropped into boiling water. Henry and Roanoke counties, Va. Rural. Reported, 1941.

scuttle: *n.* An opening in a floor for a flight of steps; a stairway. Pamlico. Occasional.

wink, not able to see a: *phr.* Unable to see anything at all. Pamlico. Common.

senagambian: *n.* A Negro boy ten to fifteen years old. Salem, as late as 1890. Reported, 1940.

shav [ʃæv]: *n.* The shaft of a cart or buggy. Pamlico. Common.

shelloats ['ʃɛl'ots]: *n.* *Shallots.* Pamlico. Formerly common among gardeners.

shite poke: *n.* A heron. ((W. L. McAtee in his *Nomina Abitera*, p. 25, lists thirty-four names for this bird. He gives the etymological meaning of the name.)) Salem, 1940.

shoed: *vb.* Past tense and past participle of *shoe.* Pamlico. Common.

shool [ʃul]: *vb.* To waste time doing a task. Pamlico. Occasional.

shuck: *n.* and *vb.* The husk of corn; to husk corn. *Husk* means the cover of a grain of corn, wheat, etc. A *grain* of corn is never called a *kernel*. Oysters are *opened*, and not *shucked*. Pamlico.

side-kick: *n.* A partner, bosom friend, escort. Mainly with reference to men and boys. Humorous. Pamlico. Common.

sight of the eye: *phr.* The pupil of the eye. Pamlico. Common.

sight unseen: *phr.* Unseen. Used chiefly by schoolboys when trading knives. Pamlico.

'simmern beer: *n.* A beverage made of persimmons, water, and a few flavoring ingredients. Pamlico.

sissy-britches: *n.* An effeminate man. Salem, 1940. Rare.

sizzly-sozzly: *n.* Very light garden-variety rain. Jocular. Pamlico. Occasional.

skift of snow: *phr.* A skimpy snowfall. Salem. Common. Reported, 1940.

skig [skɪg]: *n.* *Skeg.* Pamlico. Common among boatmen.

slashways: *adv.* Diagonally. Pamlico. Common.

sleep in: *vb.* To oversleep on the morning one is to work. Camp Lee, Petersburg, Va., 1944. Rare.

slip: *n.* A sweet potato sprout used for transplanting. Pamlico. Common.

slip bed: *n.* A plot of land about five by fifteen feet where sweet potatoes are bedded for production of slips. Pamlico. Common among farmers.

slipe: *n.* A piece of arable land enclosed by ditches. Usually much longer than wide, say 20 by 250 yards. Pamlico. Common.

slit: *n.* and *vb.* A cut (slit) made in the ear of an animal to identify it; to make such a cut. Pamlico. Common.

smearcase: *n.* Cottage cheese. Salem. Reported, 1942.

snap the whip: *phr.* To rotate a line of children horizontally and "snap off" (loose the hands of) the child on the end. ((In s. Va.: *to crack the whip*.)) Pamlico. Common among boys.

snide: *vb.* To bamboozle. Salem, 1942. Occasional.

snipe hunting: *n.* A trick played on unsuspecting freshmen about forty years ago at Roanoke College. A freshman would be induced to accompany a group of boys to a distant spot in the mountains where he would be left alone by the group to hold the bag in which to catch snipe, which the other boys were supposed to drive to him.   The snipeless but enlightened boy returned to college, alone, the best way he could.   This sport was once widely practiced in the colleges and private schools of Va. ((and N. C.)). ((*Hunting the gawk* in w. N. C. is a similar sport.))

so: *adv.*   An emphatic word added to a mild contradiction. "I didn't do it."   "You did *so*."   Salem, 1927–43.   Common.

solid: *adv.*   Certainly.   "I *solid* did do it."   Carteret Co., N. C., 1940–42.   Semi-illiterate.

son: *n.*   An affectionate term applied to a small boy and sometimes a small girl, usually in times of crisis.   Pamlico, around 1900.   Once common, now obsolete.

sooy ['suɪ]: *vb.*   A command used to drive hogs away.   ((In s. N. C. the Editor has heard it used to call hogs to one.))   Pamlico. Common.

souple ['supļ]: *adj.*   *Supple.*   Pamlico.   Common.

spar-bird [spɑr]: *n.*   The sparrow.   ((Cf. Chaucer, *Sir Thopas*, 56: "The briddes singe, it is no nay, The *sparhauk* and the papejay ...")) Pamlico.   Common.

spell one off: *phr.*   To take turns at doing something for another.   "We *spelled each other off* in driving the car."   Petersburg, Va., 1944.

spider: *n.*   A frying pan.   Pamlico.   Common.

split: *vb.*   To plow out middles or balks with a cotton plow, throwing one furrow to the left and the other to the right.   The terms *run cut* and *bust out* are sometimes used instead of *split*. Pamlico.   Common.

spring chicken: *n.*   A person in the teens or early twenties. Pamlico.   Common.

squall: *n.*   A thunderstorm.   Pamlico.

stair steps: *n.*   A flight of steps.   Pamlico, 1900—.

stave: *vb.*   Mainly in past tense and past participle, *stove:* to stab with a knife; to throw angrily.   "He *stove* a knife in him." "He *stove* a brick at him."   Pamlico, around 1905.   Negroes.

stick corn: *phr.*   To plant corn in holes dug by a grubbing hoe in unplowed ground.   ((In s. Va. a stick was sometimes used to make the hole.))   Pamlico, early 1900's.

stirrup cup: *n.*   The last drink of wine, whisky, etc., before one leaves a drinking party.   Salem, 1938–42.

stockhouse: *n.*   A building provided with stables on each side of a central passageway and with a hayloft in the upper part. Pamlico, 1900—.   Common.

stoop: *n.* A sort of stepladder used by women in the 1890's for mounting a horse. Salem. Reported, 1942.

stool chair: *n.* Any chair without rockers; usually an ordinary hard-bottomed, straight-backed chair. Pamlico. Common.

story and a jump: *phr.* A story and a half (of a house). Pamlico. Common in 1900, now obsolete.

stove up: *adj.* Feeling bad. Pamlico. Occasional among farmers.

struck on, to be: *phr.* To be very fond of one. Pamlico. Common.

study one, not to: *phr.* To ignore one; to wish to have nothing to do with one. "I *ain't studyin'* you." Pamlico. Negroes.

such a matter: *phr.* Approximately (usually of time). "I been here a week or *sich a matter.*" Pamlico. Old persons. Obsolete.

summons: *vb.* To summon. "I was *summonsed* to court last week." Pamlico. Common.

Sunday baby: *n.* A bastard. Pamlico. Common.

Sunday-go-to-meeting clothes: *n.* Best bib and tucker. Pamlico. Occasional among young people.

swage down: *vb.* To become smaller (said of swellings). Pamlico. Common.

swamp dollar: *n.* A large copper cent having about the diameter of a silver dollar. Pamlico. Common about 1890.

sweet: *adj.* Sufficient, unhurried. "Take your own *sweet* time!" (Light sarcasm.) Pamlico.

sweet gum ; sweet gum wax: *n.* The fragrant resin of the sweet gum, used for chewing gum. Pamlico. Common.

swill bucket: *n.* A bucket for holding leftovers and orts from the kitchen. Pamlico. Common.

swither, in a: *phr.* In an emotional storm; excited. "He was all *in a swither* this morning." Salem. Reported, 1940.

swivel: *vb.* Shrivel. Pamlico. Common.

swivet, in a: *phr.* In a short time. ((Also in a nervous hurry.)) Randolph Co., N. C., 1940.

swivet, in a: *phr.* Excited. Richmond, Va., 1944.

syringe: *n.* and *vb.* Always accented on last syllable. Pamlico. Common.

T, to a: *phr.* Exactly. "He impersonated him *to a T.*" Pamlico. Occasional.

taddick: *n.* A small amount—coffee, sugar, etc., not water or money. Pamlico. Old people.

take: *vb.* To submit to (an insult). Pamlico. Common.

take in: *vb.* To begin school by ringing a bell or calling the children in. "School *takes in* at nine o'clock." Pamlico. Common.

take up for: *vb.* To defend one in an argument or a fracas. Pamlico. Common.

taking: *n.* and *adj.* Impatience; ingratiating, fetching. "Don't be in such a *taking*." "She has *taking* ways." Pamlico. Rare.

tallow-faced barker: *n.* An epithet hurled by Negro children at white children. *Barker* may be a form of "po' *buckra*." Pamlico, 1900–.

tallyho: *n.* A substantial blow with the fist. Pamlico. Heard a few times from a man teacher concerning a tough student. Pamlico, 1907.

tame: *adj.* Cultivated and domesticated. "This is a *tame* honeysuckle." Pamlico. Common.

tap: *n.* A nut (for a bolt). *Nut* was never used. ((Is this another instance of verbal modesty?)) Pamlico. Common.

tarkle bed; tarkill bed: *n.* A tarkiln. Pamlico. Common.

teeninsy [ti'naɪntsɪ]: *adj.* Very small. Pamlico. Girls' word.

that: *adv.* So. "I was *that* tired I couldn't walk." Rowan Co., N. C., 1922.

think: *vb.* To remind. "*Think* me to go by the post office tomorrow." Pamlico. Common.

thought [θɔt]: *n.* *Thwart*, the seat that one sits on when rowing a small boat. Pamlico. Common.

throw up at: *vb.* To recall spitefully to one one's shady dealings or actions in the past ((or a favor done one)), usually in a hot argument. Pamlico. Common.

thumb-bolt: *n.* The finger switch on a doorlock. Pamlico. Common.

thunder mug: *n.* A euphemism for *chamber pot.* Pamlico. Common among boys and men.

tile a gun: *phr.* To place a gun in position to fire automatically when a door or window is opened, as by a thief. Pamlico, 1902. Rare.

timber cart: *n.* A log cart with wheels about five feet high used for hauling logs about one foot in diameter. The tongue is used for a lever in loading. Pamlico. Common.

tin snips: *n.* Shears for cutting tin. Salem. Reported, 1942.

to-do, a great: *n.* Doings, excitement, exaggeration. "He made *a great to-do* over the news." Pamlico. Common.

tomwalkers: *n.* Stilts. Pamlico, 1900–05.

tooth and toenail: *phr.* Business-like, seriously. "He went after him *tooth and toenail*." Pamlico. Occasional.

toothbrush: *n.* The mop chewed on the end of a blackgum twig, usually for snuff-dipping but sometimes for cleaning the teeth. Pamlico.

top of the pot: *phr.* The highest social or economic class. Pamlico. Common.

touchous: *adj.* Ill-tempered; resentful of being touched or interfered with. Pamlico. Common.

Trogdon treat: *n.* A Dutch treat. Randolph Co., N. C. Reported, 1941.

try oneself: *phr.* To make a nuisance of oneself when company is around. Applied mainly to children. Pamlico. Common.

try(up): *vb.* "To melt or produce in a pure state, as oil, tallow, lard, etc."—Webster. Pamlico. Common.

tub: *n.* A measure for oysters, four and a half to five pecks. Pamlico. Common.

turn: *n.* An armful of objects to be carried in the arms. Pamlico. Common.

turn aloose: *vb.* To let go of (usually with the hands). Pamlico. Common.

turn down: *vb.* To cut down in a spelling class. Randolph Co., N. C. Reported, 1941.

turn loose: *vb.* To cut up; to make a great deal of noise and to commit other mischief purposely. Used only in the past tense. ((The Editor has heard other tenses used in s. Va.)) Pamlico. Common.

two-by-four: *n.* A person of no importance. Used disparagingly. Pamlico. Occasional.

underbite: *vb.* To cut a triangle (or some other shape) from the under part of the ear of a hog or bovine animal. Pamlico. Common.

under the weather, (somewhat): *phr.* To be (somewhat) ailing. Pimlico.

underholt: *n.* Underhold—arm under opponent's arm in a side-by-side tussle. *Topholt* is the opposite. Pamlico. Common among schoolboys.

up in G: *phr.* Prosperous and proud. Used derisively of a person who has become somewhat prosperous and proud. Pamlico. Common.

used to: *phr.* Formerly. "*Used to*, we had thick ice in winter." Pamlico. Common.

virtue: *n.* Food value or strength of fertilizer. Pamlico. Common.

wait on: *vb.* To pay court to. Pamlico and Salem. Obsolete.

walk a chalk line: *phr.* To behave circumspectly. Pamlico. Occasional.

walking papers: *n.* Discharge papers; dismissal. "I got my *walking papers* from the boss this morning." Humorous. Va. and N. C.

water-sobbed: *adj.* Heavy with water, soaked with water. Said of potatoes dug after a rainy season. ((Also applies to wood.)) Pamlico. Common.

way yonder: *adv.* Very much. "He's *way yonder* bigger'n you are." "This is *way yonder* more'n I need."

wed: *vb.* Past tense of *weed.* Pamlico. Common among farmers.

whang up: *vb.* To patch or repair a garment hurriedly. Salem, 1943. Occasional.

what for: *phr.* What kind of. "*What for* time did you have?" Pamlico, 1908. ((Still somewhat common in parts of Va. and N. C.))

what and (in) all: *phr.* What. "*What and (in) all* did you do?" ((See *who and (in) all.*)) Pamlico. Common.

what'n all: *phr.* What in general. ((Evidently a variant of *what in all.*)) Pamlico. Common.

whelp: *n.* A welt, wale. Pamlico. Common.

whicker: *n.* and *vb.* Whinny; to whinny. *Whinny* is never used. Pamlico. Common.

whing: *n.* Wing. See *whirp.* Pamlico. Used by a few families.

whirp: *n.* and *vb.* Whip. Used by the same families that use *whing.* Pamlico. Rare. ((Also in s. Va.))

whitecap: *n.* A thief. ((The Editor has heard *whitecaps* used in s. Va. as meaning persons who took some supposed offender from his home at night and whipped him.)) Salem, 1890–. Reported.

white grape: *n.* The scuppernong. (*Muscadinia rotundifolia.*)

The scuppernong is called *white grape* in contrast to *black grape* or *fox grape*. Pamlico.

who and (in) all: *phr.* Who. *"Who and (in) all* was at the party?" Pamlico. Common. ((Perhaps an abbreviation of some such form as *"Who in all* the crowd was there?" The Editor has heard three forms of this expression: *who in all, who 'n' all,* and *who and all.* He believes that *and* here is merely an incorrect restressed form for *'n'*, the common unstressed form for both *in* and *and.* The same situation holds for *what and (in, 'n') all.* For a good discussion and illustrations of restressing, see John S. Kenyon, *American Pronunciation*, 6–11 eds., secs. 137 and 139. Another common example of an incorrect restressing is *and* from *'n'* whose original stressed form was *than.* We hear: "I am bigger *and* you."))

whole swadget: *phr.* A large amount. Randolph Co., N. C. Reported, 1941.

whoop and hide: *phr.* Hide and seek. Pamlico. The usual term among children.

wild cotton: *n.* A salt-marsh weed that produces blossoms resembling cotton blossoms. Pamlico, 1900–. Occasional among old people.

window light: *n.* A window pane. Pamlico. Common.

wing-footed: *adj.* Slue-footed. Pamlico. Common.

woods colt: *n.* A bastard. Salem. Reported, 1940.

woods mold: *n.* Leaf mold. Pamlico. Common.

would-come: *n.* Something like a blackhead. Salem region, 1940.

woooooooy ['wu:ɪ]: *interj.* A hog call used for calling hogs a quarter of a mile or more away. Pamlico. Among farmers.

work on: *vb.* To castrate a male animal. Pamlico. Common.

wut [wʌt]: *n.* A mistake, blunder. Slang. Pamlico, 1900. Obsolete.

yepping stretcher: *n.* Quarry sought on a college snipe hunt. Roanoke College, around 1900.

yew shoes: *n.* New shoes. Banks near Atlantic Beach, N. C. Reported, 1942.

B. SAYINGS

To be **able** to crack corn. (To be alive and feeling well. Humorous reply to "How are you?") Craven Co., N. C.

Better be **alone** than in bad company. Va.

The reddest **apples** are always on the highest bows. (Good things are hard to get.) Va. ((Cf. Sappho's lyric 93 (150):

Οἶον τὸ γλυκύμαλον ἐρεύθεται ἄκρῳ ἐπ' ὕσδῳ
ἄκρον ἐπ' ἀκροτάτῳ· λελάθοντο ϑὲ μαλοϑρόπηες·
οὐ μὰν ἐκλελάθοντ', ἀλλ' οὐκ ἐϑύναντ' ἐπίκεσθαι.

Rosetti gives the following translation of the lyric:

"Like the sweet apple which reddens upon the topmost bough,
A-top on the topmost twig,—which the pluckers forgot, somehow,—
Forgot it not, nay, but got it not, for none could get it till now."))

Well, this ain't buying the **baby** any clothes ((shoes)). (Well, I must be going; I have a little work to do.) Pamlico. Occasional.

To **bark** up the wrong tree. (To be mistaken in one's suspicions; to flatter the wrong person.) Pamlico. Occasional.

Like a **bat** out of hell. (Very fast.) Pamlico. Common.

Not to know **beans** about anything. (To be ignorant of the matter under discussion.) Pamlico. Occasional.

Not to know **beans** when the bag is open. (To be ignorant.) Granville Co., N. C., 1944.

Not to say **beans** about anything. (To keep silence on some matter.) Pamlico. Occasional.

Give him two bottles of **beer,** and he'll take down his hair. (*In vino veritas.*) Salem, 1942.

To get too **big** for one's britches. Pamlico. Occasional.

That's **blackgum** against thunder ((Lightning)). (Strength against strength.) Salem.

In the kingdom of the **blind** the one-eyed man is king. Va.

To run a **blind** calf over one. (To bamboozle.) Pamlico, 1910.

The moment you are **born** you're done for. (This expression occurs in the autobiography of William Lyon Phelps, who heard it several years ago in Asheville, N. C.) ((The Editor heard a man at Manteo, N. C., use this epitaph for a child:

"If I was so soon to be done for,
What was I begun for?"

This may come from the epitaph for a three-weeks old child, Cheltenham churchyard, England:

"It is so soon that I am done for,
I wonder what I was begun for."))

He's so **bowlegged** he couldn't change socks.   Salem.

He's so **bowlegged** he couldn't head a pig in an alley (ditch). Salem.

Like the little **boy** that fell out of the cart—strictly out.   Pamlico.   Humorous.

If his **brains** were in a bird's head, he'd fly backwards.   Salem.

Whose **bread** I eat his song I sing.   S. C.

To have a **bridge** across one's nose.   (To be easily offended.) Salem.   Reported, 1940.

To butt the **bull** off the bridge.   (To do wonders, according to the speaker.)   Pamlico.   Occasional.

As **busy** as a bee in a tar bucket.   Granville Co., N. C., 1944. Occasional.

As **busy** as a cow's tail in flytime.   Salem.

The last **button** on Gabe's coat ((shirt)).   (The limit of a person's patience.)   Randolph Co., N. C., 1941.

To **buy** one for what he is worth (in the opinion of the speaker) and sell him for what he thinks he is worth (in the opinion of the person referred to).   Pamlico.   Occasional.

If the **cap** fits, you'll have to wear it.   Va.

A **caress** is better than a career.   Petersburg, Va.   Of recent coinage.

She runs around like a **cat** after its tail.   (Said of a chattering gadabout woman.)   Salem.   Reported, 1940.

There are more ways of killing a **cat** than choking it with butter. Salem.   Reported, 1940.

The **cat's** got his tongue.   (He is too shy to talk; generally said of children.)   Pamlico.   Common.

Charge it to the sand ((dust)) and let the rain settle it.   (Charge it on the books, but it may not be paid.   Generally said jokingly.) Salem.   Reported, 1940.

A warm **Christmas** makes a fat graveyard.   Va.

To show one's **cloven foot.**   (To reveal one's true character unintentionally.)   Pamlico.   Occasional.

Take off your **coat** and roll up your sleeves, for Jordan's a hard road to travel.   (Prepare yourself to do some hard work, a difficult task, or an embarrassing defense of a shady act.)   Pamlico. Occasional.

Common sense is that sense without which all other sense would be nonsense.   N. C.

They planted the **corn** before they built the fence. (The woman became pregnant before she was married.) Salem. Reported, 1940.

As **crooked** as a barrell of fish hooks. (Untrustworthy.) Pamlico. Occasional.

He's **crooked** enough to sleep on a corkscrew. (Untrustworthy.) Salem. Reported, 1940.

He's so **crooked** he has to sleep in a roundhouse. (Untrustworthy.) Salem. Reported, 1942.

He's so **crooked** they'll have to bury him in a cheese box. (Untrustworthy.) Salem. Reported, 1940.

He's so **cross-eyed** the tears run down his back when he cries. Salem.

Every **crow** thinks its own crow the blackest. Va.

A fellow that would take a **dare** would push blind bitties (biddies) in the creek. (Used by a schoolboy who dares another one to fight.) Pamlico.

A fellow that would take a **dare** would steal pennies off a dead man's eyes. (Same as for the saying just above.) Pamlico.

A fellow that would take a **dare** would suck a rotten egg. (Same as the two above.) Pamlico.

There's no telling what the **day** will bring forth. (Said to encourage the dejected.) Salem, 1940.

The longest **day** you (he, etc.) live. (Always. "You'll remember that *the longest day you live*.") Pamlico. Occasional.

You **deserve** well of your country. (Playfully complimentary. Said to a person who has just told of something important which he did.) Salem. Occasional.

Not willing to eat with the **devil,** but willing to drink his broth (Not willing to take part openly in a dishonest affair from which profit will result, but willing to aid indirectly and secretly.) Salem, 1941.

The **dickens** and Tom Walker! (Exclamation of amazement at something told.) Salem. Reported, 1940.

We're old enough to **die** before we learn how to live. Va.

After **dinner** sit a while;
After supper walk a mile. N. C.

Give a **dog** a bad name and everybody will want to kick him. N. C.

A **dog** gnaws a bone because he can't swallow it whole.   Va.

A **dog** that will bring a bone will carry a bone.   (A person who will bring gossip will carry gossip.)   N. C.

If you lie down with **dogs,** you will get up with fleas.   Salem.

She **drinks** her milk from a saucer too.   (Said of a woman who makes "catty" remarks about someone, generally another woman.) Salem and Petersburg, Va.

Under the **drippings** of the sanctuary.   (Up close to the speaker; near the amen corner, etc.)   Salem.   Occasional among the *cognoscenti*.

God looks after **drunkards** and fools.   Va.

Not **dry** behind the ears.   (Young, ignorant, and inexperienced.) Pamlico.   Occasional.

Shakespeare says 'tis **education** that forms the common mind— With a stick they beat it in behind.   Pamlico, 1900–05

((The first line appears in Pope's *Moral Essays, Epistle* I, 149. The second line is similar to a passage in Carlyle's *Sartor Resartus,* II, iii: "The Hinterschlag Professors knew syntax enough; and of the human soul thus much: that it had a faculty called Memory, and could be acted-on through the muscular integument by appliance of birch-rods."))

Dug off one's heel with a sang hoe.   (The *spit image* of.   "He looks as much like his daddy as if he was *dug off* his heel with a sang hoe."   *Sang hoe* is used to dig ginseng with.)   Salem.   Reported, 1940.

Dull as a froe.   (Very dull—a knife, an ax, a person's mind.) Pamlico.   Occasional.

If **F** hadn't been in the way, *G*'d 'a' been a gentleman.   (Retort to a person who gives *iffy* excuses for some questionable action or inaction.   Many older persons pronounce *if* as *ef.*)   Pamlico, 1900–05.

His **face** looks like a spanked behind.   (Red from overindulgence in alcohol.)   Salem and Petersburg, Va., 1946.

To **feel** ((look)) like five cents' worth of soap after a week's washing.   (To feel embarrassed; to feel ((look)) worn out.) Pamlico.   Occasional.

To **feel** like a three-cent piece with a hole in it.   (To feel worthless and do-less.)   Pamplin, Va., and Pamlico.   Occasional.

Fimdiddle for a dingbat. (An evasive answer to "What is that? What are you making?") Salem, 1938. Rare.

Fingers were made before forks. Va.

To kill dead **flies.** (To do research work that has already been done by someone else.) Chapel Hill, N. C., 1925.

To go up **fool's hill.** (To live a care-free life. Said mainly of young people.) Salem, 1936 .

As fine as **frog hair.** ((Excellent.)) Salem.

To come to the goat's house for wool. ((To ask a person for something which he would not be expected to have.)) Randolph Co., N. C., 1941.

Good-by, if you call that gone. ((Said to a person just leaving.)) Va. and N. C.

I hain't seen **hair** nor hide of him. Salem, rural areas, 1940.

You have to pull his **head** off to get him to the trough and his *tail* off to get him away. (It is difficult to get one to begin doing something and difficult to get him to stop once he has begun.) Pamlico. Occasional.

Make your **head** save your heels. Salem. Reported, 1940.

A **heap** sees and a few knows;
A heap starts and a few goes. Salem. Once by a Negro, 1943.

Hell broke loose in Georgia. Pamlico. Occasional.

Hell to split for Boston. (In great haste.) Pamlico, 1900–.

To ride a **high horse.** (To be arrogant.) Salem, 1942. Occasional.

A **hog** returns to his wallow. Va.

Hold your horses. (Don't become excited.) Pamlico. Occasional.

Hold your taters. (Don't become excited.) Pamlico. Occasional.

She's a **honey,** but the bees don't know it. (Said by boys about some well-dressed silly girl out for a "killing." Disapprovingly.) Pamlico. Occasional.

Clean as a **hound's tooth.** (Said of the reputation of a man, who perhaps is running for some local office.) Salem. Reported, 1940.

A **huckleberry** above someone. (Wiser or more sophisticated than someone.) Salem. Reported, 1942.

"Joy, temperance, and repose
Slam the door on the doctor's nose." Va.

Keep your shirt on. (Don't become excited.) Pamlico. Occasional.

A high **kick** for a low calf. (A big action, word, etc., for a small, insignificant person.) Salem. Reported, 1942.

Looks like he was **kicked** out of hell for sleeping in the ashes. (He looks slovenly and dirty.) Salem. Reported, 1940.

Kitty, kitty, kitty! (Same meaning as *She drinks her milk from a saucer.*) Salem and Petersburg, Va.

Not to **know** anything from a hill of beans. (Ignorant.) Pamlico. 1900–. Common.

Not to **know** B from a bull's foot. (Ignorant.) Pamlico, 1900–. Common.

I'd **know** him if I saw his hide in a tanyard. Salem. Reported. 1942.

He wouldn't **know** me from Adam's house cat ((Adam's off ox)). Salem. Reported, 1942.

Lack o' mercy on me, this is none of I. (Used when something pleasant and unexpected happens to the speaker.) Bridgewater, Va., region. Fairly common.

I'll make you **laugh** on the other side of your face. (That is, make you cry.) Pamlico.

Lazy as a tarred hog. (Extremely lazy and indifferent. Hogs that have been castrated or spayed become listless and indifferent. The incision is usually smeared with tar at the end of the operation.) Pamlico. Occasional.

Least said, soonest mended. Va.

If your **left hand** itches, you are going to get pleased. Salem.

He that is **left-handed** owes the devil a day's work. Salem.

He hath a short **Lent** who oweth money to be paid at Easter. Salem.

To **lick** with the rough side of the tongue. (A sarcastic way of threatening to "polish a person off.") Pamlico. Common among bullies.

You'll have to **lick** your calf over. (Parental reproof to a child who has slighted his work and must do it over.) Salem. Reported, 1942.

He **lit** out down the road for who laid the rail. (Used in horse-and-buggy days of a person who got off at full speed.) Salem. Reported, 1940.

Where there's **little** known, there's little required. **Salem.**

And the farmer hauled away another **load** (— of *bois de vache*, I presume). (Retort to a braggart's boasting.) Salem. Reported, 1940.

Low enough to crawl under a snake's belly. (Said of a person of low character.) Salem, Va , rural region, 1944.

((Needles and pins, needles and pins;))
When you get **married** your trouble begins. Va.

He is **mean** enough to push blind bitties (biddies) in the creek. Pamlico. Occasional.

Don't **measure** other people's corn by your half-bushel. Va.

God gave us **memory** so that we might have roses in December. Salem.

He has **money** to burn. (He has plenty of money.) ((In s. Va.: *He has money to burn, but he doesn't like the smoke.* That is, he has money, but he is stingy.)) Va. and N. C.

He doesn't have enough **money** to jingle on a tombstone. Salem.

Monkey see, monkey do. Salem.

You must have stuck a **nettle** in your foot. (Said to a person who gets up in the morning cross.) Pamlico.

Wherever **North Carolina** sits is the head of the table. ((Cf. "Where Macgregor sits, there is the head of the table." Ascribed to "Rob Roy," the Scottish outlaw Robert Macgregor, 1671–1734.)) Pamlico. Rather common.

Down in **North Carolina,** where men are men, and women are glad of it. N. C.

Down in **North Carolina,** where men are men and women climb trees. Pamlico.

If your **nose** itches, company is coming. N. C.

If your **nose** itches, you will quarrel with a friend. Va.

Our **noses** are clean. (We have done all we can; our conscience is clear.) S. C.

I'd rather be an **old man's** darling than a young man's slave. Salem.

My pub[?]ic **opin**[?]on is tha[?] the eart[?] do revolve, bu[?] my priva[?] opin[?] on is tha[?] i[?] do *no*[?] revolve. (The [?] indicates something like a glottal stop. The creation of this expression of opinion—or the straddling of an opinion—was attributed to a well-read old gentleman of Stonewall, Pamlico Co. When I asked him about it in 1924, he denied originating it. The expression is sometimes now jokingly quoted or alluded to by men who wish to avoid controversy.)

To take one down a **peg** ((notch)) or two.   (To scold, reprimand or otherwise put a person in his place.)   Pamlico.   Common.

We'll put the little **pot** in the big pot and stew the dishrag. (We'll do our best to provide a meal for unexpected company). Salem.   Reported, 1942.

He is small (sorry) **potatoes** and few in a hill.   (He is an insignificant person.)   Pamlico.   Occasional.

Poverty knows no leisure.   Salem, 1940.

He that **prescribes** for himself has a fool for a doctor.   Va. and S. C.

To every **publisher** all his geese are swans of Avon.   Salem, 1940.   Heard once.

He's been drinking **razor soup.**   ((He thinks he's sharp—witty. A derisive term.))   Salem and Pamlico.

If your **right hand** itches, you are going to receive money, N. C.

This **room** is too small to cuss a cat in without getting hairs in your mouth ((teeth)).   Salem, 1940.

To be in a bad **row** of stumps.   (To be in difficulties—bad health, debts, etc.)   Pamlico.   Occasional.

To have a bad **row** to hoe.   (To have many kinds of difficulties to contend with.)   Pamlico.   Occasional.

To **run** around like a hen on a hot griddle.   (To busy oneself with trifles.)   ((Cf. *to run around like a chicken with its head cut off.* S. Va.))   Richmond, Va.   Occasional.   1944.

To ride a hot **saddle.**   (To ride rapidly.)   Salem region, around 1900.   Reported, 1940.

If you make a big **salary,** you'll swell up to it; if you make a small salary, you'll shrink down to it.   Salem, 1940.

Shakespeare never repeats.   (A reply to someone who has asked that something just said be repeated.   Jocular.)   Pamlico. Occasional.

Sharp enough to stick in the ground and green enough to grow. (Rebuke to a person fond of cheap wit and puns.)   Salem.   Reported, 1940.

Two **sheep's heads** are better than one.   Salem.   Reported, 1940.   ((S. Va.: *Two heads are better than one even if one is a sheep's head.*))

Save your last piece of **silver** to keep the witches away.   (From the folk belief that a witch could be killed by shooting a picture of her with a silver bullet.)   Near Salem.   Reported. 1942.

To keep the **skillet** greasy. (To look out for one's best interest.) Salem.   Reported, 1940.

No **skin** off one's belly ((nose)).   (To be of little concern to one.)   Salem.   Reported, 1940.

Every shut-eye ain't **sleep,** and every good-by ain't gone. Salem.   Negroes.   Heard 1942.

As **slow** as the seven-year itch.   (Exasperatingly slow.)   Pamlico.   Occasional.

To make one feel **small** enough to walk under a trundle bed with a silk hat on.   (To make one feel unimportant.)   Salem.   Reported, 1940.

As **smart** as a Philadelphia lawyer.   Pamlico.   Common.

As **smart** as a steeltrap.   Pamlico.   Occasional.

He is a **smart man** that knows he is dumb.   Salem, 1944.

Soap will drip out of a pot if there is a crack in it.   Salem, 1942.

A **son** is a son till he gets him a wife;
A daughter is a daughter all the days of her life.   Va.

To sip **sorrow.**   (To regret.)   Salem region, 1940.   Occasional.

To save at the **spicket** and lose at the bunghole.   Va.

To **split** one's biscuit and then butter it.   (To prevail in an argument or a fight.)   Salem.   Occasional.

To put a **spoke** in the wheel.   (To have something—usually authoritative—to say; to upset plans.)   Pamlico, 1900–.   Common.

As **strong** as *aqua fortis*.   (Very strong.)   Salem.   Rare.   1941.

Strong enough to bounce ((float)) an iron wedge.   (Said of coffee, tea, etc.)   Salem.   Reported, 1940.

Sweating like a Nigger going to 'lection.   (To be tired, sweaty, and out of breath.)   Pamlico.   Occasional.

Good **swimmers** are oftenest drowned.   Va.

To get one's **tail** in a split stick.   (To get into difficulties.) ((Perhaps figurative from the hunter's habit of putting a 'possum's tail in a split stick and letting him "ride" the stick while carrying him.))   Pamlico.   Occasional.

If you can't **talk,** shake a bush.   (Find some way to explain yourself.)   Randolph Co., N. C., 1941.

Ten, ten, double ten, forty-five, fifteen.   (Used in contest among school children as to which can count to a hundred first.)   Pamlico, 1900–05.   Common among children.   ((Also s. Va. and c. N. C.))

I (he, etc.) will be **there** with the bells on.   (Declaration that a person is sure to attend a party, etc.) Va. and N. C.   ((In s. Va.: *I'll be there with every foot up and toenails dragging.*))

As **thick** as hairs on a dog's back.   Salem and Pamlico.

As **thick** as three in a bed.   (Quite friendly.)   Salem, 1940. Rare.

He's as **tight** as the bark on a tree.   Salem, 1942.

He's so **tight** he can sit down on a dime and give you a nickel in change.   Salem.   Reported, 1942.

He's so **tight** he holds his money till the eagle squeals.   Salem.

He's so **tight** he squeaks when he walks.   Salem, 1940.

I don't chew my **tobacco** but once.   (Cf. *Shakespeare never repeats.*)   Pamlico.   Occasional.

Not to be able to carry a **tune** in a bucket.   Salem, 1940.

I wouldn't **turn around** on my heel for the difference.   (The difference between two persons or things is negligible.)   Salem. Reported, 1940.

Ugly enough to stop an eight-day clock.   Salem, 1940.

Unable to chew clabber.   (Very feeble.)   Salem.   Reported, 1940.

He lost his **voice** crying for buttermilk.   (The reason he can't sing.)   Salem, 1941.

Willful **waste** makes woeful want.   Va., 1940.

Whimmydoodle to wind up the moon with.   (An evasive, flippant reply given to inquisitive children or grown-ups.)   Pamlico. Probably obsolete.

Not worth two **whoops** in hell.   Pamlico.   Occasional.

A nice **wife** wife and a back door
Often makes a rich man poor.   N. C.

A bad **workman** quarrels with his tools.   Pamlico.

WORDS FROM *A GLOSSARY OF VIRGINIA WORDS* CURRENT IN MAINE

B. J. WHITING

Harvard University

The following examples from Mrs. Nixon's *Glossary of Virginia Words* were commonly used in the town of my birth, Northport, Waldo County, Maine, during the years when I was growing up there, 1904–1921. Since 1921 I have lived the greater part of each year in Massachusetts, but there has been only one year that I have not spent at least a part of the summer in Waldo County.

aim: Not obsolete.

alter.

angleworm.

andirons.

attic: More common than *garret*.

back-house: Anything but obsolete, and used for privies located in sheds and other attached out-buildings.

beholden: Very old fashioned, but still heard.

bite.

bonny-clabber.

breeze up.

bucket: A wooden vessel with a bail.

burlap bag.

calm down.

catty-cornered.

chamber: Always upstairs, and as *the chamber* a large, often unfinished or "open" room, but also *front chamber* for a finished bedroom on the front of the house.

clever: Usually of animals, but sometimes of human beings; in the latter case condescending or mocking.

coal hod: Much more common than *scuttle*.

corn bread.

cottage cheese: The common term, though *home-made cheese* and *curd-cheese* are familiar.

curtains.

cut: More common than *alter*.

fix up.

freshen.

front room.

galluses.

garret: Not so common as *attic*, but with the same meaning.

gentleman cow: Seldom heard and then usually with specific and humorous reference to an unduly mealy-mouthed woman of our township who used the term in court when testifying to the theft of her husband's bull. I never knew or heard of another Maine woman who objected to the word *bull*.

hog's head cheese.

hop-toad.

Irish potatoes.

johnny cake.

let out.

lightning bug.

living room.

(give someone) the mitten.

moderate.

parlor: The best room.

poor.

primp: Usually without *up*.

prink.

puny.

(throw a) rock: I can remember being corrected by an out-of-stater, when I was no more than eight, because I called something a *rock* which he considered too small for that word.

sack.

saw horse.

scrawny.

scrooch down.

shades.

shindig: Usually, if not always, as a humorous term.

sitting room: Carefully distinguished from the *parlor*.

snack.

somerset.

spider.

spry.

squall.

string beans.

sundown.

sunup.

tote.

whetstone.

wishbone: The only word.

((Note: The Editor is always pleased to get comments on material in *PADS*. He urges that persons who wish to send in comments do so early enough for them to be published in the issue immediately following the one being commented on.))

Continued from Cover 2

THE AMERICAN DIALECT SOCIETY

Membership in the Society is conferred upon any person interested in the activities of the Society. Dues are $2.00 a year for persons or institutions. Members receive free all publications. The price of any issue when purchased separately will depend upon the production cost of the issue.

The *Publication of the American Dialect Society* is issued twice a year, in April and November.